THE PRESENCE OF TRANSCENDENCE

ANNUA NUNTIA LOVANIENSIA
XLII

The Presence of Transcendence
Thinking 'Sacrament' in a Postmodern Age

Edited by

Lieven Boeve and John C. Ries

PEETERS

LEUVEN – PARIS – STERLING, VA

2001

CIP KONINKLIJKE BIBLIOTHEEK ALBERT I, BRUSSEL

ISBN 90-429-1082-8 (Uitgeverij Peeters)
2001/0602/97

Image on the cover: Jan Vanriet, "… en de broden."
Aquarelle and linography on Hanji paper, 42 × 30 cm.
Collection Bibliotheek van de Faculteit Godgeleerdheid, K.U. Leuven.

© Uitgeverij Peeters, Bondgenotenlaan 153, B-3000 Leuven (Belgium)

Contents

Introduction

There can be little doubt that at the heart of the Christian tradition stands a conviction that God is present in the world. Understanding and articulating this, particularly theologically, has nevertheless proved rather difficult, and often become the source of conflicts and divisions. How and/or in what sense can an infinite God – a God that truly 'transcends' every (finite) thing – actually be 'present' in the finite? While such a question could hardly be expected to lend itself to a simple answer, the depths of its inquiry shows itself to be particularly germane. For Christians this question about "the presence of transcendence" touches upon – and gives shape to – the very sense and vitality of what it means to be a Christian. Theologically, giving words to such a self-understanding shows how "incarnation" – whether in theologies of creation, revelation, grace, or in Christologies, ecclesiologies, etc. – is a mystery in which our very being a Christian is rooted.

Although theological articulation of incarnation – the presence of transcendence – has never been easy, the coming of the modern age brought even greater difficulties to Christian self-understanding. For indeed, the ascent of modern reason – demonstrated in countless scientific and technological advances – lies in its powerful ability to grasp and give an account of everything that is. Philosophically, this shows itself through the persistent endeavour to justify or ground any and all claims about reality. Insofar as this assumes the principle of sufficient reason and that everything lies within the grasp of reason, how could one hope to 'think' transcendence? The triumph of modern reason would seem to allow no place, no ground for genuine transcendence. As such, there would be no reasonable "foundations" of Christian faith, but only "myth" and "superstition." Moreover, ever-growing secularisation further and further eclipsed the possibilities of understanding "incarnation" – not only in reflective thought, but more importantly in practice and imagination.

The advent of the postmodern age – as ill-defined as it may well be – has brought forth both new opportunities and further challenges to understanding Christianity's underlying question concerning the presence of transcendence. There can be little doubt that the optimism of the modern age has now waned and that the power of reason falls under a rather ominous shadow of doubt. Philosophically, postmodern reflection has come to affirm what might be called a principle of *in*sufficient reason, realising that not everything – or perhaps nothing at all – lies within the confident grasp of reason. Indeed, for as diverse as postmodern thinking proves to be, it could well be characterised by a sustained effort to undo the pretensions of modern reason, particularly regarding its idealistic and foundationalistic assumptions.[1]

For understanding the question of the presence of transcendence at the heart of Christianity, such a postmodern undoing or 'deconstruction' of modern reason – with its, at bottom, immanentistic claims – would seem to open the possibility for genuine transcendence. Herein various thinkers, particularly philosophers, have brought to light a number of central presumptions that have come to be embedded in Western thinking – perhaps brought to their climax in modernity – which have severely limited, if not distorted, such thinking. In a fundamental sense, Heidegger's critique of 'onto-theology' – and as such any 'metaphysics of presence' – underlies so much of postmodern thinking. This "end of metaphysics" has had wide repercussions – from radical difference/alterity, to the end of grand/master narratives, from narrative particularity to the endless play of signifiers – repercussions which have pushed theology to probe its own roots.

While surely laying open a space wherein genuine transcendence might come to be understood – and not known/grasped – such "space" is still not enough. For even though postmodern thinking has gone to great lengths to point out 'difference,' 'the other,' etc., such transcendence remains only "absence" and so somehow hollow/empty for Christian theology's question concerning the presence of transcendence. For the Christian, this "other" is really present – indeed incarnate – yet not in an idolatrous sense. As Louis-Marie Chauvet has shown well, this means that "theology's critical thrust" does not lay "in a prolongation of the negative onto-theology stressing the

---

1. Of course, one must also be wary of so describing the modern and postmodern ages. For example, even though Kant and Hegel are surely both "modern" thinkers, their differences concerning the reach of reason should not be neglected. While in Hegel the 'real' and the 'rational' are explicitly identified, in Kant one finds critical limitations of reason, limitations which allow for something real outside the bounds of human understanding. Still, Kant's modern character remains, for even if there are such things which in principle cannot be known ('noumena'), their reality is still critically limited to what must be assumed by reason. And indeed, religion in Kant ultimately comes to be emptied of any genuine transcendence.

unknowability of God but rather in the direction of the believing subjects themselves."[2]

As such, a truly fecund *place* – and not simply a space – wherein the deepest of Christian questioning would be "enfleshed" would lay in the human being. As "enfleshed," the presence of transcendence is neither an idea to be thought – like a metaphysical entity – nor reduced to the confines of materiality – like an idol. Rather, the incarnationality of Christianity means that the transcendent God is indeed present, yet in such a way that this presence does not lie in our grasp, but we in its.

While theological reflection upon sacrament (i.e. "sacramentology") has tended to place sacrament within the context of a theology of incarnation, or even to instrumenalise its role therein, what "takes place" in sacrament has now come to the fore in theological reflection. "Thinking sacrament," however, has not simply gained a more prominent position in theological discourse in the postmodern age, rather it questions and challenges the very core of theologising. Therefore, contemporary theology seems profoundly 'Sacramento-theology'. The "enfleshment" of sacrament not only refuses to be reduced to a mere application of (metaphysical) ideas, it incarnates the presence of transcendence in such a way that one is moved more deeply than one can move oneself.

But exactly what is the "sacramental presence" of transcendence? And what does it reveal about our understanding of God, the world, and even ourselves?

The variety of questioning, methods and answers presented in this volume all make manifest the crucial, even if unsettling, role that thinking 'sacrament' – or better, re-thinking sacrament – comes to play in theology's persistent endeavours at Christian self-understanding.

In the first place, (re)thinking sacrament in a postmodern age brings us to difficult questions concerning method. How should one approach sacraments? How exactly should such thinking proceed? What are its grounds, particularly in a postmodern age? In the contributions of Part One (Approaching Sacrament in a Postmodern Age: Questions of Method), Jeffrey Bloechl and Lieven Boeve seek to probe this problematic. The first sets out to draw out the limits and possibilities which

---

2. Louis-Marie Chauvet, *Sacrament and Symbol: A Sacramental Reinterpretation of Christian Existence*, trans. Patrick Madigan and Madeleine Beaumont (Collegeville, MN: The Liturgical Press, 1995) 41 [*Symbole et Sacrament: Une relecture sacramentelle de l'existence chrétienne* (Paris: Les Éditions du Cerf, 1987)].

postmodern thinking brings to thinking about sacrament, particularly concerning how the intersection of immanence ("the horizontal") and transcendence ("the vertical") is dealt with. The second seeks to display a fruitful theological method for thinking transcendence and immanence, a method that finds resonance in postmodern thinking insofar as it refuses to rely upon metaphysical "grounds" or "grand narratives," but rather remains an "open narrative" wherein the "irruptive event" can break in.

The questions and challenges brought forth by the postmodern age bring our (re)thinking of sacrament to consider the past – to revisit yesterday. By looking again at theologians like Rahner and Schillebeeckx, or considering ways of re-appropriating past approaches, the contributions in Part Two ("Yesterday Revisited: Recovering the Past in the Face of the Challenges of the Postmodern Age") attempt to see how Christianity's past self-understandings might be thought again, both finding insights which had gone unnoticed and questioning their current plausibility.

By engaging postmodern thought today, (re)thinking sacrament has turned from more metaphysical understandings of sacrament and uncovered the profoundly "ethical" character of sacrament. In Part Three ("Today's Imperative: Uncovering the Transformative Power of Sacrament in a Postmodern Age") the contributions make this character manifest, recasting the sense of sacrament as demanding something of us: radical self-transformation – from outside.

In and through engaging postmodern thought, many have sought to re-think sacrament in such a way that the incarnationality or "enfleshment" of sacramental presence could be discovered in new places. In Part Four ("Tomorrow's Possibilities: Discovering new *Loci* of Sacramental Presence in a Postmodern Age") the contributions seek out some new possibilities that such a re-thinking of sacrament can bring forth. Herein the Church as sacrament, both as a whole and in the particularities of a specific context, is critically examined. There are also explorations of modern art and the body as "enfleshments" wherein the presence of transcendence might be more fecundly conceived.

While none of these contributions puts an end to the myriad of philosophical and theological debates that have been precipitated in the postmodern age, they each work from a sense – one might say a *quaerens* – that thinking 'sacrament' in a postmodern age not only affords both fecund opportunities and potential dangers, but a question of incarnation that Christianity must continually and ever-more deeply address.

The contributions of this volume stem from a common origin – an occasion that sought to probe the question of "sacramental presence in a postmodern context." From the 3rd through the 6th of November 1999, scholars from various countries gathered in Leuven to participate in the second biannual 'Leuven Encounters in Systematic Theology' (LEST II), entitled: "Sacramental Presence in a Postmodern Context: Fundamental-Theological Approaches," organized by L. Leijssen and L. Boeve, together with J. Bloechl, G. De Schrijver and S. Van den Bossche. This event was devoted to reflecting upon the conditions and possibilities for thinking the 'presence of transcendence' in the present 'postmodern age'. It was part of a more extended research project, called 'Postmodern Sacramento-theology' (1996-2000), sponsored by the K.U. Leuven Research Fund and the Fund for Scientific Research of Flanders (FWO-V). The subject under investigation in this project has also been selected for the programme of collaboration between the Faculty of Theology, K.U. Leuven, and The Netherlands School for Advanced Studies in Theology and Religion (NOSTER). Within the framework of this agreement, NOSTER co-sponsored the organisation of this congress, in particular the Junior Scholars Conference (3 November 1999), which preceded the main Congress, as well as the present volume.

Finally we owe special thanks to Johan Ardui, research assistant to the Research Group 'Theology in a Postmodern Context', and Leo Kenis, editor of ANL, for their valuable editorial assistance.

Lieven Boeve
John C. Ries

PART ONE

APPROACHING 'SACRAMENT' IN A POSTMODERN AGE:
QUESTIONS CONCERNING METHOD

The Postmodern Context and Sacramental Presence
Disputed Questions

Jeffrey Bloechl

The focal point of the discussion before us lies in an encounter between the two expressions "postmodern context" and "sacramental presence." If this conjunction is immediately interesting or even provocative, this is probably due to the way each expression has a sense that places the sense of the other in doubt. I will address this mutual confrontation primarily from one direction, moving from some thoughts on what the "postmodern context" might be to what that implies for reflection on religion. This choice of procedure leaves me no way around the difficult task of defining the nebulous term "postmodern." Fortunately, the assignment of confronting this term with the theme of "sacramental presence" permits me to focus attention on the well-restricted theme of religious practice and experience. There is thus, for instance, no pressing need to venture far into the fields of metaphysics or the history of theology, where – it must be said – the record of many postmodern thinkers is uneven at best. There is also no need, in my estimation, to yet ask whether the exercise at hand is philosophical, theological, or perhaps even sociological – not because the differences between these modes of thinking are either meaningless or unimportant, but simply because there is nothing in what follows that any one of them could not think or say precisely as a preliminary step toward arguing about the implications. What I propose to do instead of entering into those other, no doubt pressing discussions is simply trace some main lines of postmodern thinking, sketch what they would require us to think about sacramentality (while occasionally questioning their inner coherence), and then ask whether they present us with plausible accounts of the phenomena in question.

This already brings me to my first, and most banal point of interrogation: the expression "postmodern context" can evoke either of two general spheres – on one hand, the mindset and self-understanding of contemporary culture (and here it would be necessary to ask whether this can be said univocally for *all* contemporary cultures), and on the other hand, an intellectual current that in some way argues that we must now think in terms no longer essentially bound to those of "modernity" (itself a notoriously vague term). Here I can only state a basic reservation: In deciphering the relation between these two spheres – between contemporary consciousness and a single form of rationality claiming to explain it – what is especially to be avoided is the idea that all of the critical claims of that rationality must be granted *only because it reflects or agrees with popular sentiment*. In the area of method, this means that the search for what is essential to a practice or experience must see past what belongs only to prevailing opinion, however pervasive it may be. As pertains specifically to theology, this requires close reflection on the relationship between basic sociological data and the healthy growth of Christian tradition[1].

1. The Vertical Dimension

Having set before ourselves the theme of "sacramental presence," it is inevitable that we will come quickly to the theme of religious experience. However, it should not escape our attention that the very logic of postmodernity itself would also have made this a concern. The two principles most commonly associated with thinking that claims to have gone through and beyond modernity are (1) a radicalization of historical consciousness to a point where historical consciousness itself is said to be historically conditioned, and (2) an interpretation of all foundationalism in terms reducing it to anthropomorphism. These two principles have been brought most closely together in the work of Nietzsche, for whom human consciousness works like a spider that sees everything from the center of a home that is in fact spun out of its own inner make-up. This vision of ourselves is then to function like a wake-up call, telling us what we have been doing with a clarity that makes it impossible to return to it. And what awakens is precisely the will to occupy that place at the center of the universe, as if its focal point and master. What awakens, in short, is a will to power suppressed even before we had caught sight of it. Nietzsche's awakening – the dawn of the will to

---

1. I have previously given more time to questioning the capacity of postmodern theology to address this distinction in "Theology and the Postmodern Condition: The End of Christian Truth-Claims?," *Liberation Theologies on Shifting Grounds: A Clash of Socio-Economic and Cultural Paradigms*, ed. Georges De Schrijver (Leuven: Leuven University Press/Peeters, 1998) 284-295.

power – is thus also, he says, a moment of liberation. For too long, he tells us, we have lived in the naive assurance that our perspective is objective and enduring, and too long have we looked directly past the fact that that very assurance is driven by a deeper will to power; let us stop deceiving ourselves, and indeed depriving ourselves of the visceral energy driven underground where it festers in resentment rather than coarsing into tired flesh and tepid blood. Nietzsche's aim is thus to uncover the naked thrust he considers to underlie the whole of human expression, from individual thought and speech to the historical and cultural pattern of behavior shared by entire communities and their lineage. It is this nerve of self-assertion and self-creation that Nietzsche always has in view as he claims to see beneath every objective foundation or universal framework, to the radically individual source where they really emerge and exercise their appeal. This is where a thinking that is truly, wholly *post-modern* begins: to deny the possibility of grounding subjects or objects in a transcendent principle, so that properly speaking they would only *appear to be* subjects and objects, is to turn away from an epistemological concern with fixed definitions toward an aesthetics of dissimulation, where literally everything is a matter of perspective and appearance.

Few thinkers have claimed this vision as their own while still pretending to any positive relation with theology. To celebrate, as Nietzsche does, surfaces over depth and masks over hiddenness – to embrace the former and eschew the latter – can seem to express nothing less than a denial of everything fixed or lasting, and thus an affirmation of sheer flux. Yet it may be that this assessment, however accurate it may be, moves too quickly past the *desire* evident in such full-blooded nihilism. One might well ask: Is there not something akin to mysticism in the nihilism which rejects any and all definitions of who we are because they close us from a greater reality that is indefinable? After all, nihilism is no more content to stop at images or ideas than is most mysticism. What does plainly distinguish the two, however, is the absence of any confession of heteronomy in nihilism – of any willingness to admit that one's existence depends on something other than its own drive and its own devices – presumably because this would immediately nullify the nihilist's effort to liberate naked passion from each and every qualification allegedly imposed on it.[2] Nietzsche speaks always of a faith that is

2. This difference is noticed often by Gabriel Marcel, in *The Mystery of Being*, Vol. I (Chicago: Regnery, 1950) 24ff. It is also a central concern of an essay by Henri de Lubac

invested first and only in oneself, of a Yes to the blind rustle of life, and nothing else.[3]

The most consequent attempt to embrace that perspective *and* continue to think through the field of theology appears in the work of Mark C. Taylor, where the death of God and the end of history open the time and space of what he calls "graceful erring,"[4] a wandering without aim except to hold itself open to the play of appearances, of – in a recent formulation – "skin rubbing at skin, skin, skin…"[5] What one misses most in this epidermic thinking is of course an adequate analysis of symbol, which has a depth that is difficult to reduce to the flat circulation of adjacent and overlapping surfaces. Yet how can Taylor avoid precisely this reduction, once he has decided with Nietzsche, or rather a Nietzschean Derrida, to challenge every instance where such binary oppositions as "latent" and "manifest" – essential to the symbol – are arranged so as to raise one of them over the other?[6] Whereas a *symbol* is generally understood to consist in non-literal manifestation of something which is itself out of reach, Taylor is bound to speak of a relationship between two *signs*, the first of which gives the second while the second for its part grounds the first. This much of the analysis is fair enough, but it is also incomplete. Intent on defining even the symbol strictly within the scope of surface, fold and skin, Taylor emphasizes the way it binds two meanings together according to the structure of similarity, and he *de*-emphasizes the way it nonetheless also holds the two meanings apart according to the structure of *dis*similarity. Never mind the fact that this 'structure of dissimilarity,' this 'holding apart,' is exceptionally pronounced in, above all, religious symbolism; Taylor says so little about it that it is not always clear how – or even *if* – he can distinguish between symbol and *metaphor*.[7] What is lost in this move to graft a theory of symbol into a Nietzschean philosophy of language is not merely the right to speak of the inherent depth of the symbol but,

entitled "Nietzsche as Mystic." This essay was originally published in *Affrontements Mystiques* (Paris: Éditions du Témoignage chrétien, 1950), and became the final entry in all subsequent editions of *Le drame de l'humanisme athée*, thus beginning with the fourth edition in 1951.

3. "The concealed Yes in you is stronger than any No or Maybe, stronger than everything that has made your times ill and languishing. And if you must go out to sea, you wanderers, it is a *faith* that drives you there…" Friedrich Nietzsche, *Wille zur Macht*, ed. Giorgio Colli; Kritische Gesamtausgabe, 12 (Berlin: de Gruyter) 168.

4. Mark C. Taylor, *Erring: A Postmodern A/theology* (Chicago: University of Chicago Press, 1984) 150.

5. Mark C. Taylor, *Hiding* (Chicago: University of Chicago Press, 1997) 11.

6. Catalogued at Taylor, *Erring*, 8-9.

7. See Taylor, *Erring*, 56-58.

more broadly, the means to adequately address the vertical dimension of all religious experience, of which that depth is only one example. At stake, in short, is the presence of a verticality transcending the existential context in all religion, both as a matter straightforwardly of the belief that we are all dependent in our very humanity on some higher power or force, and as a matter of the specific form of experience – symbols – where that dependence is encountered.[8] This question need not become a matter of giving a metaphysical place to the God encountered in the symbol, but simply asks whether Taylor can provide an adequate representation of the experience of symbols. This difficulty touches directly on the conjunction of "sacramental presence" and "postmodern context": without a sense of dependence, of a relation with what transcends human identity positively, exceeding it and supporting it, it is extraordinarily difficult to do justice to the theme of *sacrament*, consecration of the divine mystery.

With that much firmly in place, it should also be asked whether this problem confronts all religions in the same way or to the same degree. As a category in the study of religion, "dependence" can not have the same content in monotheism, where there is one dependence on one God, as it does, for instance, in the polytheism which disperses the dependence among distinct relations with many gods and goddesses. In the case of polytheism, where each symbol and ritual will be directed to a deity whose powers are specific and therefore limited, it seems certain that the relation of dependence will also be encountered only in parts or perhaps in a series. Whether or not this significantly changes the role of sacrament requires separate attention. And this is to say nothing of the matter of Buddhism, or at least those schools of Buddhism which do not have a strong sense of a relation with the wholly Other – at least not in a manner easily admitting the personification we find in the Abrahamic religions. Here it is no longer clear that the notion of sacrament has any pertinence.

2. The Religion of the Event

Does this mean that sacramental theology and the notion of the divine that it entails have grown implausible or even been discredited –

---

8. The importance of this "vertical dimension" is established in Antoine Vergote, *Interprétation du langage réligieux* (Paris: Seuil, 1974) 95ff.

or, conversely, that modern and postmodern thinking, should we elect
to follow them, threaten to deprive our humanity from its sacramental
bond with the divine? One might well object that this question proposes a false dilemma. Perhaps Nietzsche was correct when arguing that
human nature is spontaneously narcissistic, so that theology is actually
indebted to him for having reminded it of just how far it is necessary to
go in order to protect the image of God from anthropomorphism and
thus, in the technical sense, idolatry. This line of thinking thus comes
inevitably to the apophantic strand of theology, as it reflects on what
I have just called the "vertical dimension" of religious experience. One
recalls the prayer of Anselm: "Are my eyes darkened by weakness, or
dazzled by your glory? […] The truth is, I am darkened by myself and
dazzled by you. I am clouded by my own smallness and overwhelmed
by your greatness…"⁹ And indeed, this sort of thought would seem to
recur in, for instance, Jean-Luc Marion's phenomenology of the icon
which shines from wholly beyond the limits of a gaze still imprisoned in
what Anselm called our own smallness, thus transforming us by opening us to a transcendent glory.¹⁰ What these two positions share is a
vision of human smallness defined by a relation with the greatness of
God, as the latter announces itself from beyond comprehension. However, before assimilating them – and this would be another question for
any reflection on sacramental presence in a postmodern context – it will
have to be asked whether Marion's navigation through the arguments of
Nietzsche and, by extension, Heidegger, has not in fact put him at some
distance from the tradition he claims to resurrect. This task can be formulated in a question aimed at the theme of verticality: do the works of
Anselm and of Marion in fact promote the same sense of transcendence
and glory?

   Anselm's perspective is well-known: "Lord, you are then not only that
than which nothing greater can be thought; you are something greater
than that which can be thought."¹¹ Perhaps we can better approach the
heart of this thought by taking up its variant in Thomas doctrine of
creatio ex nihilo. The advantage of Thomas' argument begins with his
sense of the difference between the *nihil* of the God who neither gains
nor loses by creating and the other *nihil* out of which that God creates:

   9. Anselm, *Proslogion* al. 14, in *Anselm of Canterbury The Major Works*, ed. Brian
Davies and G. R. Evans (Oxford: Oxford University Press, 1998).
   10. See Jean-Luc Marion, *Dieu sans l'être* (Paris: Fayard, 1982) 35.
   11. Anselm, *Proslogion* al. 15.

creation out of nothing does not mean creation out of God but creation without need or desire on the part of the Creator, creation without the Creator having lacked anything. The Creator who creates without having lacked anything – without needing or desiring something from the creating – is a Creator who is beyond the difference between creation and non-creation. By saying that God created out of nothing, Thomas says that God created from a divinity with no lack, with no prior requirements and driven by no higher necessity. This way of wholly transcending the inner necessities governing the world and everything in it reminds us that Thomas' sense of God as First Cause is only analogical, pointing from within human understanding toward what by definition exceeds human understanding. The glory of this God does not diminish as one proceeds back from effect to cause until arriving at a First Cause, but only magnifies as one is compelled to give a name to what surpasses every name. God, says Thomas, has a simpleness inaccessible to the thinking that always works with distinctions and connections.[12] This is already found in Anselm before him: "What purity, what simplicity, what certainty and splendor [...] It is more than a creature can comprehend!"[13] The closer thinking comes to apprehending the limitations in its understanding of God, the more it realizes that God can not be understood.

For his part, Marion defines God by a transcendence so great that no image or concept can cross the "distance" separating us. This concept of "distance" – crucial to Marion's work until well into the 1980s – designates an "asymmetry" between us and the divine so great that it even consumes – as Marion does not hesitate to argue – the very name "distance."[14] At first blush, this may appear close to Anselm and Aquinas: after all, a sense of our "distance" from the divine would thus seem to designate insight into the fact that our finitude (modern expression) or creaturliness (classical expression) makes our understanding inherently limited. And naturally, this insight can not be produced from within that understanding itself, but must rather be attributed to an intervention from outside and beyond: it must be given to us, in a revelation that breaks into our finitude and overpowers the limited understanding

12. Thomas Aquinas, *Summa Theologiae*, I-I, q. 2. Thus precisely *before* the celebrated Five Proofs.

13. Anselm, *Proslogion* al. 14. It should be noted that Thomas' basic agreement with this part of Anselm's thought does not prevent him from criticizing the latter's view, at least as Thomas understood it, that we have direct access to the existence of God.

14. See Jean-Luc Marion, *L'Idole et la distance* (Paris: Grasset, 1977) section 17.

that comes with it. It is here that Marion responds to the Nietzschean concept of will to power with his phenomenology of the iconic gaze of God. It is also here that he claims to have found the way back to a theology – fundamentally sacramental – free of the idolatry characterizing all metaphysics. What Marion calls "icon" is the rupture of being and becoming by what has no need of either being and becoming, tearing open the envelop of immanence in which we narcissists tend always to wrap ourselves, so that it is, as we then confess with that word "distance," always already interrupted by the glory of the transcendent.

In *Dieu sans l'être*, Marion's example for how and where this occurs is the Eucharist, which he is thus intent on protecting from anthropological and metaphysical analyses. These two possibilities are condemned for functioning by projection, and therefore serving self-idolatry; Marion suspends them, and attempts to let the Eucharist determine the conditions of its own reality starting from itself and itself alone. This leads him to speak of the Eucharist as a gift of superabundance, of a presence that always overflows what either the individual or the community may make of it. The fact that such a gift, by definition arriving without conditions, is explained only by the divine love expressed in and by Christ points the way toward a non-ontological and non-representational theology that Marion immediately links with phenomenological neutrality: theology is the crown of philosophy because it alone can think the gift which truly defines the event of the Eucharist – an event which philosophy ignores only at the price of conceding incompleteness; conversely, the philosophy which can indeed satisfy the demand for completeness must in the first instance be phenomenological because only phenomenology possesses the means to purge thinking from metaphysical prejudices otherwise distorting our understanding of this unique event.

Without questioning the good faith of this surprising conjunction of phenomenological neutrality and theological affirmation,[15] it can still be asked whether it does not represent a decisive concession to the sort of thinking already seen in Nietzsche. This concession, if I am right, lies in Marion's definition of "idolatry," which he readily reduces to, at heart, self-idolatry: one believes in idols because idols can be understood and in that sense managed; idolatry lives from an urge for security, for closure into oneself. This is a recognizable translation of Nietzsche's will

---

15. See Dominique Janicaud, *Le tournant théologique de la phénoménologie française* (Paris: Éditions de l'Éclat, 1991) and *La phénoménologie éclatée* (Paris: Éditions de l'Éclat, 1998).

to power into the language of religion, but with the significant limita-
tion of immediately contrasting it with the iconic. François Dagognet
has summarized how the icon works in the field of aesthetics: the field
of appearance is reduced in order to let more into it from outside.[16]
Transferred into the sphere of philosophy and speculative theology, this
way of reducing the idol to an effect of narcissism and then contrasting
it with the icon which is entirely without that narcissism yields a dualism in which everything we do is either defined by either a tendency
toward self-idolatry or complete abjection before the iconic gaze. One
difficulty with applying this interpretation to Marion comes from the
fact that he usually argues from the side of revelation, that is from a
starting point in God as pure gift. This enables him to speak, for
instance, of the "patience" *in the icon* itself, as it only asks us to receive
what it gives of itself,[17] but does not force itself wholly into experience
and identity. Still, until he speaks more explicitly of the original goodness of our freedom to choose for or against accepting the icon, everything else in his argument requires us to think that receiving the icon is
a matter of a sharp opposition between speaking for oneself and bearing
witness to the Other. Furthermore, that opposition sometimes appears
so sharp that it is difficult to see how one can maintain one's own identity as a speaking subject without betraying the God revealing itself in
Marion's icon. Even the first words of prayer will already put one on the
path to forgetting God.

   If Marion can therefore be said to build up a sense of our separation
from God at the price of undermining our attachment to God – if, in
other words, he promotes a sense of dependence so radical as to defy
understanding it well or holding it long in view – then it is certainly to
be expected that his argument will reserve a crucial place for our concrete encounter with that God: after all, without a reliable conception
of God in hand, we must rely entirely on God's own initiative, and in
God's own time. Of the many hesitations arising at this thought, the
pastoral one is perhaps the most telling: if theology is to denounce the
entire history of metaphysics as the source of a false sense that God is
indeed what we would like God to be – namely, present and supportive
even in our frailest moments, and if theology is then to limit valid
contact with the true God to isolated moments of participation in the
sacraments and rare moments of mystical consolation, how will it avoid

   16. François Dagognet, *L'écriture et iconographie* (Lyon: La Manufacture, 1973).
   17. Marion, *Dieu sans l'être*, 37.

the impression that divine love is in fact dispensed only occasionally and under particular conditions? How, if this is to be the message, will theologians convey the idea that that more reassuring God was defined by our own immaturity without having many people lose their faith entirely, rather than progressing to maturity? For a great many who hear this message, the result will be as it was for the young Proust, whose mother once gave her kisses freely and in abundance but who one day tarried longer with other affairs, and thereafter sometimes did not appear at all. In *Jean Santeuil*, Proust recounts that for a long time after his mother's first refusal he met each subsequent kiss from her not with gratitude for a new and unexpected gift, but hatred for all the depriva-tions both earlier and still to come. How can a theology of love resting on sudden, disruptive events avoid stirring this same bitterness in a populace long used to at least the dram of a love which is uninter-rupted? Does it not risk incurring the very sort of resentment in which Nietzsche saw the beginning of the end of monotheism?

3. The Horizontal Dimension

There is of course a complex history of misfortune behind this diffi-culty. No one will deny the negative consequences of the widespread loss of orientation to a biblical God who joins us in working for a common future, in favor of the modern theistic God who guides our every act according to a plan unfolded, as it were, from above. There is no need to take up this chronicle, which would have to explain the victory of a voluntaristic God and then the rise of atheism and deism, to suppose that a considerable measure of what went wrong for theology has to do with the dialectical process of a history that saw, first, an attempt at recuperating anthropological reflection into theology, but then, in an inevitable reaction, anthropological reflection visit itself on theology in the same way.[18] All of this is also familiar enough to recog-nize that it is part of Marion's intention to skirt the entire issue by permitting contemporary philosophy to deconstruct every candidate for an origin or foundation – and then insist that precisely this re-opens the way to a proper understanding of the Transcendent. If the pastoral problem arises from an extreme definition of the Transcendent, seeming to risk a de-sacralization of the world and indeed the humanity which

---

18. For historical documentation, see Michael J. Buckley, *The Origins of Modern Atheism* (New Haven: Yale University Press, 1987).

welcomes it, then it also rejoins a more speculative concern with the price of purging God of any contact with the concepts and images formulated by us humans. This speculative concern must in the first place lead back to the proper nature of Christian metaphysics, which would now seem called on to re-think the relationship between creatures and Creator without founding either one of them on the other. As I have suggested, it is not clear that Thomas did not attempt precisely this with his doctrine of *creatio ex nihilo*, which qualifies every effort to think about God with the reminder that no thought can grasp God *as* God. As a concept "*ex nihilo*" is not a principle grounding the Creator in the creature or the creature in the Creator, but rather a statement of the fact that in the special case of God, the language of grounds is at once unavoidable and in an important sense inadequate.

Marion is not alone in radicalizing religious transcendence to the point of investing immanence with an essentially negative definition – as what qualifies, resists, or contaminates our authentic religious identity. Nor is he alone in characterizing our experience of that transcendence by an encounter with extreme "height." In such cases, the appearance of metaphysical dualism is matched by experiences of overwhelming, bedazzlement, dispossession, and shock, all of which do not merely transform a person's inner bearing but go so far as to reverse it, from deep self-absorption or self-idolatry into unlimited openness. It deserves notice that this perspective can be found elsewhere than in reflection on the Christian liturgy. In the work of Levinas this encounter is located in the face of the other person, the self-expression of an otherness at once so opposed to my sameness and so undeniable as it breaks into that sameness, that its sheer presence commands me from to change myself, to rise up from my previous narcissism into a responsibility able to see beyond animal impulses. The "Highness" (*hauteur*) of the other whose presence alone represents an imperious command is, for Levinas, the necessary condition of the upright posture which defines each of us as responsible subjects. It stands to reason, of course, that Levinas then speaks of the good fortune of the subject thus freed from enslavement to his or her animality, but he also does not fail to state – in a remarkably Kantian moment – that what is truly noble about it is precisely its indifference to any sense of satisfaction or relief. "And yet Lord, I am not happy..."[19] In the philosophy of Levinas, this is never a complaint.

19. Emmanuel Levinas, "Transcendence et hauteur," *Liberté et commandement* (Paris: Fata Morgana, 1994) 67.

To the contrary, the Highness of Other demands vigilance against wrongly assimilating it, against interiorizing the revelation of what is by definition *ex*terior. It therefore also stands to reason that this extreme position leads Levinas away from any positive interest in myth, mysticism, and the category of the sacred, all of which he suspects of promoting metaphysical "participation" rather than religious plurality – unless underwritten by responsibility for the other person.[20]

The striking lesson to be taken from this line of thought, and above all from Levinas, is that any magnification of the vertical dimension of religious experience seems to imply a proportional diminishment of what can be termed the *horizontal* dimension, which would include all the elements of existential engagement – history, language, and corporeality. On this point, Marion's position can be directly opposed to that of Taylor: whereas Taylor seems ill-prepared to recognize the vertical dimension opened by religious symbol, Marion's strong definition of transcendence renders the horizontal dimension secondary at best. And yet, the two positions flirt with a similar danger. Taylor's opposition to any vertical dimension in religious experience hands everything over to an itinerant creativity in which what was once called "God" is dispersed in the cloudy water of subjectivism; when Marion's contrary emphasis on verticality removes God from the reach of any name or image rooted in our lived situation, he comes perilously close to the subjectivist illusion in which *one no longer possesses an adequate conception of the Other – God – for the simple reason that all we know with any confidence is that the Other is not-me.*[21] And the Other who is defined ultimately as not-me is an Other whose definition is still ultimately imaginary. One has not yet reached the real.

In order to understand this unexpected confluence of an austere philosophy of religion with fervent nihilism – and to take a large step back toward the theme of sacramentality – it is not enough to think only that Marion has adopted the Nietzschean vision of subjectivity and then failed to open it to divine revelation. Alongside this, his tendency to define the horizontal dimension of religious experience – again: history, language, corporeality – solely according to the question of capacity or incapacity to accommodate the gift given in the Eucharist, is

---

20. Emmanuel Levinas, "Lévy-Bruhl et la pensée contemporaine," *Entre nous: Essais sur le penser-à-l'autre* (Paris: Grasset, 1991) 53-67.

21. On the subjectivist illusion as the result of an exaggerated definition of the "vertical dimension," see Vergote, *Interprétation*, 100-101.

also a tendency to forget that the separate and original existence of the world is an important element in religious experience itself. For Marion, the world is the environment of my narcissism and self-idolatry, until the icon shatters that illusion by entering that world from infinitely afar. At that moment, the same distance defines the world as either "vain" or "beautiful and good," depending on whether it is viewed from my perspective or the inaccessible perspective of God.[22] In other words, there is nothing good in the world as I myself, *alone with myself*, live it, and what goodness can eventually be said of the world illumined by the icon comes from a source so far beyond me as to defy comprehension. Here again is a reminder of the inclination to dualism, this time in the implication that we can know nothing of how God relates to the world, which is to say not merely nothing about the interior life of God, the God beyond all revelation, but also God's exterior life here and now, in the present world. All that is possible is the reception of the eucharistic gift which, to be sure, transforms our own relation to the world by attuning us to the divine – but this falls well short of meeting God on some middle ground, in the world where, according to Scripture, God and people *work together* toward the coming of the Kingdom (see above).

It is necessary to insist on this aspect of Marion's thought in order to highlight the moment where he misses the possibility to better avoid the subjectivist illusion I mentioned earlier. After all, what is it that permits us to understand another person as more than not-me, if not the different way he or she inhabits what is nonetheless the same world? Perhaps what phenomenologists have long argued about interpersonal relations should also be extended to the relation with God: without the background of a common world belonging exclusively to neither of us, it is impossible to see more in the Other than a negation of oneself. (And this, it must be stressed, is a difficulty not yet overcome by the capacity to explain personal language about God as a response to the encounter with a distance which nonetheless consumes that language.) This difficulty can not be made to go away simply be saying that the world itself has meaning for me only in and as my response to the Transcendent – as Marion often implies, and Levinas argues explicitly. Unless our speech is always woven between a relation with the world and a relation to God – unless prayers and symbols have a history and culture – we will lose the means to relate to God as anything more than what is strictly wholly

22. Marion, *Dieu sans l'être*, 187.

Other. It is here that we would do well to heed the hermeneut's warn-
ing against mistaking a philosophical form – in the religious discourse
of postmodernity, Otherness – with the theological content it is meant
to interpret it: a personal God.[23]

Between these two poles, extreme nihilism on one hand and radical
apophansis on the other, the need to think the vertical and horizontal
dimensions of religious experience together directs us to the themes of
ritual and sacramentality. Among recent developments, it has been the
particular merit of Louis-Marie Chauvet and Jean-Yves Lacoste to call
new attention to the significance of corporeality in liturgy (I do not pre-
tend that they are in agreement on many important points). For
Lacoste, it is a matter of the gestures and the posture proper to the
liturgical relation; Lacoste thus reminds us that acts of worship are irreducibly corporeal, and that the proper sense of prayer does not aim at
forgetting the mortality that this entails.[24] Chauvet is more concerned
with the way the body is inscribed by language taken in the broadest
sense, as the network or symbolic order invested with the defining fea-
tures of culture and community; the latter sections of the First Part of
his *Symbole et sacrament* add to Lacoste's reminder the further notice
that one's senses of corporeality and mortality are themselves embedded
in a history, both personal and cultural.[25]

It matters little whether these two theologians can rightly be called
"postmodern" or, failing that, whether the canons of postmodernity can
be adjusted to include them. What ultimately deserves notice, however,
is the fact that each of them, according to markedly different proce-
dures, refuses to decide the issue of belief and unbelief in one direction
or the other. Chauvet's modest intention is only to protect the specific
integrity of the life of faith and practice of theology, alongside – *but not
raised over* – other ways of life and the practice of other disciplines.
Lacoste's argument exercises a similar restraint, utilizing phenomenology
to isolate anchoring points for a theology planted in the world described
by existential philosophy, *but without claiming the capacity to defeat it.*
One sees immediately that beyond an obvious methodological caution,
there is also a visible commitment to reinstating a conception of human
nature which admits continuity between belief and unbelief, and thus

---

23. I owe this thought to a conversation with Ben Vedder of the K.U. Tilburg.

24. See Jean-Yves Lacoste, *Expérience et Absolu: Questions disputées sur l'humanité de
l'homme* (Paris: P.U.F., 1994) 72, cf. 45-48.

25. Louis-Marie Chauvet, *Symbole et sacrament: Une relecture sacramentelle de l'existence
chrétienne* (Paris: Cerf, 1987).

perhaps of a theology no longer flatly opposed to disciplines starting from elsewhere than faith and revelation. And while it is probably too soon to rest in optimism at the promise of such ventures, one might at least take some consolation in the thought that not only does the world have something good about it, but faith and theology can afford to think so – even at the heart of their concerns.

Method in Postmodern Theology
A Case Study

Lieven Boeve

In his paper "The Postmodern Context and Sacramental Presence: Disputed Questions,"[1] J. Bloechl points to some important questions to be answered by theologians willing to think the structure of sacramentality today. These questions concern first of all (1) the definition of 'postmodern context,' whether this is a descriptive or rather a programmatic term, (2), the methodological relation between the data and reflections drawn from an in-depth analysis of the present context and the 'healthy growth of Christian tradition,' which includes theology, and (3) the status of religious experience in theology today.

Secondly, in his analysis of the work of Mark Taylor, who presents us a theology in a Derridean fashion, and of Jean-Luc Marion, who superposes a theological interruptive rationality upon philosophy, Bloechl reproaches the first for undervaluing verticality, and the second, the theologies of the 'event,' for severely neglecting the horizontal dimension in theology. But what is the place of language, history, bodiliness, and corporeality in thinking the mediation of God's active presence? In the whole of this debate the question remains which perspective finally sets the criteria for evaluation: a philosophical one (i.e. criteria stemming from a philosophy of religion) or a theological one? It is this last question on which I focus this contribution, although the other ones are touched upon in the course of it.

1. Philosophy and Theology: Whose Criteria?

It is clear that a crucial item for further discussion is the relation between philosophy and theology. Different positions on the field have been taken and defended.[2] So-called postmodern philosophies (philosophies of

---

1. See pp. 3-17 of this volume.

2. More recently, the encyclical of Pope John Paul II, *Fides et ratio*, has intensified this discussion. See Lieven Boeve, "The Swan or the Dove? Two Keys for Reading *Fides et Ratio*," *Philosophy and Theology* 12 (2000) 3-24.

difference) are welcomed by theologians for various reasons. Whereas a
first theological position – so to say – baptises these philosophies, and in
a way, reduces the Christian theological discourse to a seemingly mere
doubling of the philosophical, other positions precisely stress the difference between theological and philosophical discourses. Among the latter,
however, one still can distinguish between two manners of dealing with
this difference. Some theologians appreciate the latter for criticising the
exaggerated claims of modern thinking but perceive it only as a unique
opportunity to reintroduce Christian thinking patterns from of old.
Others in one way or another positively relate to postmodern thinking,
and strive for a fruitful interaction.

a. Who Rules Whom?

The work of Mark Taylor serves as an example of the first position.[3]
The philosophical deconstructive rationality by Derrida completely dic-
tates the way in which theological rationality should work, and results
in an immanentistic play of signs. As such, theology would seem to be
merely doubling cultural and philosophical sensibilities. In the same
vain, another theologian, Don Cupitt, pleads, e.g. in *The Time Being* for
a redefinition of Christianity: not for its secularisation but its imma-
nentisation and temporalisation. Herein, there is no reality behind the
appearances. All duality is based on secondary fiction: "there is only the
transient flux of language-formed, feeling coloured experience,"[4] and
nothing is behind it. There are no grounds to maintain the ideological
distinctions between fact and interpretation, mind and matter, things
and words, reality and appearance, religion and culture, revelation and
reason, divine truth and human theory. There is no other world than
our already verbalised world. Thinking is nothing but the moving chain
of signs and marks. Personality and self-consciousness are the eclectic
connection of parts of the flow, not the result of the spiritual activity of
the soul, and is *in se* totally immanent. The myth of transcendence has
to be broken down as a narrative construction. Religion has to be identified with its stories, its practices, its images. All is constructed out of

---

3. Cf. e.g. Mark C. Taylor, *Erring: A Postmodern A/theology* (Chicago: University of
Chicago Press, 1984); Mark C. Taylor, *Nots* (Chicago: University of Chicago Press,
1993). See the comments by Bloechl in "The Postmodern Context," and the reading of
Taylor offered by Georges De Schrijver in "Postmodernity and Theology," *Philippiniana
Sacra* 27 (1992) 439-452, pp. 443-449.
4. Don Cupitt, *The Time Being* (London: SCM, 1992) 15.

the flux of language-formed events. Cupitt's programme then for an new liberating, therapeutic Christianity against all dualism intends to convert religious theorising and vocabulary. On the waves of postmodernism he pleads for a totally immanent religion and gives up all transcendence, and thus theology engaged in thinking its mediation, e.g. in terms of sacramental presence. Immanent Christianity, identified with its stories and images, remains important for Cupitt, because it can offer a life-style adapted to postmodernity by helping people to live with their temporality, with the general and absolute contingency, preventing collective flight reactions into the fixed securities of fundamentalism and nationalism...

Theologians involved in *Radical Orthodoxy*,[5] on the contrary, welcome postmodern thinking only insofar as it makes apparent the devastation caused by secular modernity, resulting in anxiety, because of its lack of values and meaning. Radical Orthodoxy sees – and I quote from the *Introduction* to the volume – "the nihilistic drift of postmodernism (which nonetheless has roots in the outset of modernity) as a supreme opportunity ... to reclaim the world by situating its concerns and activities within a theological framework." "What emerges is a contemporary theological project made possible by the self-conscious superficiality of today's secularism." It gives up the project of modern correlation theologies which seek – as it were – an internal link with 'universal accounts of immanent value.' It criticises as well a (postmodern) theological "baptism of nihilism in the name of misconstrued 'negative theologies.' Instead, in the face of the secular demise of truth, it seeks to reconfigure theological truth."[6] Hereto it proposes a return to Augustinianism, a Christian framework of conceptuality, in which the modern aporias brought to the fore by postmodern nihilism, are resolved. The central key in this regard is the category of 'participation.' The finite only preserves its own integrity – in fact even its worldliness – when it participates in its infinite eternal source, whereas in modern epistemology and postmodern nihilism the integrity of the finite ultimately dissolves. Presence – thus also Eucharistic presence – therefore does not

---

5. See John Milbank, Catherine Pickstock and Graham Ward (eds.), *Radical Orthodoxy: A New Theology* (London/New York: Routledge, 1999) as well as John Milbank, *Theology and Social Theory: Beyond Secular Reason* (Oxford: Blackwell, 1994); Catherine Pickstock, *After Writing: On the Liturgical Consummation of Philosophy* (Oxford: Blackwell, 1997); Graham Ward (ed.), *The Postmodern God: A Theological Reader*, Blackwell Readings in Modern Theology (Oxford: Blackwell, 1998); Phillip Blond (ed.), *Post-secular Philosophy: Between Philosophy and Theology* (London/New York: Routledge, 1998).

6. "Introduction" in Milbank, Pickstock and Ward (eds.), *Radical Orthodoxy*, 15.

vanish in an immanentistic play of signs, only preserved in a concatenation of fragmentary and temporary 'now'-moments. Nor is it reduced to a traumatic, eventful breaking in of transcendence in a world enclosed in itself. Both these strategies think presence by accentuating and isolating the present as a 'now-moment.' In terms of a radical orthodox strategy, the presence in the 'now' is immediately related to the eternal: "The present is not a discrete and isolatable entity, as Augustine reminds us." For such a view implies a 'violation of time.' For Augustine, the now always recollects the past and looks ahead to the future – it participates in an encompassing continuity, exceeding the present. Moreover, the modern and postmodern isolation of the 'now' render it impossible to think liturgical presence. "For the Eucharist participates in a temporal plenitude that gathers up and rehearses the past, while drawing upon futural expectations and significations of the act in the present."[7] In the words of the *Introduction*: "the theological perspective of participation saves the appearances by exceeding them."[8] Good philosophy, one could say, finds in a radical orthodox perspective its completion in the Christian *vera philosophia*.

It would be worth asking, however, whether one could not read the broadening of the scope of phenomenology in what has been called 'the theological turn of French phenomenology,' along the same lines – with a different outcome, no doubt. By this I mean the insertion of philosophy in a theological configuration as the criterion for good philosophy.[9] Jean-Luc Marion,[10] as well as Jean-Yves Lacoste,[11] analyse Heidegger's phenomenological account of the world as closure. The world constitutes a horizon of meaning without God. The logic of the gift (Marion) and of the liturgical attitude (Lacoste), however, break open such a closed horizon and reveal its posteriority. The world, beings and Being, is

7. Graham Ward, "The Church as the Erotic Community," *Sacramental Presence in a Postmodern Context: Fundamental-Theological Approaches*, ed. Lieven Boeve and Lambert Leijssen; BETL, 160 (Leuven: Leuven University Press/Peeters, 2001) 167-204.

8. "Introduction," in Milbank, Pickstock and Ward (eds.), *Radical Orthodoxy*, 4.

9. Cf. Dominique Janicaud, *Le tournant théologique de la phenoménologie française* (Paris: Éditions de l'Éclat, 1991).

10. Jean-Luc Marion, *Dieu sans l'être* (Paris: Fayard, 1982). In *Étant donné: essai d'une phénoménologie de la donation* (Paris: P.U.F., 1997) Marion claims to be able to show phenomenologically (and not any longer only theologically) the priority of the logic of gift over the logic of Being. For a sympathetic theological evaluation, see S. Van den Bossche, "God Does Appear in Immanence after All," *Sacramental Presence in a Postmodern Context* (n. 7), 325-346.

11. Jean-Yves Lacoste, *Expérience et Absolu: Questions disputées sur l'humanité de l'homme* (Paris: P.U.F., 1994).

already given (Marion); its closure is radically opened up from the encounter with the Absolute (Lacoste).

b. Recontextualisation and the Intrinsic Bond of Theology with Philosophy

The third position mentioned above accentuates both the difference as well as the internal link between philosophical and theological discourses. Such a connection of theology with philosophy (and other disciplines reflecting upon, and from, the contemporary condition), however, does not imply that the former ultimately supersedes the latter and would dictate its proper rationality, nor the reverse. Both discourses here do not enter a competition, but, from the theologian's perspective, relate intrinsically to each other.

The investigations of Kevin Hart concerning whether the method of deconstruction can help theologians to understand the relation between apophatic and kataphatic theologies illustrate this methodological position.[12] It is Hart's aim to bring "deconstruction into conversation with Christian theology, rather than confirming Derrida's individual programme." Deconstruction, according to Hart is not a refined version of Nietzsche's 'God is dead,' neither a crypto-'negative theology.' What is at stake in deconstruction is not the delegitimising of theology as such, but of metaphysics – meaning that only theologies grounding their claims upon metaphysics, are addressed. Deconstruction helps theologians to trace back the metaphysical "reflexes" in theology, and also to see the limits of any attempt at non-metaphysical theology. From this perspective, Hart shows how deconstruction as a method – not as a negative theology in disguise itself – helps to perceive the tradition of negative theology as the deconstruction and, at same time, condition of positive theology:

> In general terms, deconstruction helps to clarify the concept 'non-metaphysical theology,' while its strategy of using language 'under erasure' lluminates particular moves and attitudes in mystical texts.[13]

A major example of such fundamental theological reflection about sacramentality within this methodological perspective is the theological work of Louis-Marie Chauvet. In the first part of his *Symbole et sacrement*,[14] Chauvet explains that thinking sacramentality within an onto-theological

---

12. Kevin Hart, *The Trespass of the Sign: Deconstruction, Theology and Philosophy* (Cambridge: Cambridge University Press, 1989).

13. *Ibid.*, xi.

14. Cf. Louis-Marie Chauvet, *Symbole et sacrement: Une relecture sacramentelle de l'existence chrétienne* (Paris: Cerf, 1987).

framework involving productionist schemes of causality (i.e. departing from foundational metaphysics), ends up in idolatry. He shares Heidegger's criticisms of onto-theology, in remembering the ontological difference. Moreover, to proceed theologically, Chauvet claims that there is a 'homology of attitudes' between Heidegger's anthropological thinking and a contemporary theological anthropology. The relation between a human subject ('Dasein') and Being is homologous to the relation of the believer to God. God's presence to the believer is thought of in a similar thinking pattern to that of Heidegger's thinking the manifes-tation of Being, which is also and at the same time the withdrawal of Being, i.e., in revealing God constantly withdraws. This positing of a homology in no way tends to identify the two; on the contrary, it implies that neither is reducible to the other.[15] Heidegger's account of 'Dasein' and the Christain faith are both distinct ways of living, anchored within two irreducibly different, co-existing, symbolic orders. For, with Heidegger, Chauvet accepts that, because of the fact that Being always has already withdrawn, we are left, abandoned in a histor-ically determined particular context. As such, we are embedded in a narrativity which is anterior to our identity; we belong to a symbolic order that irreducibly surrounds and determines us.[16] Methodologically, philosophy serves theology both in situating the Christian faith in an anthropological and epistemological perspective, and in helping to express theologically what faith is. Philosophical clarification and theo-logical motivation go hand in hand here: a specific particular narrativity is developed in its normativity.

The basic assumption of these positions is the acceptance of a legiti-mate plurality of discourses. Philosophy and theology are discourses in their own right, and the latter is not reducible to, nor dominated by the former. Theology, however, cannot simply dismiss philosophy – and this for reasons proper to theological methodology. At work in on-going theo-logical reflection, as in Christian tradition in general, is a process of *recon-textualisation*. When contexts shift, theology, because of its inherently

---

15. Chauvet, *Symbole et sacrement*, 78-79.

16. Chauvet finds his resistance to metaphysical theological foundations and his open-ness for symbolic thinking as a way for theology to escape from onto-theology also con-firmed in psychoanalysis. In the perspective of Lacan every foundation of absolutely secured identity belongs to the imaginary. Living from this insight, i.e. coping with the insatiable desire for secured identity, without attempting to give into it by wishing to sat-isfy it completely, implies entering a (particular) symbolic order, circling around what is revealed in the desire. Identity construction, therefore, is coping with the rupture in one's identification, to learn to live with the desire of desire, without filling it in completely.

contextual footing, is challenged time and again to re-engage in its dialogue with contemporary critical consciousness, which often takes shape in the philosophy of the time. For theological plausibility is always contextual plausibility, embedded in particular horizons of meaning. From its beginnings, theology has adopted philosophical categories and conceptual frames to structure its own dialogue. These have entered the theological discourse, not to be baptised as crypto-theology, but to assist in constructing a theology which was reflexively plausible for Christians living in those days. Once integrated in a theological discourse, these categories and frames have become irreducibly theological, fitting within the rules of a discourse meant to be *fides quaerens intellectum*.[17] When contexts change, however, theology is pressed to reconsider its relation to the context. That is the reason why in our time of postmodern criticism of metaphysics and grand narratives, theology needs to recontextualise. This implies not only (1) engaging in a confrontation with contextual critical consciousness (self-criticism) but also, and more importantly, (2) searching for a contextually anchored understanding of our Christian faith, i.e. developing a theology for today. In both, philosophy's assistance is both necessary and welcome.

c. Thinking Sacramental Presence as Interruptive Event

In "Postmodern Sacramento-Theology: Retelling the Christian Story,"[18] I have shown that from the dialogue with contemporary critical consciousness (which stresses the radical plurality of discourses, the irreducible particularity of our narratives and the heterogeneity which surrounds and challenges all attempts at identity[19]), the relation between transcendence and immanence can be reconceived. Transcendence then no longer denotes a pre-modern, Neo-platonic 'presence' or a modern, as it were Hegelian, 'identity.' In the postmodern context of plurality, transcendence rather is conceived in accord with the interrupting event of heterogeneity which confronts us with the particularity and contingency of our own (Christian) engagement with reality. Transcendence,

---

17. I have elaborated on this recontextualisation perspective in Lieven Boeve, "Bearing Witness to the Differend: A Model for Theologizing in the Postmodern Context," *Louvain Studies* 20 (1995) 362-368.

18. Lieven Boeve, "Post-Modern Sacramento-Theology: Retelling the Christian Story," *Ephemerides Theologicae Lovanienses* 74 (1998) 326-343.

19. In this regard, see also my "Critical Consciousness in the Postmodern Condition: A New Opportunity for Theology?," *Philosophy and Theology* 10 (1997) 449-468.

as event, interrupts and disturbs the on-going particular narrative, challenging this narrative to open itself to the heterogeneity which breaks through in that event. The religiously experienced and interpreted relationship to the transcendent can thus no longer be conceived as premodern 'participation' in salvific presence, or as modern 'anticipation' of the ultimate identity. The Christian narrative which has become conscious of its own particularity and contingency can only adequately relate to the transcendent by, on one hand, *opening itself up* – cultivating a sort of contemplative openness into which the transcendent as interruptive event can enter – and on the other hand, by *witnessing* in a non-hegemonic way to the transcendent with the help of its own, always fragmentary words, images, stories, symbols and rituals. The sacramentality of existence does not offer us insight into some underlying foundational order, legitimating the existing narrative. Nor does it provide the redemption manifestly lacking in an unredeemed world. To the contrary, it opens up precisely that unredeemedness, that moment of interruption, to which no closed narrative does justice. This sacramentality points toward neither an ahistorical ontological depth inviting human similitude, nor a history whose fulfilment is insured through a process of maturation, but instead undermines such self-assuring human constructions.

These theological elaborations are – in line with the recontextualisation paradigm of theology – due to an intense dialogue with the philosophy of Jean-François Lyotard (both his language pragmatics and his esthetical thinking[20]). The tension created by the constant and inevitable escape of heterogeneity – or in esthetic categories: the sublime – from each particular attempt to give it expression – or to (re)present it – serves as the basis for a reconceptualisation of the dialectical relationship between transcendence and immanence, a relationship that is fundamental for the Christian tradition. Using Lyotard's thinking strategy, transcendence then is clarified as an ineffable, unpresentable moment of disruption or interruption in the midst of the immanent reality (of language and artistic presentation). But such an endeavour does not go uncriticised. In what follows we present, as a kind of case

---

20. Cf. Jean-François Lyotard, *Le différend* (Paris: Minuit, 1983); *L'enthousiasme: La critique kantienne de l'histoire* (Paris: Galilée, 1986); and *Tombeau de l'intellectuel et autres papiers* (Paris: Galilée, 1984); for his aesthetics, apart from *Le postmoderne expliqué aux enfants: Correspondance 1982-1985* (Paris: Galilée, 1986) see especially *L'inhumain: Causeries sur le temps* (Paris: Galilée, 1988), and his study of Kant's aesthetics of the sublime in *Leçons sur l'analytique du sublime* (Paris: Galilée, 1991).

study, a discussion on the legitimacy of using Lyotard's thinking patterns to theologise[21].

2. A Case-study: Lyotard and Theology

Is it possible to fruitfully receive Lyotard's thinking in theology? The German theologian Saskia Wendel, having devoted herself to a study of Lyotard's aesthetics[22], is not convinced. In 1993 she published her judgement on the useability of his thinking for theology[23]. Her negative evaluation is not without importance for theology wishing to recontextualise itself in a postmodern context, in particular our attempts in this regard.

a. Lyotard: Inspiration for Theology? Wendel's 'No'

Both title, "Ästhetik des Erhabenen – Ästhetische Theologie?" and subtitle, "Zur Bedeutung des Nicht-Darstellbaren bei Jean-François Lyotard," reveal the focus of Wendel's research: How far does Lyotard's aesthetics of the sublime open perspectives for theologians to speak of God?

In her discussion, Wendel first deals with Kant's conceptualisation of the sublime, in contrast to his aesthetics of the beautiful, and later on, with the reception of Kant's 'Analytik des Erhabenen' in Lyotard. Subsequently, she wonders whether a surreptitious theology lies behind Lyotard's aesthetics of the sublime. She even sketches four starting points for such a theology – starting points that could tempt the theologian to

---

21. Also on other occasions I have dealt with this dialogue: see, for example, "Bearing Witness to the Differend;" "Critical Consciousness in the Postmodern Condition;" "J.-F. Lyotard's Critique of Master Narratives: Towards a Postmodern Political Theology?," *Liberation Theologies on Shifting Grounds: A Clash of Socio-Economic and Cultural Paradigms,* ed. Georges De Schrijver; BETL, 135 (Leuven: Leuven University Press/Peeters, 1998) 296-314; and "Postmoderne politieke theologie? Johann Baptist Metz in gesprek met het actuele kritische bewustzijn," *Tijdschrift voor Theologie* 39 (1999) 244-264.

22. Cf. Saskia Wendel, *Jean-François Lyotard: Ästhetisches Ethos* (München, 1997).

23. Cf. Saskia Wendel, "Ästhetik des Erhabenen – Ästhetische Theologie? Zur Bedeutung des Nicht-Darstellbaren bei Jean-François Lyotard," *Das Ende der alten Gewißheiten: Theologische Auseinandersetzungen mit der Postmoderne,* ed. Walter Lesch and Georg Schwind (Mainz: Grünewald, 1993) 48-72. She has elaborated on the feasability of a 'postmodern theology' in a similar fashion in "Postmoderne Theologie? Zum Verhältnis von christlicher Theologie und postmoderner Philosophie," *Fundamentaltheologie: Fluchtlinien und gegenwärtige Herausforderungen,* ed. Klaus Müller (Regensburg: Pustet, 1998) 193-214 (for bio-bibliographic data on Wendel, see *ibid.,* 458).

identify the non-presentable (the sublime, that which presents itself in the experience of the non-presentability of the non-presentable) with the divine, with God.

(a) The partnership of pleasure and displeasure ('Lust und Schrecken') in the experience of the sublime reminds one, according to Wendel, of Rudolf Otto's 'holy' as '*mysterium fascinosum et tremendum*.'

(b) The non-presentability of a (the) non-presentable could be related to mystical negative theology, and thus the sublime feeling to mystical experience.

(c) In Lyotard's considerations regarding the 'event' as a non-temporal now-moment, reminiscences of epiphany are present: "die Offenbarung des Göttlichen im Augenblick, im Blitz der mystischen Erfahrung."[24]

(d) Likewise the paradox between, on the one hand, the reaction to the event of amazed and powerless silence and, on the other, the demand to give witness, can be fleshed out religiously from mysticism.

All of these starting points, as already mentioned, could result in the identification of the sublime feeling with the experience of the divine – of the non-presentable with God. Lyotard would then be recognised as the (philosophical) representative of the tradition of Jewish mysticism, just like other French thinkers like Levinas and Derrida. Postmodern thinking would then be made fruitful for theology – the end of theology has been too prematurely proclaimed.

But such conclusions are made too hastily. According to Wendel, theologians commit two mistakes when they proceed in this way.

> The religious interpretation of both the non-presentable and the sublime feeling, according to me, is due, first, to a shortened explanation of the sublime already in Kant [1a], which is then transferred to Lyotard [1b], and also, secondly, to a similarly shortened interpretation of Lyotard's texts [2].[25]

Wendel even goes further in her rejection of the fruitfulness of Lyotard's thinking for theology. Also a modified reception of his aesthetics in what could then be called a postmodern aesthetic theology is dismissed by Wendel. For this claim, she sees three arguments: the specificity of Lyotard's aesthetic inquiry [3a], the negation of the question on meaning in Lyotard [3b] and the impossibility of a thinking

---

24. Wendel, "Ästhetik des Erhabenen – Ästhetische Theologie?," 58.
25. *Ibid.*, 59.

together of Lyotard's purpose with the Christian concept of God [3c]. Below, we follow Wendel's argument and shed light on her critical reflections (1a-b, 2 and 3a-c, respectively) as regards the presuppositions of theologians intending to integrate the thinking of Lyotard. Afterwards we provide a critical commentary and correction.

[1a] What do theologians do when they interpret the experience of the sublime and the non-presentable, as brought to the fore in *Kant*, in *religious terms*? Either, when the sublime is equated with God, they hypostatise the sublime feeling to a being, while for Kant it is purely about a subjective feeling. Or they hypostatise the non-presentable – which is in Kant's view characteristic for the Ideas of the *Vernunft*, from which the non-presentability in the sublime feeling is revealed – to a non-presentable divine being. For Kant, 'God' is, to be sure, a necessary Idea of the *Vernunft*, but herewith nothing is said of its objective reality. Or they ultimately do not respect what is intrinsic to the aesthetics of the sublime. The latter instead bears witness to the 'sublime in our nature,' to the Idea of freedom and morality, rather than to something that can be identified with the 'powerless religious subjugation of a people that bends its knees in worship before its Godhead.'

[1b] Wendel concludes: if theologians already misunderstand the aesthetic thinking in Kant attempting to interpret it religiously, how much more do they *misunderstand* the point of *Lyotard's* aesthetics of the sublime. Lyotard as well is discussing the status of Ideas when he brings up the non-presentable.

[2] Moreover, concerning the non-presentable Lyotard is especially interested in the *event*: namely 'that it happens, that something happens.' His thinking is not about content, or significance, but about pure 'occurrence.' Lyotard does not enter into the question 'why is there something rather than nothing?' but deals with the question 'is there indeed something rather than nothing?' It is not the significance of being, but the being or not of being itself which is the focus of the question.[26]

To make clear what Lyotard is concerned with, Wendel directs herself – remarkably – to Lyotard's language pragmatics, his philosophy of phrases. By doing so, she hopes to demonstrate the contingency and immanence of the event in Lyotard. The event, after all, is the happening of a phrase and precisely this happening of the phrase as event cannot be grasped in the phrase. The happened phrase can only negatively present the event, which 'precedes' the happened phrase, along with the

---

26. Cf. Wendel, "Ästhetik des Erhabenen – Ästhetische Theologie?," 62.

presentation that happens in the phrase. This 'preceding' of the event cannot be interpreted as the non-presentable origin of the presentation, as a reality on the other side of the phrase-events. "Language has no origin," no expressible principle from which meaning ensues. *The* language as a unity does not exist, but rather only the plurality of phrases and genres of discourse. And further: "The non-presentable and absolute thus, in as far as it is the event and summit of Being itself, is not the One, the Universal, nor the Whole."[27]

Mindful of Lyotard's application of 'paralogy,'[28] Wendel labels his philosophy – which is based on heterogeneity, contrast and openness – as 'paralogical thinking.' Such thinking can never be reconciled with traditional Christian theology and the metaphysical thought involved in it.[29] The event can in no way be understood as an epiphany, as a revelation of the divine. The non-temporal now-moment is only an 'epiphany of the immanent event.' When Lyotard does use religiously connotated categories, then these function purely as "analogies for a secular state of affairs."[30] In short, Lyotard is no 'crypto-theologian,' nor a philosopher of religion.

[3] But given these conclusions, is it not thinkable that Lyotard, in a modified version, could nevertheless offer some inspiration for theology? One could aim, suggests Wendel, for a reception of Lyotard, analogous to the way in which Marx's thinking has been received in liberation theology. Liberation theologians were not afraid to turn to Marx, while at the same time criticising and correcting his atheistic presuppositions. Similarly one could revise Lyotard's thinking and construct an aesthetic theology on the basis of his aesthetics of the sublime. As said, Wendel rejects such a reception on three grounds: the distance of Lyotard from Kant (the primacy of the aesthetic) [a], the negation of the question on meaning in Lyotard [b], and the problematic definition of the concept of God [c].

---

27. Wendel, "Ästhetik des Erhabenen – Ästhetische Theologie?," 63.

28. In reference to Jean-François Lyotard, *La condition postmodern: Rapport sur le savoir* (Paris: Éditions de Minuit, 1979) 98-99.

29. We cite this not unimportant thesis: "Christian tradition defines God with reference to metaphysical thinking, at the one hand, as Origin and Creator, transcending the immanence of the world, and, at the other, as Trinity, and therefore as Difference, be it a triune of Unity. From this follows that Lyotard's non-presentable, which one definitely can not perceive as a transcendent, original Unity, is simply in contradiction with the concept of God in traditional theological thinking" (Wendel, "Ästhetik des Erhabenen – Ästhetische Theologie?," 64-65).

30. Wendel, "Ästhetik des Erhabenen – Ästhetische Theologie?," 65-66.

[3a] First of all, Wendel returns to Kant.[31] With him, religion belongs to the field of ethics. The existence of God is not a theoretical matter but is postulated practically. For Kant, the aesthetic is 'eine Vorstufe' towards ethics and religion. Both the esteem one has for the moral law (and for God), as well as the religious mood, are considered by Kant as analogous to the sublime feeling:

> In the sublime feeling is aesthetically revealed what is practically ensured. The sublime is, therefore, not only a praeambulum to morality, but to religion as well.[32]

In this way, the aesthetics of the sublime surely has theological relevance and can be received in the practical perspective of ethics. This argumentation does not hold true, however, says Wendel, when the aesthetics of the sublime is studied in the context of Lyotard's thinking; and this for two reasons: first, in Lyotard the aesthetic finality is no longer interpreted from the ethical (but the other way round); secondly, in Lyotard there is also no more ground for postulating a God. First of all, the non-deducibility of the ethical obligation (and specifically the event as well) is also present in Lyotard. Both, obligation and event, go hand in hand with a feeling of esteem (as a negative presentation of the non-presentable, be it the law, or the event[33]). But despite this parallel between Kant's ethical law and Lyotard's event, both cannot simply be identified. The law is homogenous and singular; the event, however, points to the irreducible heterogeneity of the genres of discourse. Moreover, the ethical in Lyotard needs to be interpreted precisely from the event: "The ethical [...] corresponds not in the least with the homogenous law, but with the heterogeneous event."[34] This leads us to the second reason: holding onto this irreducible heterogeneity precludes any possibility of ultimate reconciliation. Virtue and beatitude, however, demand the possibility of reconciliation. Therefore, given the absence of such reconciliation, the postulate of God is cancelled, because in Kant this postulate finds its ground precisely in the connection between virtue and beatitude.

[3b] A second reason to reject the theological relevance of Lyotard's thinking is the conscious absence of the question on meaning in his

---

31. For this, Wendel makes use of, aside from Kant's *Kritik der Urteilskraft*, *Die Religion innerhalb der Grenzen der bloßen Vernunft*.
32. Wendel "Ästhetik des Erhabenen – Ästhetische Theologie?," 68.
33. Cf. *ibid.*, 68.
34. *Ibid.*, 69.

philosophy: Lyotard inquires into the possibility of being ('is it happening?'), not into the grounds of this possibility and thus into the meaning of being. Here, the theologian could blame Lyotard for two things, says Wendel. On the one hand, Lyotard dogmatically excludes the question on meaning; in other words, he questions about the possibility of being, without actually pondering the possibility of nothing. On the other hand, if a last ground cannot be indicated somewhere which does not belong to the series of events, Lyotard is in danger of ending up in an unending regression of events. Wendel parries the first theological reproach with Kant: the one who is dogmatic is precisely the one who is not aware of the boundaries of knowledge and thinks he/she is able to demonstrate the objective reality of the transcendental Ideas, in this case the Idea of God. As regards the reproach on the unending regression, Wendel admits that this does not disturb Lyotard but precisely seems an opportunity for a thinking that is paralogous and goes beyond the established frameworks.

[3c] As a last reason, Wendel mentions the problems involved in the definition of God for theologians wanting to theologise proceeding from Lyotard. In this regard, she wonders whether God should be conceived of necessarily as unity, necessity, origin; and whether God cannot be understood as event. Wendel adds that the Christian concept of God has already been exposed to criticism repeatedly and its attributes have been questioned. She points for instance to feminist theology in which the fatherhood, the omnipotence, the Aristotelian presentation of God as the unmoved mover, etc. are criticised. But such critique does not go so far that the conception of (the essence) of God as unity, necessity or origin is rejected.

> From a Christian-theological perspective, the criticism of the traditional God concept finds its limits where the essence of the Divine is questioned. And precisely this happens when the definition of God as origin, as unity in Trinity, as transcendence in immanence, is cancelled.[35]

Theologians can possibly mitigate the identity thinking at the background of the Christian concept of God and make more space for difference (e.g. seeking alliances with Emmanuel Levinas), but they can never give up identity thinking itself. This means that they could never follow Lyotard. Theologians are posed with a choice: either theology, or postmodern thinking (*à la* Lyotard).

---

35. Wendel, "Ästhetik des Erhabenen – Ästhetische Theologie?," 71.

b. Critical Rejection of Wendel's 'No'

According to Wendel, Lyotard's aesthetics of the sublime does not open any perspectives for theologians. In her evaluation, his work is not considered relevant for contemporary theology. We, however, do not agree with her assessment. In our view, Wendel problematises from the very beginning, already in the way she poses her questions, any dialogue with Lyotard. In our evaluation of her position, (a) we first treat the (too) important place the thinking of Immanuel Kant enjoys in the discussion of the theological relevance of Lyotard's aesthetics. This will lead us to two deeper reflections, resp. (b) on Wendel's presentation of Lyotard's thinking (the place of aesthetics) and (c) the relationship between theology and philosophy, as this is implicitly contained in Wendel's argument. Where necessary, we will refer in our discussion to the numbers we have used to indicate the different arguments by Wendel.

(a) For her argument Wendel returns time and again to *Immanuel Kant*. She does this not only in order to shed light on Lyotard's aesthetics of the sublime, which is not misplaced due to the fact of the latter's dependence on Kant, but likewise to evaluate the theological plausibility of Lyotard's thinking. First Kant serves, so to speak, as the referee to enable to impute dogmatism to Lyotard [3b]. Wendel also employs him in order to make clear that the aesthetics of Lyotard does not help in solving the question of the problematic of the existence of God. Kant's aesthetics is after all only a 'Vorstufe' of ethics and religion, and actually does not immediately – but only analogously – have anything to do with the problematic of God; the sublime feeling cannot be hypostatised (1ab). More important still: seeing that in Kant religion is brought into the discussion out of ethics, and in Lyotard, according to Wendel, ethics cannot possibly lead to the postulating of God, a theological reception of his aesthetics is already out of the question (3a). In other words, the connection between religion (theology) and philosophy is continuously fleshed out in a Kantian way: if one does no longer meet the Kantian conditions in order to speak reasonably about religion – and this is apparently the case with Lyotard – then such thinking cannot possess any theological relevance. The least one can say, is that this conclusion is a rather problematic; and this due to two reasons, which are now touched upon, but will be further developed, later, as a second and third element of critique.

A first reason by which Wendel's employment of Kant's philosophy as a referee is problematised, resides in the fact that Lyotard himself uses

Kant for his own ends. Lyotard teaches us to read Kant from his own standpoint, namely as a thinker of heterogeneity. Kant offers him the conceptual instruments to reflect on the present sensitivities. In his philosophy, Lyotard thus attempts to bear witness to the event by reflecting on it. When theologians, engaged in processes of recontextualisation, then wish to link up with Lyotard's postmodern thinking, the appropriate way does not seem to be the reading of Lyotard through Kantian lenses – but exactly the opposite. Moreover, Wendel's position has its own difficulties, which is shown by the awkward obfuscation of the importance of the reversal which Lyotard carries out in the relationship between ethics and aesthetics [3a]. If, in Kant, aesthetics ensues as 'Vorstufe' from ethics (the sublime feeling ultimately bears witness to the greatness of the person, the Idea of freedom), then the experience of the ethical obligation receives, as Wendel also states, an interpretation analogous to the feeling of the event. If this is so, would the change introduced by Lyotard to the Kantian pattern not problematise in advance every attempt at precisely demonstrating, from Kant, the impossibility of the reception of Lyotard in theology? Especially when one takes into consideration that the Kantian scheme – where aesthetics leads to ethics and religion is thought of out of ethics – is abandoned by Lyotard himself?

Secondly, the preferential place enjoyed by Kantian thinking in Wendel likewise follows from the relationship she implicitly holds between theology and philosophy – and which brings her own argument again into difficulties. For whoever reflects on religion only within a Kantian framework extends primacy to philosophy: religion becomes 'Vernunft-religion,' theology receives only its place within the boundaries philosophy has set. However, it may be expected of those having read Lyotard's language pragmatics, that they all the more respect the irreducible diversity of the genres of discourse, in this case of the philosophical and the theological discourse. Even then it is still possible – in respect to this irreducibility – to speak of mutual dependence, as we have made clear in our methodological considerations. The ambiguity of Wendel's position is shown again when she, as a theologian, refers to the concept of God. Here she immediately derives this concept from the classical Christian-theological tradition and obviously forgets about the Kantian perspective (as regards, among others, the objective reality of God) she presented otherwise as normative [3c]. This move makes us at least pose the question as to the nature of the theological hermeneutics she wishes to employ.

But as already mentioned, in our second and third points of evaluation of Wendel's position, we now add two reasons why the Kantian slant in Wendel hampers her assessment of the relevance of Lyotard's thinking for theology. We first (b) contest Wendel's reading of Lyotard and afterwards (c) question her presuppositions concerning the relationship between theology and philosophy.

(b) *Wendel's perception of Lyotard* proceeds from his aesthetic philosophy. Her inquiry into the feasability of a postmodern theology (is Lyotard's aesthetics theologically relevant, so that it is meaningful to speak of a postmodern theology?), makes it clear, moreover, that she does not go beyond his aesthetics. But, surprisingly, when she unfolds this further, she suddenly appeals to Lyotard's language pragmatics [2]. She uses the latter to clarify the aesthetic. In our opinion, however, whoever wants to investigate the relevance of Lyotard's 'postmodern' thinking for theology will do better by proceeding the other way round and read Lyotard from his language pragmatics. After all, that is precisely where he develops his 'postmodern' critique of the grand narratives (and thus also of Christianity). Precisely there he comprehensively sheds light on the phenomenon of the 'event.' And – in light of Wendel's preference for Kant – it is in his language pragmatics, that Lyotard disolves the philosophy of the subject through a 'philosophy of phrases.'[36] Hence, exactly in the opposite way, we would opt to proceed from Lyotard's language pragmatics to unfold the significance and importance of the 'event.' Only in a second step would we illuminate on the 'event' from Lyotard's aesthetical considerations – a procedure that is, for that matter, completely legitimate, given Lyotard's thesis that the aesthetic and the historico-political are analogously constituted.[37] In the light of this thesis, it is moreover surprising that Wendel holds onto the aesthetic perspective so exclusively, and the historico-political is mentioned only fragmentarily and supplementarily, while the latter is not subordinated to the aesthetic.

36. Cf. Jean-François Lyotard, *L'enthousiasme: la critique kantienne de l'histoire* (Paris: Galilée, 1986) 111-112. See our reflections upon this in "Theologie na het christelijke grote verhaal: In het spoor van Jean-François Lyotard," *Bijdragen: Tijdschrift voor filosofie en theologie* 55 (1994) 269-295 (with a summary in English).

37. For this claim, see Jean-François Lyotard, *Pérégrinations: loi, forme, événement* (Paris: Galilée, 1990) 45-46. "Undoubtedly both belong to the process of thinking that Kant called reflective judgment, which implies the ability of the mind to synthesize data, be it sensuous or socio-historical, without recourse to a predetermined rule." Furthermore, the chronology of Lyotard's work demonstrates that his more important aesthetic studies were published after the unfolding of his language pragmatics.

We certainly do not deny that the aesthetic is important for whoever
wants to understand what Lyotard wants to say with the term 'event';
what we do think is that for a correct understanding of it, it is better –
and for a possible reception in theology, more rewarding – to start from
language pragmatics, to indicate there the crucial role of the event and
later to shed light on this term from Lyotard's aesthetics of the sublime.
Wendel's aesthetic exclusivism is all the more obvious when one observes
that Lyotard's philosophy of the historico-political (the field of praxis)
would have been more helpful for discussing religion from a Kantian
(ethical) perspective. Even one who does not think in a Kantian way,
could preferably situate religion within the historico-political.[38]

Much more than in his aesthetics, Lyotard unfolds in his philosophy
of phrases perspectives to reflect on 'reality' within language. As we
have already pointed out, Lyotard there offers a way of thinking about
transcendence and immanence. Indeed, Wendel is right when she says
that the event is language-immanent [2]. But for Lyotard, that is also
the case for the 'subject' (as an instance in the phrase universe). One,
however, has to ask the question: what is 'language'? In the first place,
it is a concatenation of phrases in genres of discourse whereby the linkage is problematised each time and betrays (reveals) something that is
transcendent with regard to the happened phrases and regulating genres
of discourse. Whoever stands open for the event being thus revealed
feels propelled to bear witness to it and to thus develop an open discourse. Nonetheless, the event is never a phrase among phrases, or to be
traced back to a phrase, but always remains, even though it is 'language-
immanent' – transcendent with regard to the preceding and the following phrase, and with regard to the genres of discourse.

Furthermore, whoever broadens Lyotard's thinking into a model of
the 'open narrative,' in contrast the the structure of the 'grand' or 'master
narrative,'[39] has the opportunity to deal with theology as a narrative –
i.e., on the area of the historico-political – alongside Lyotard's philosophical narrative (i.e., his open discourse). The latter's new way of

---

38. Whoever proceeds from language pragmatics moreover realises that the aesthetic
is but *one* genre of discourse, while the historico-political is precisely the playing field of
the genres of discourse, the field where the linkages take place. Cf. Jean-François
Lyotard, *Le différend* (Paris: Éditions de Minuit, 1983) n. 190. In our model of the open
narrative, the narratives are to be situated in the historico-political field, where religions
profile themselves *par excellence* as narratives.

39. See my "Critical Consciousness in the Postmodern Condition," *Philosophy and
Theology* 10 (1997) 449-468.

reflecting about transcendence, then, not only becomes something with which theology is internally confronted, but likewise something that questions it, from the outside, as a different narrative. This brings us to the third element of our critique.

(c) *The relationship between theology and philosophy.* Why would theologians seek starting points for theologising precisely in Lyotard? Are they seduced to do so only in order to be able to call themselves – fashionably – 'postmodern'? And what do they look for in Lyotard? Wendel makes it seem as if Lyotard could offer – as Kant did with his 'Vernunftreligion'? – theologians a workable whole which enables them to practise their discipline, or at least she gives the impression that theologians expect this from Lyotard. Wendel surely is right in affirming that Lyotard does not provide this support initially – he is indeed neither a theologian nor a philosopher of religion – and that theologians cannot expect this of him. But is the question whether Lyotard can be made relevant for theology thereby settled? Is the choice – after having read Lyotard – either remaining a theologian or becoming a postmodern?

Actually, Wendel herself offers the key to solve this dilemma. She herself pointed to the methodological approach of liberation theology [3], especially to its interest in the Marxist socio-economic (and in Marxist frameworks, also cultural) analysis-tool (as this took shape in historical materialism). What did Latin American liberation theologians look for in Marx? To be sure not his radical rejection of religion as 'opium of the people.' They sought rather a method to bring their social context into the theological forum, especially the wast socio-economic inequality. In short, they wished to enable themselves to theologise plausibly and relevantly about the historico-political. These Marxist tools (already corrected by the neo-Marxists) offered them the possibility for recontextualising theological discourse. Marxist critical consciousness, which originally venture a hefty critique of religion, challenged theology to recontextualise its own specific religious consciousness, so that the confrontation of theology with the Marxist critical consciousness did not lead to the sublation of theology, but gave form to a specific Latin American liberation theology. This theology not only tested itself against this contemporary critical consciousness, but also corrected the latter within its own discourse. (It should not be surprising that today, because the then accepted Marxist critical consciousness has lost its plausibility, liberation theologians are challenged to further their recontextualisation and to look for new forms of contemporary critical

consciousness[40]). What, then, do theologians look for in Lyotard? Not for
an implicit (whether negative or not) theology which they wish to develop
further in their own name. They rather hope to encounter a plausible
form of current critical consciousness with which theology can confront
itself to its own benefit. In this respect In this respect Lyotard offers the
theologian a language for speaking about reality (in this case: language).

Within this broader framework of the relationship between philosophy and theology, the problem of Wendel's theological hermeneutics
also becomes clear. She ties down the God of the Christian tradition
to concepts, like those that were developed in the recontextualisation of
the Christian narrative at the time of the philosophical dominance of
metaphysics [2]. When Wendel then affirms that whoever no longer
thinks of God as origin, unity, identity, fundamentally does harm to the
'essence' of God [3c], this certainly raises serious questions from a
methodological perspective in terms of recontextualisation. During
times when classical metaphysics determined the frameworks of thought,
metaphysics indeed helped give shape to the reflexive clarification of the
Christian faith in God. But when one forgets the distinctness of theological discourse, i.e. that the terminology and thinking patterns theology borrows from philosophy are applied only within the discourse of
theology in order to refer to the God believed in, and when one wrongly
thinks that these categories borrowed from philosophy (cognitively)
describe the essence of God, then one opposes the hermeneutic consciousness that religion develops from its standing-in-relationship with
the holy itself.[41] In other words, metaphorical language which refers to
what in fact is (still) not grasped in the current discourse – and God can
never be grasped – is then literally understood and so loses all possibilities for making reference. 'God' then begins to function within a particular discourse, as an instance of this discourse, and no longer as transcendent with regard to it. And this is precisely made clear by a theory
of the open narrative grafted onto the postmodern thinking of Lyotard.[42]

40. Cf. among others, Frei Betto, "Did Liberation Theology Collapse with the
Berlin Wall?," *Theology Today* 41 (1994) 109-112; Duncan B. Forrester, "Can Liberation
Theology Survive 1989," *Scottish Journal of Theology* 47 (1994) 245-253. For a serious
attempt in this regard, see: Raúl Fornet Betancourt, *Filosofía intercultura*, Subsidios
didácticos, 3 (Mexico, 1994); and *Liberation Theologies on Shifting Grounds: A Clash of
Socio-Economic and Cultural Paradigms*, ed. Georges De Schrijver; BETL, 135 (Leuven:
Leuven University Press/Peeters, 1998).

41. See Richard Schaeffler, *Religion und kritisches Bewußtsein* (Freiburg: Alber, 1973).

42. See in this regard my "Postmodernism and Negative Theology: The A/theology of
the 'open narrative'," *Bijdragen: Tijdschrift voor filosofie en theologie* 58 (1997) 407-425.

It is indeed the case that certain terms in the theological narrative have become established, e.g. Father, Creator, Trinity, Logos... (3c). But it likewise counts here, that these terms actually cease to function when they really become literal. They thus form not so much a standard for rejecting every other language use that attempts to refer to God. One can perhaps better turn the relationship around. Such terms only retain their established status when their referential power is illuminated upon, or restored by new references, new metaphors. Whether the referential power of the term 'creator' to signify God is maintained in our times by further interpreting this concept as 'origin' is likewise a most pressing question. Perhaps, a perspective on the creative demand that ensues from the event offers better possibilities for referring to the being-creator of God.[43]

The same holds true for a theological reflection on sacramentality. To escape from metaphysical patterns which have become implausible to reflect upon our contemporary condition, one can attempt thinking God's mediation in terms of interruptive event. A postmodern sacramental perception of time, then, no longer reflects a pre-modern eternal continuum in which the actual 'now' participates. But neither is sacramental time embedded in a modern perspective of progress that cancels the 'now' in function of the future. Rather, sacramental time is the time of the interruptive, apocalyptic 'now-moment' ('kairos'), the event which opens up the particular and contingent, placing it in the perspective of the transcendent God, but without nullifying or cancelling its particularity and contingency. The event of grace – or the grace of the event – consists in precisely this: self-enclosed narratives are opened up, and this openness is remembered, experienced and celebrated. Living by this openness to what happens, the Christian narrative loses its hegemonic characteristics and becomes truly an 'open narrative.'

---

43. Together with Kurt Feyaerts, I have developed this further in "Religious Metaphors in a Postmodern Culture: Transverse Links between Apophatical Theology and Cognitive Semantics," *Metaphor and God-talk*, ed. Lieven Boeve and Kurt Feyaerts; Religions and Discourse, 2 (Bern: Peter Lang, 1999) 153-184.

PART TWO

YESTERDAY REVISITED:
RECOVERING THE PAST IN THE FACE OF
THE CHALLENGES OF THE POSTMODERN AGE

The Poetry of Transcendental Thomism
Postmodernity Anticipated and Challenged in Karl Rahner

Craig A. Baron

Postmodernism is a critique of foundationalism, such as the rational-ism, universalism, objectivism and certitude about truth and knowledge in the Enlightenment mind-set. It is a radical questioning of all estab-lished beliefs and ideas. The postmodern consciousness constitutes a radical break with the assumptions of previous generations.[1] Thomas Guarino characterizes it as a "type of thought that revolts against any totalizing understanding of reality."[2] Postmodernism is extremely critical of the tendency of modernism to claim an Archimedean point upon which to judge, as if beyond space and time, all things. It is specifically critical of the notion of universal truth, universal revelation and univer-sal experience. Postmodernism only recognizes truth relative to the community in which a person participates.[3] There are many human societies, hence there are many truths. As such, relativism and pluralism become central to the postmodern approach.

Karl Rahner was not a postmodern thinker in the technical sense. He was a modern thinker who was aware of the shortcomings of modernity. He knew only too well that modern thinking was in need of some refurbishment from the recent developments in existentialism and phenomenology. In this essay I would like to explore the adapt-ability and fecundity of Rahner's Transcendental Thomism to the post-modern context. There seems to be a 'poetic streak' in Rahner's work that seems to equip him to meet the philosophical challenges of today. My convictions are based on Rahner's exposure and incorporation of the seminal ideas of postmodernism in their embryonic stage while he was studying with a godfather of postmodernism, Martin Heidegger. My analysis will consist of four parts: (1) a situating of Rahner's work

---

1. Stanley Grenz, *A Primer on Postmodernism* (Grand Rapids, MI: Eerdmans, 1996) 13.
2. Thomas Guarino, "Postmodernity and Five Fundamental Theological Issues," *Theological Studies* (1996) 654.
3. Grenz, *A Primer on Postmodernism*, 14.

generally for postmodern explication; (2) a review of the basic postmodern insights of Heidegger to demonstrate the level of impact he
had on Rahner's theology; (3) an overview of the poststructuralism of
Jacques Derrida and some suggestions for how Rahner could be gently
chastised by the patron saint of deconstruction; (4) a few suggestions
will be given as to how Rahner's Transcendental Thomism, especially
when read in light of his ground breaking essay, "Priest and Poet," can
prepare Rahner to speak in an eloquent way about revelation that is
responsive to the 'play of signifiers' in postmodern linguistics but is still
faithful to the idea of revelation as manifestation and witness.

1. Karl Rahner and Postmodernism

Karl Rahner was evidently aware of this significant shift in the course
of intellectual history. In his essay, "Modern Piety and the Experience of
Retreats," he says that men and women are in a new historical and spiritual context, the end of the modern period, and one in which Christians will find some discomfort.[4] Rahner begins his only explicit essay
about postmodernism with the insights of Romano Guardini, as exhib-
ited in his book, *The End of the Modern World*, assumed as an intellectual backdrop. This discussion prompts Rahner to muse about what the
church will look like in the postmodern age. Specifically, he sees a
change in how the church will achieve self-realization as an ecclesial
body in the future. The stress will be on the local community.[5] Rahner's
forecast is that the church should be structured and active more along
the lines of the 'pilgrim people of God'. This model will be more democratic with each part or member involved in a shared process of decision
making and discernment. The Church of the postmodern age will not
just be an objective reality that one has to deal with, explains Rahner,
but rather an active subject finding expression in a specific community
of believers. Rahner continues his method of continuity and change by
stressing that in the 'new age' one cannot lose sight of the radical subjectivity of modernity when actualizing the communal model of the
church. With his new stress on the particular and the community, Rahner admits he is now working in a postmodern age.

---

4. Karl Rahner, "Modern Piety and the Experience of Retreats," *Theological Investigations,* Vol. 16 (New York: Seabury Press, 1983) 135.
    5. Rahner, "Modern Piety," 150.

2. Karl Rahner and the Postmodern Martin Heidegger

Heidegger demonstrates that the human being is always an 'interested' party. It is always immersed in the entertaining of the things of the world and the world itself. It is situated in a particular time, with many relations and attitudes to various things. The right way to get to know a range of entities is contingent in part upon the nature of those entities. Heidegger wants to focus on entities not on discerned information about entities.[6] Heidegger points out how often Western Philosophy has treated the entities of the world as "present-at-hand," as objects for easy categorization into theoretical knowledge. This unfortunate tendency is to homogenize beings by forcing the diverse beings and contexts of knowing into ready-made categories to facilitate systematic thinking. What could be called a worldview with a static nature. For Heidegger, Polt explains, all things are dependent for their existence on the fact that they are produced, asked, used and interpreted by human beings.[7] Heidegger unveils the primordial fact that Dasein is not one being among others but is at the center of beings. It brings all of them together. It creates world and world creates it. Or, one could say that Dasein is singular in that it is ontological, that is, it asks about and understands Being.[8]

Dasein is not a definite actual thing, but the possibility of various ways of being in the world. The human being can be religious, scientific, or artistic in one's thinking and living but whatever one decides it is always reached by way of a personal decision about how to be. Jack Bonsor explains,

> there is an intrinsic relationship between world and freedom. A world is an environment where things are functionally deployed for the human beings' projects (becoming). In turn these various projects (education, recreation, profession, etc.) reflect Dasein's being as freedom. And, in turn once more, Dasein is free to become because it finds itself in a world which offers possibilities, most fundamentally to be itself or not.[9]

Since Dasein is a possibility that can bestow actuality through its choices, Heidegger will not speak of categories but rather of human

---

6. Michael Inwood, *Heidegger* (New York: Oxford University Press, 1997) 10-12.
7. *Ibid.*, 17.
8. Martin Heidegger, *Being and Time* (New York: Harper and Row, 1962) 32.
9. *Ibid.*, 33.

existentials.[10] In other words, the human being along with all other things in the world do not possess a definable nature.

Dasein is in the world. It is not a self-enclosed subject with an immutable structure impervious to its external surroundings that just happens to inhabit a place. It is always engaged with beings and their world. Heidegger demonstrates how all knowing and understanding is contextualized and a product of its environment. The example of the 'table' shows what Heidegger has in mind. He explains how the table (or any object for that matter) is not first seen as an extended object (static reality with a definable nature) and later as for some human use. It is always first and primarily as something to be used by the human being. The human significance it carries is what matters. It is 'ready-to-hand'. The table is never viewed as distinct from its setting.[11] What the table 'means' is that it is a place where a human being writes his books and eats his meals, or is in the right place to meet one's needs or not.

Dasein's approach to the world is a practical one of circumspect concern.[12] Dasein and world are in complementarity to one another. World is not something we have; world is what we are. Heidegger dispenses with the notion that the subject is an independent substance existing above time and human society and dwelling intellectually in some detached transcendental realm.[13] Rather Dasein finds truth within a context; it is there that one finds out what things are. Truth and meaning are part of the public realm of Dasein's there. The language, customs, values, and family structures are created by the world in which Dasein dwells.[14] The subject-object distinction is not totally abandoned by Heidegger though. He moves it out of the primordial event of knowing to the derived state of knowing in judgment. The distinction between self and object only occurs when the object fails to meet the expectations assigned to it within its given contexts.

Heidegger is a rugged realist. He insists on the embeddedness of Dasein in the world. This becomes the basis for his challenging criticism of the philosophy of 'presence' in western thinking. Here, Being is confused with presence. The only things that are considered to exist are those that are present in the here and now. This is dualism. Heidegger

10. Inwood, *Heidegger*, 19-20.
11. *Ibid.*, 26-28.
12. *Ibid.*, 30-32.
13. Grenz, *A Primer on Postmodernism*, 105.
14. Jack A. Bonsor, *Athens and Jerusalem: The Role of Philosophy in Theology* (New York: Paulist Press, 1993) 126-129.

shows how being can be understood in connection with all dimensions of temporality: past, present, future. This realization will bring to light that being includes 'absence' as well as presence. According to Grenz, "an existing thing is not merely what presents itself to us in the present; it also includes what is not present to us because it is either past or future."[15]

Heidegger is interested in 'presencing the absent.' He wants to uncover those inconspicuous but constitutive structures that are determinative of thinking and being: historicity, throwness, possibility, otherness, linguisticality, and immersion.[16] By paying proper attention to such existential facts Heidegger brings about a fuller appreciation of the radical finitude of the human being. Dasein is being onto death, an orientation to nothingness. Here again Heidegger is undermining the western preoccupation with substance.

Karl Rahner was deeply influenced by the philosophy of Martin Heidegger. He was exposed to the seminal ideas of postmodernity in its embryonic stage while he was Heidegger's student at the University of Freiburg. Rahner attempted to incorporate the postmodern horizons of historicity, finitude, socio-cultural particularity, the contextualization of knowledge, otherness, difference and absence into his fundamental theology:[17] method and anthropology.

In his essay, "Reflections on Methodology in Theology," Rahner lists eight challenges that confront modern theology and they seem a partial response to his teacher. These issues must be included in any future theology if it is to be successful and in touch with reality. First, dogmatic definitions need to be interpreted, translated and transposed into a different theological language in order to be assimilable in any effective way in the present world. Second, there is a chronic pluralism in philosophy, theology and culture that is so vast that it is impossible for any one individual to master. There has been a knowledge explosion.[18] This is the major reason why a direct and positive approach to theology can no longer work. Third, we are particularly aware today about how difficult it is to be able to distinguish between the genuinely binding message of scripture and the conceptual models and modes belonging to

---

15. Grenz, *A Primer on Postmodernism*, 106.

16. Thomas G. Guarino, *Revelation and Truth: Unity and Plurality in Contemporary Theology* (Scranton PA: University of Scranton Press, 1993) 63.

17 *Ibid.*, 63.

18. Karl Rahner, "Reflections on Methodology in Theology," *Theological Investigations,* Vol. 11 (New York: Seabury Press, 1982) 72-73.

dogma, because of the conditioning of history. Fourth, theology must engage consistently in a direct dialogue with the natural and social sciences and it can no longer be communicated just through philosophy. Fifth, the theologian must realize that self-understanding is not communicated just through words, but also by original sources of knowledge that consist of images and practical reason.[19] Speculative reason is always limited in how much it can provide. Sixth, the theologian's ideas, premises, and preconceptions are realized today more than ever before to be all subjected to historical conditioning and the limitations of the particular epoch. Seventh, the theologian today must realize that our views are immediately in danger, by our own subjective inclinations, the moment they are no longer confronted by the convictions of society in an effective dialogue.[20] Truth has something to do with institutional life and practice says Rahner. Human knowledge cannot be achieved in isolation. Eighth, it is proper to theology to foster a 'return to mystery' in its work. The multiplicity of realities, experiences and ideas must be related to the one absolute mystery-God.[21] The doctrine of the incomprehensibility of God is enough to demonstrate that comprehensive knowledge is a deficient mode of knowing.[22] The formulations of faith need to be more modest since they always fall short of expressing the full reality as it actually is. There is no such thing for Rahner as a simple correspondence between ideas and reality.

Rahner is also indebted to Heidegger for his fundamental anthropology. The basic experience of being human is finitude. All people know they are not self-sufficient. Rahner says that this general experience has a specific character in the intellectual realm. Whenever a person experiences oneself as finite and therefore experiences oneself, one does so through an encounter with an 'infinite horizon'. Rahner's epistemology really is grounded in this act. He says that to be able to have the experience of finitude, one must have already transcended the self and moved into the infinite. We have to have some sense of the whole first before we can deal with the parts. Rahner explains that the infinite horizon of human questioning is experienced as a horizon which recedes further and further the more answers a person can discover.[23]

---

19. Rahner, "Reflections on Methodology," 74.
20. *Ibid.*, 80.
21. *Ibid.*, 102.
22. *Ibid.*, 104.
23. Karl Rahner, *Foundations of the Christian Faith: An Introduction to the Idea of Christianity* (New York: Crossroad, 1992) 32.

The involvement with the infinite horizon is necessary for all human knowing. The pre-apprehension of being is also called the *Vorgriff* by Rahner, which he got from Heidegger. The *Vorgriff* is not the infinite per se. It is only a trace of the infinite or an anticipation. This mandatory component for human knowing is usually known unthematically or unconsciously.[24] This experience of the vastness of being is considered a positive reality. It is not an encounter with the 'nothingness' of space or the emptiness of a vacuum. Rahner says the natural compulsion to reach out in movements of hope and curiosity to the other cannot be grounded in illusion (nothingness).[25]

The transcendental movement occurs through the mediation of the categorical objectivity of the objects of the world. The unthematic or thematic encounter with the *Vorgriff* can only take place through sensible contact with the people, places and things of the material world. The *Vorgriff,* as a metaphysical backdrop, only shows itself against a sense image and the abstracted concept in human intellection. The human being's 'being-in-the-world' is mandatory for self-actualization. It is through the world that one comes to be who/what one is. Time, world, and history mediate the subject to oneself.[26] The person's life is bound up with world history. One is "thrown" into a culture and time period over which one has little control. These factors determine human nature to a great extent. Therefore, one is dependent on the historical situation and is always aware of the historical limitations, historical origins, and the contingency of origins of human existence.[27] In this way, Rahner begins to step away from the static view of human nature being beyond time and space.

3. Heidegger and Language and Rahner's Appropriation

The later Heidegger was captivated by language and poetry, not that he never dealt with these things before, but he approached them in the advancing years of his career with more diligence. Heidegger believes that languages are alive. They change, grow, develop and are always

---

24. A. Carr, "Starting with the Human," *A World of Grace: An Introduction to the Themes and Foundations of Karl Rahner's Theology,* ed. Leo J. O'Donovan (New York: Seabury Press, 1989) 21.
25. Rahner, *Foundations of the Christian Faith,* 33.
26. *Ibid.,* 40.
27. *Ibid.,* 42.

open to new possibilities of meaning with each passing age. This means for him that words can never have fixed meanings. Language should never be viewed as a enduring tool for the exact representing of things or ideas. Language is really the 'unconcealment of beings'. The representational function of language always occurs in a particular or historical situation. The meaning understood for words is the product of the communal context. This means that truth can only be claimed depending on the interpretation of the time. This interpretation is forever evolving.

Often times it is claimed that an idea can be expressed unalterably by several different languages. The words change but the essence of the idea remains intact in all expressions. Heidegger would disagree. He said this could not be so because beings and facts present themselves differently depending on the culture/historical situation. There is no way to speak in a universal way in which all people will understand the message; even the most gifted translator cannot accomplish such a feat. It is impossible because of the deep connection between words and meaning.

Heidegger has a deep reverence for language. He is in awe at its power to reveal the world. Language is not at the disposal of the human being, says Heidegger, rather the human being is at its disposal. Language is the 'House of Being'. This is appreciated best in the case of poetry. Many thinkers have concluded that the most fundamental use of speech is everyday speech. But that is not the case for Heidegger. For him, everyday speech is dull and without flavor. The commonness of regular speech makes it just idle chatter with no ability to really 'speak' to people; it has lost its power to reveal or unconceal being. However, poetry has not fallen into such a base state. Poetry always has the potential to release new possibilities and transform the existence of Dasein.[28] Heidegger considers it the most fundamental form of language. Poetry is fundamental because it is the "elemental emergence into words, the becoming uncovered of existence or being in the world: saying as showing."[29] It communicates possibilities of 'moodness'. Moods are different ways of finding oneself in the world. The poetic moment is indeed rare but when it does happen it can lead to a radical transformation. Poetry touches reality more deeply and faithfully than other forms of language.

---

28. Richard Polt, *Heidegger: An Introduction* (Ithaca, NY: Cornell University Press, 1999) 176-177.

29. Martin Heidegger, *On the Way to Language* (San Francisco: Harper and Row, 1971) 122-123.

It has the ability to recapture the illuminating power that secretly resides in common words, unleashing a view of the world that may never have been seen before. Therefore, poetry is the essential unfolding of language. Language speaks, says Heidegger, through the human being and Being takes hold of Dasein through language.[30] Dasein has to listen for what the language has to say about Being.[31] This is a mystical event that shows that language is neither objective nor subjective.[32]

For Heidegger, the human being moves constantly within the distinction between beings and Being. This distinction sustains the relationship.[33] The tradition of the West has focused its attention on *what is disclosed* by the distinction. It has offered different versions of how Being and beings are different. Heidegger wants to think about the distinction itself. 'Dif-ference' names what is differing in the difference. The term signifies how Being and beings are carried outside of one another while at the same time carried to one another. The 'difference' is fundamental to Dasein, explains Heidegger. It is in the difference, in the distinction that Dasein comes to be, the clearing made available of the difference between Being and beings. The novelty of Heidegger's approach is in his attempt to 'step back' into the difference between Being and beings. He wants to think about the unthought. He thinks the unthought which is the oblivion where difference recedes. Heidegger considers this a returning to the essence of metaphysics: the rising up. Differentiating is a two-fold process. First, beings arrive in appearance with the coming over of Being. Second, the arrival of beings leads to concealment of Being.[34] Therefore, differentiating is the 'revealing-concealing-dif-fering' of being in language. According to Caputo:

> In the difference there is a granting of the historical horizon within which any given metaphysics takes place. It is the origin of every metaphysical epoch. In the opening up of the difference which prevails at any given time, the difference determines the whole horizon of manifestness the whole shape of the appearance in the given epoch.[35]

30. Polt, *Heidegger*, 177-178.

31. Martin Heidegger, *Poetry, Language and Thought* (New York: Harper and Row, 1971) 190.

32. Grenz, *A Primer on Postmodernism*, 108.

33. John D. Caputo, *Heidegger and Aquinas: An Essay on Overcoming Metaphysics* (New York: Fordham University Press, 1982) 147-148.

34. *Ibid.*, 151.

35. *Ibid.*, 156.

Heidegger claims that language itself produces meaning.[36] However, it is still true that language does perform communication, but it is more fundamentally the 'way' in which things emerge into presence. Speaking is the human response to the call which is addressed to the human being by the difference.[37]

Karl Rahner makes the postmodern turn to lingusticality most clearly in his essay "Priest and Poet." I am contending that his relationship to Heidegger has made this possible. While it is true that Heidegger's mature and developed conception of language is after *Being and Time*, there seems little doubt that in his earlier work there are at least pointers to what is to come later.[38] Rahner says that the word is more than thought; it is thought that has become incarnate.[39] The word is more than the mere externalization of thought by sound. The word is the corporeal state in which what is expressed in the present 'first' begins to exist by fashioning itself into this world-body. Rahner is tacitly critiquing the traditional understanding of language. His contention is that the word as embodied thought is more than thought, more original than thought. Rahner is adjusting to the postmodern view of language. He is saying that language has a life of its own. It breaks through speech or writing into many possibilities and allows itself to be open to fresh interpretations and meaning. Language is event for Rahner. It mysteriously reveals more than just thought. When brought to expression an excess of meaning or unconcealment is taking place. Rahner carries this initial insight into the relationship he sees between the different languages: No language can substitute for another. Language should never be considered a row of external facades behind which dwells simply one and the same thought. Rahner seems to suggest that the language event is an intrinsic component in the unveiling of Being. Rahner could be transcending the form/content distinction rejected by all postmodern thinkers since Gadamer.

Rahner shows a deep appreciation for the miracle of language. He says language is not at the disposal of humanity; its not a tool for the human to dominate; rather, language brings light to humanity. It is a gift from God. Rahner also is sensitive to different levels of unconcealment in language. There are the everyday words of the common life of

---

36. Caputo, *Heidegger and Aquinas*, 159.
37. *Ibid.*, 162.
38. Inwood, *Heidegger*, 8.
39. Karl Rahner, "Priest and Poet," *Theological Investigations*, Vol. 3 (New York: Seabury Press, 1982) 295.

Dasein. Rahner says these are shallow words without mystery; they are the words the humans can control. The words that are well-worn, familiar and obvious. However, there are other words that are not transparent. They are obscure but powerful in possibility and rich in meaning. These are primordial words. They are words capable of clearly rendering the infinity of reality. They evoke mystery. They bubble up from the deep recesses of Dasein. Rahner could be understood as saying that between Being and beings, within the difference, there is glimpsed that which makes the difference possible-eternal being. This is the 'obscure' that makes the event of appropriation possible.

Language is alive for Rahner and so words are not static realities. They change, reveal, conceal, sometimes say one thing, sometimes another. What the 'saying' says depends on the context and the particular language. Consequently, words have a history. Dasein is the only being who speaks and Dasein changes over time. He suggests this when he says, "words have a history...and as in the care of the history of man himself, there is only one true master of history: God."[40] There are no fixed meanings because of the historicity of being. For Rahner, God alone escapes in the eternal Triune essence. However, the incarnate God is conditioned like all other beings to time. The primordial words are words that cannot be defined according to Rahner. Attempting to force them into pre-fabricated meanings, kills the language. His postmodernism is clear here: "all definitions have constant recourse to new words, and this process must come to a stop with the ultimate words, whether there are absolutely the last possible words or merely those that constitute in fact the final point of man's reflexive self-interpretation. And yet these ultimate words possess only the 'simplicity' which conceals within itself all mysteries. These are the primordial words which form the basis of man's spiritual existence!"[41] Following what appears to be Heidegger, he says these primordial words say "something about everything" (Being), within which all things dwell. Therefore, Rahner eschews giving words definite meanings because of Dasein's historicity and the fluid nature of language.

One of the major criticisms of Western metaphysics by Heidegger is its bifurcation of reality. Rahner has absorbed that aversion here as well. He explains that there is a knowledge which stands before the mystery of unity and multiplicity, of the essence in appearance, of the whole in

40. Rahner, "Priest and Poet," 296.
41. *Ibid.*, 297.

the part and the part in the whole. This knowledge uses primordial words. The uttering of these words carries Dasein into the difference, into the in-between of subject and object. One is carried into the gap by the primordial words of the poet.

Rahner believes that every primordial word signifies a piece of reality. A door is mysteriously opened for humanity into the unfathomable depth of true reality. This makes the word more than a mere word. The primordial word does communicate its literal meaning but it also simultaneously reveals a spiritual meaning.[42] This spiritual component transcends the literal confines of the meaning of the word. Rahner may very well be suggesting here that words not only have indefinite meaning, but also words say more than the speaker/writer intends or audience expects because of its expressing of Being. This approach gives Rahner the ability to detach author and text as postmodernism demands.

4. The Deconstruction of Jacques Derrida and Karl Rahner

The major thrust of the work of Derrida is the deconstruction of the 'logocentricism' of the Western philosophical tradition, which amounts to a critique of language. Derrida challenges the "realist" understanding of language that has dominated thinking since Plato and Aristotle. This is the view that words and language themselves are capable of representing the world as it exists in objectivity. Or, to come at it another way, in language, specifically spoken language, meaning is present to the speaker through a process of self-reflection which assures an "intuitive fit" between intention and utterance.[43] This version of language says that reality is static and can perfectly mirror and/or represent the external world through the intercession of words and concepts. Additionally, the words used to describe what is external are considered fixed in meaning so as to be able to accurately capture reality for all those who use them and assure clear communication between dialoguing individuals. This is the correspondence theory of truth.

Derrida wants to lift this veil of misconception about language. He is interested in bringing to attention the fact that the written word is open to many hermeneutical possibilities and here is where Derrida's critique of logocentricism comes in. Logocentrism is the philosophical method in

42. Rahner, "Priest and Poet," 298.
43. Christopher Norris, *Deconstruction: Theory and Practice* (New York: Routledge, 1993) 23.

Western thinking that looks to the logos or the word or language or reason as the communicator of meaning and truth. The presupposition is
that language is founded on a 'presence of being' or essence that humanity can come to know. Presence, essence, and truth are the ultimate terms
used to express this foundation and Derrida categorizes this approach as
'onto-theological'; because it advocates something beyond language, and
even in some cases beyond the human being, as the foundation and
anchor for thought: God, being, and world-spirit. These extra-linguistic,
extra-mental referents, Derrida calls "transcendental signifiers."[44]

Derrida attacks the veracity of presence and he explains why this is a
faulty view when he points out that language is based on the dynamism
of 'differing' and 'deffering'. Meaning does not reside in the intention of
the isolated, self-reflected consciousness. The meaning of words is contextual, that is, it is produced by a process of interaction between the
various juxtaposed words that together form the sentence. What a word
means is based on what is mentioned in connection with it. One can
'infer' the sense from the linguistic particulars of the utterance. Derrida
would say in that way meaning is 'produced'. These positive and negative relationships between the components of language are the play of
'difference'. Additionally, Derrida also says that words 'defer'. There is a
distinction to be made between spoken words and the corresponding
idea or concept. Meaning does not arise out of connecting a word and
an idea. It is never the case, says Derrida, as has so long been held, that
speech is in a more direct connection with reality or meaning because
the speaker's intention can be discerned and function as a foundation
for meaning, with writing being treated as a symbol of absence and a
depreciated capacity to presence because of its distance from its source.
Rather, meaning comes into being solely from within the textual-
linguistic context. This means that, says Derrida, speech and thoughts
are disconnected. The binary oppositions between the components of
the linguistic sign, the signified and the signifier, are deconstructed by
Derrida. He says that there is no difference between the signifier and
signified. Both are merely representations of representations,and so,
ideas are signs of images, and words are signs of ideas. For Derrida,
then, the world is known by the representation of images and not
correlation.[45]

44. Jacques Derrida, *Of Grammatology* (Baltimore, MD: Johns Hopkins University
Press, 1976) 49.
45. David B. Barrett (ed.), *The Discerning Reader: Christian Perspectives on Literature
and Theory* (Grand Rapids: Baker Book House, 1995) 123.

And yet, Derrida does not say that all language is meaningless. He claims that some dependable meaning is present in what he calls 'the trace'. The trace is the meaning of a now absent reality that has left the mark of connection with former elements. This means that the text is open to a plethora of interpretations with only hints of former meanings. No definitive reading of a text can be given. For Derrida, there is nothing beyond the text. He wants to replace logos with trace: the trace is in fact the absolute origin of sense in general which amounts to saying that there is no absolute origin of sense.[46]

The theology of Karl Rahner in general and his views on language in particular bear the marks of someone trying to come to grips with the central tenets of postmodernism. However, he does not go so far as to anticipate the radical version advocated by Derrida. He remains engaged in an earlier and more gentle form of postmodernism. And yet, there is room for more radical postmodern upgrading. Rahner could be tutored about selected themes in Derrida, such as those just outlined, to enhance his postmodern leanings and in the process extend the longevity of his theological influence.

For all of Rahner's theological and philosophical acumen, he does remain rather steadfastly locked in the transcendental view of human knowing as a universal structure. There is a foundationalism in his thinking. The postulating of a nonlinguistic encounter with the *Vorgriff* is an example of a metaphysics of presence. Relatedly, there is a conviction in Rahner of an enduring sense of self or subjectivity that functions as the basis for all of human activity. It is foundational not so much as an encased ego with an absolutely defined essence, but one with an enduring core personality shaped by its interactions with the other.

Rahner's philosophy of symbol could also be upgraded. He believes that symbols participate in the reality they represent and this participation is to such a great degree as to be able to make present the signified by the signifier. The Eucharist is a trans-signified symbol that makes the incarnate God present in the consecrated bread and wine. Therefore, Rahner does not see a gulf between thoughts/images and words/expressions.

For some postmodern thinkers, Rahner seems sensitive enough to the historicity of being.[47] He acknowledges its intrinsic temporality and its

---

46. Barrett (ed.), *The Discerning Reader*, 124.

47. Kevin Hogan, "Entering into Otherness: The Postmodern Critique of the Subject and Karl Rahner's Theological Anthropology," *Horizons* 25 (1998) 181-202.

mutability as it encounters different situations in the world. The human being is formed by the choices one makes from among the particular possibilities that present themselves in that context. However, Rahner does seem to fall short from incorporating the linguisticality of being in all of its dimensions. His notion of language could be enhanced by the introduction of difference. Sensitivity to difference would soften the philosophical anthropology of Rahner. The lessening of dependence on a metaphysics of subjective presence would logically lead to a reduction in his realistic linguistics.

5. Karl Rahner, Derrida and Revelation

I believe the article "Priest and Poet" is an essay that tacitly tries to balance the extreme confidence of modernism with the skepticism of postmodernism. Rahner speaks eloquently about the role of the priest, as the proclaimer of God's word as it has been entrusted to the church, and that of the poet, who playfully shows that all language opens up to a rich variety of interpretations because of the mystery of creation. Rahner hints in his analysis of language at what a poetically inspired theology of revelation would look like in this essay. Language is at the heart of the 'word event' known as revelation, he explains. All human knowing is intrinsically connected to language; even the infinite God is found most perfectly through the expression of words. Rahner actually says that and then immediately begins to pull back from the capacity of language to communicate and bring things into presence. He is cautious about emphasizing too strongly the ability of language to express matters so definitively. Rahner describes why he is so hesitant, "were it not to sound exclusively negative, destructive, one could say that negation alone lives in it." He continues, "the word alone is the gesture which transcends everything that can be represented and imagined, to refer us to infinity."[48] One possible interpretation of Rahner on this point would be to say that he is cognitively troubled by the 'trace' character of language and its inability to capture reality and render it totally present. His use of the word 'gesture' could be substituted for trace. Language is never for Rahner just presence but always includes the negative moment of absence as well. All words have this tendency – a tendency to lose or

---

48. Rahner, "Priest and Poet," 302.

defer or differ in meaning. If we were to stop here, Rahner's view of
language would produce something very similar to Derrida, which
would annul the possibility of revelation. Rahner would never totally
accept this. He sees the possibility for words to reach a place of "unsur-
passable fulfillment" when the words of the longing poet find the possibility of an answer in the word of God proclaimed in Jesus Christ and
in his apostolic successors.[49] The word of God was spoken and salvation
made available in the Incarnation, the "absolutely particular."[50] This
word ends the remoteness of God as the creator of the world and
abstract 'first cause'. The loving being of God is revealed in the word of
Jesus in a unrepeatable way. A Christian Theology of revelation must
take stock of the Christological component of the faith or else it will be
left with revelation as the unconcealment of being or the play of signifiers left by the trace without any ethical and doctrinal content.[51]
Rahner's work suggests a more balanced theology of revelation that
takes the play of signifiers seriously but still maintains its possibility to
emerge as manifestation and witness. Rahner says that it is the saints
who sustain the Church. It is not the truth of propositions, rather the
intimate truth of deified hearts that sustains the Church and Faith. It
witnesses to what transformation by the message would look like. Even
Derrida, when speaking about justice and the modeling of it, hints at
the truthfulness of recognizing the dignity of the other when he says
that justice is the relation to the other. Justice has to do with the other
and is always unequal to the other.[52]

A Rahnerian theology of revelation as witness and manifestation
would allow for great flexibility in expression because revelation has a
true history and God really does not say and do the same thing in
exactly the same way all the time. God speaks a unique word through
the many particular events in epics, in history and in individual
lives.[53] Human historicity makes this necessary even for God. Therefore,
I would suggest that the story of Jesus Christ, which is really the story
of God's definitive communication, is the Christian paradigm for being-
in-the-world that is of such a nature, since it means loving all people as

49. Rahner, "Priest and Poet," 316-317.
50. Karl Rahner, *The Practice of Faith: A Handbook of Contemporary Spirituality*
(New York: Crossroad, 1986) 11.
51. John Macquarrie, *Heidegger and Christianity* (New York: Continuum, 1994) 92.
52. John D. Caputo (ed.), *Deconstruction in a Nutshell: A Conversation with Jacques
Derrida* (New York: Fordham University Press, 1997) 17.
53. Karl Rahner, "Theos in the New Testament," *Theological Investigations*, Vol. 1
(Baltimore: Helicon Press, 1961) 87.

oneself, that it functions like any symbol and opens up unforeseen possibilities of meaning given its elastic structure. One would never want to say we have exhausted God by any event or text. But, the basic text can promote an enduring guidepost for all. Written narratives are free to break from the plot, says David Power, to be rewritten in different sequences, interjections, and metaphors, without disturbing the sense of passing on the foundational story.[54] For a christologically attuned theology of revelation as witness, it would mean love of neighbor in accordance with diversity of human beings and their historical situation. History, therefore, is full of surprises for Rahner.[55]

Karl Rahner would accept this analysis to a certain degree because it protects the 'mysterious' nature of God which always presents itself as 'heterogeneous' and as often confounding our theological discourses. However, careful attending to this fact cannot take place at the expense of the event of the incarnation. Unfortunately too many postmodern theologians sacrifice their Christology for a public fundamental theology. The reasons for this are many and complex. I would like to highlight one. The aversion to the doctrine of incarnation may to be partly fueled by a fear of intimacy. The thought of a deep relationship with God or another person is evaded because of the great demands this would place on the person and the constant threat of disappointment and challenge that his relationship would create. For all of its talk about community, few postmodern thinkers are willing to submit to the intimacy and self-reform this would entail. All that we get from postmodern thinkers is traces of intimacy or personal presence. Rahner would correct this idea. While he would never say that absolute presence is possible, he would say that the life of grace and faith is available because of the intimacy achieved between the Logos and humanity in the Incarnation. This revelation and relationship is always offered as a form of communion with God as history continues to flow and change. For Rahner, the postmodern enterprise can never be accepted in any unqualified way. Its applicability to Theology is significant, but limited. Christian Theology in the Rahnerian enterprise is always guided by the Incarnation even as new perspectives of appreciation of the mystery present themselves in the changing flows of history and language.

54. David N. Power, *Sacrament: The Language of God's Giving* (New York: Herder and Herder, 1999) 69.
55. Karl Rahner, *The Love of God and the Love of Neighbor* (New York: Crossroad, 1983) 73.

Experience, Language and Sacramental Theology George Steiner and Karl Rahner on the Postmodern Critique

Thomas M. Kelly

1. The Problem

At first glance it may seem odd that a critical theorist writing about aesthetic experience might have anything useful to say to the contemporary theologian concerned with sacramentality in a postmodern world. I will argue in this paper that it is precisely in the encounter between 'word' and 'world', that sacramentality becomes intelligible. Of course what we mean by 'word' and 'world' will become critical for this inquiry. The purpose of this paper is to understand the nature of one postmodern critique of theology – to bring a sacramental theology to bear upon the core of that critique – and to synthesize both moments in a way that respects the critique, learns from it, but moves beyond it. George Steiner provides an understanding of one postmodern critique both in its linguistic and anthropological dimensions. Karl Rahner provides a theological method that can serve as one response to such a critique. Thus, this paper will attempt to synthesize the main concerns of postmodernity and Catholic sacramentality by suggesting a metaphysical anthropology informed by kerygmatic theology.

Recent scholarship in the arts and humanities (as well as religious studies) has questioned the possibility "of any significant relations between word and world."[1] This intertextual turn has occasioned the emphasis – *our* 'word' is *the* 'world'. This, of course, has direct consequences for sacramental theology – a theology that has as its main concern how the finite encounters the infinite. If human subjectivity is confined to its own origins, so is human experience. A response to this challenge for sacramental theology is the topic of this paper.

---

1. George Steiner, *Real Presences* (London: Faber and Faber, 1991) 86-87.

2. Postmodernity

In his work *Real Presences*, George Steiner asserts that in any meaningful human interaction there is a correspondence between language and
that which it signifies. Language references not only other words, but can
correspond in some way to external reality as well. This correspondence
is made possible through a trust in the reality of such reference – the
same unthematic trust that is the condition of possibility for communicating anything to anyone. Unfortunately, such correspondence can no
longer be assumed. "Skepticism has queried the deed of semantic trust."[2]
The very nature of the language-act as something which can correspond
to a real referent, an 'external' reality – an object, an idea, a person – has
in some circles been entirely rejected. Prior to this break of semantic
trust, a break, according to Steiner, that occurred in Europe and Russia
in the latter part of the nineteenth century, even the most radical skep-
tics never questioned the ability of language to function as a vehicle for
the real, as a vehicle for meaningful argument, "even the most astringent
skepticism, even the most subversive of anti-rhetorics, remained commit-
ted to language. It knew itself to be 'in trust' to language."[3]

What precipitated the challenge to the possibility of real reference in
language?[4] Steiner implies that radical, though futile philosophical efforts
aimed at totalizing visions were, in part, responsible for the deconstructive response.[5] These developments instantiated "a terminal lunge towards
totality, towards a controlled in-gathering of all cultural-historical values
and legacies."[6] The reaction to such an all-encompassing "fundamentalism" (as David Tracy would identify it) severed the covenant "between
word and world." The result was a totalizing vision of another kind.

> A fully consequent skepticism will make language a primarily internal-
> ized, conventional shadow-system whose autistic rules and figurations
> have nothing verifiable to do with what is 'out there' (itself a childish,
> meaningless phrase).[7]

---

2. Steiner, *Real Presences*, 91.

3. *Ibid.*, 92.

4. This focus on "reference" in language is clear in Steiner's development of the
problematic. See *ibid.*, 94-95.

5. While Steiner implies this on page 94, it becomes clear that Mallarmé and Rimbaud are freeing language and human subjectivity *from* one or another totalizing vision
they believe stifles the nature of both.

6. Steiner, *Real Presences*, 94. Steiner specifically cites attempts made by Hegel,
Schelling, and Comte.

7. *Ibid.*, 91. In the Leslie Stephen Memorial Lecture delivered to the University of
Cambridge in 1985 and later published as "Real Presences," Steiner argues that the

The origin of the rupture between 'word and world' emerged from the thought of Stephané Mallarmé and Arthur Rimbaud. It occurred specifically with "Mallarmé's disjunction of language from external reference and in Rimbaud's deconstruction of the first person singular."[8] Both reject a correspondence theory of language, i.e., for language to cohere with any reality 'out there', as not only illusory, but actually deceptive. A 'correspondence' of language to reality makes language a lie. "Mallarmé's repudiation of the covenant of reference, and his insistence that non-reference constitutes the true genius and purity of language, entail a central supposition of 'real absence'."[9] Consequently, all language becomes only an internal word-game. Words refer to other words, and signify no reference to any determined reality.[10]

Mallarmé's linguistic epistemological alteration combined with Rimbaud's anthropological deconstruction of the first person results in a chasm dividing language from external reference – the dissolution of the self knows only real *absence*.[11] First comes a break in the trust of semantic correspondence, second comes the denial of an 'I' and an affirmation, instead, of many selves. This effectively severs any possibility for receiving or maintaining a 'meaning' that is capable of being 'shared'. Neither the nature of language nor the nature of human subjectivity admits of the kind of stability necessary for the reception of externally given meaning through an externally accessible referent. "We do not, via language, transcend the real towards the more real. Words neither say or un-say the realm of matter, of contingent mundanity, of 'the other'."[12]

Similar treatment is given to human subjectivity: "Where 'I' is not 'I' but a Magellanic cloud of momentary energies always in process of fission, there can be no authorship in any single, stable sense."[13] This

deconstruction of language occurred through four stages. George Steiner, *No Passion Spent: Essays 1978-1996* (London: Faber and Faber, 1996) 21-24.

8. Steiner, *Real Presences*, 94-95.

9. *Ibid.*, 96.

10. "The word *rose* has neither stem nor leaf nor thorn. It is neither pink nor red nor yellow. It exudes no odour. It is *per se*, a wholly arbitrary phonetic marker, an empty sign. Nothing whatever in its (minimal) sonority, in its graphic appearance, in its phonemic components, etymological history or grammatical functions, has any correspondence whatever to what we believe or imagine to be the object of its purely conventional reference." *Ibid.*, 95.

11. *Ibid.*, 100-101.

12. *Ibid.*, 97. Steiner continues, "Language speaks itself or, as Heidegger, in direct reprise of Mallarmé, puts it, "*Die Sprache spricht*" (but just this, as we shall see, is Heidegger's initial step out of nihilism and towards a counter-Mallarméan ontology of presence.)

13. *Ibid.*, 100. See also *No Passion Spent*, 22.

dissolution of the self grounds the impossibility of any reference to a "common humanity," i.e., to an appeal to any "meaning" that might transcend space and time and be accessible to all. And though many authors use language to critique language,

> it is not what is said that is being queried: it is the nature, formal and substantive, of the ascription of meaning, of intelligible signification, to the act and medium of the saying.[14]

One might conclude from this very limited summation of postmodern assertions that its foundational arguments are essentially grounded in particular understandings of epistemology and anthropology that inform an understanding of the nature and role of language.

Some contemporary postmodern approaches to religious experience and theological inquiry in the United States presume an understanding of language, evident for example, in a regulative view of doctrine or a conceptual theory of emotion. In these approaches, language and human experience are understood as historically, culturally bound – formative – and finite in possibility. Taken to its inevitable conclusion, any linguistic 'reference' that is external, prior to, or beyond a particular linguistic paradigm becomes inaccessible. This, of course, becomes a critical issue for doing sacramental theology.

What is needed is an approach to language and its relation to experience that is located somewhere between a "systematic exhaustive hermeneutic" and a "gratuitous, arbitrary play of non-sense."[15] This determination of how language functions is correspondingly informed by the understanding of the limit and function of 'experience'. The relation of 'experience' and language determines much of the possibilities for sacramental theology. So it is to the unique character of 'experience' emerging from Steiner's understanding of language that we now turn.

3. Experience and Language

The character and function of 'experience' for Steiner figures prominently in that encounter with meaning in art or literature that is an experience of the "aesthetic," of "selective interactions between the constraints of the observed and the boundless possibilities of the imagined."[16] It is

14. Steiner, *Real Presences*, 102.
15. *Ibid.*, 165.
16. *Ibid.*, 11.

not simply a coming into contact with some thing that exists, rather it is a meeting, an acknowledgment of the claims and demands of an 'other'. Aesthetic experience can be the experience of 'real presence', i.e., "the encounter with the aesthetic" can reveal the 'other' through a work of art. [17]

"There is language, there is art, because there is 'the other.'"[18] There is something that is not language, and not art, to which language and art respond.

The 'other', consequently, is the reason and possibility for communicating. "It is out of the fact of confrontation, of affront in the literal sense of the term, that we communicate in words, that we externalize shapes and colors, that we emit organized sounds in the forms of music."[19] First there is the experience of the other, i.e., the "confrontation", second is the communication or re-collection of that encounter, in art, music and language, etc. "The meaning, the existential modes of art music and literature are functional within the experience of our meeting with the other."[20] Aesthetic experience, for Steiner, is therefore understood dialectically. "All representations, even the most abstract, infer a rendezvous with intelligibility or, at the least, with a strangeness attenuated, qualified by observance and willed form."[21] Rendezvous and representation – "the continuum between both, the modulation from one to the other, lie at the source of poetry and the arts."[22] Encounter with the "other" and the embodiment of this encounter in language, art or music leads to a third moment – the recognition that such embodiment of encounter bespeaks and ultimately leads one both to a deeper understanding of the 'self' and to an approximate experience of the original encounter.

Notice the aboriginal nature of self-transcendence; there is a knowledge of self that comes from the movement toward that which is not the self. "Beyond the strength of any other act of witness, literature and the arts *tell* of the obstinacies of the impenetrable, of the absolutely alien

17. "Whatever its stature, the poem speaks; it speaks out; it speaks to. The meaning, the existential modes of art, music and literature are functional within the experience of our meeting with the other. All aesthetics, all critical and hermeneutic discourse, is an attempt to clarify the paradox and opaqueness of that meeting as well as its felicities." Steiner, *Real Presences*, 138.

18. *Ibid.,*, 137.

19. *Ibid.*, 138.

20. *Ibid.*

21. *Ibid.*, 139.

22. *Ibid.*

which we come up against in the labyrinth of intimacy."[23] When the artist or thinker give their "findings" (encounters) the "persuasion of form" (art, music, literature), they tell us both about "us" and of that original meeting, "of the irreducible weight of otherness, of enclosedness, in the texture of and phenomenality of the material world."[24] While the meaning of this encounter may be intertextual, i.e., it is intelligible through other terms used in language – the reference is a separate and external reality not constructed from the subject's worldview. Literature, art and music allow one to transcend such boundaries and encounter the 'Other'.

This encounter occurs in a context, but is not reducible to any or all factors of that context. "Context is at all times dialectical. Our reading modifies, is in turn modified by, the communicative presence of its object."[25] Causality is mutual. The subject and the work of art are mutually dependent on each others' freedom. The work of art could have *not* been. The subject *can* say 'no'. Where 'freedoms meet', when a work is freely given and freely received in the context of our own liberty, an encounter, an 'experience' of real presence has occurred.[26] One can accept or reject the work of art, and it is such a possibility of real absence, of rejection, that gives presence to the force of any work. While this encounter never results in a complete knowledge, this does not mean "that intelligibility is either wholly arbitrary or self-erasing. Such deduction is nihilistic sophistry."[27]

For Steiner, the infinite reach and context of language prohibits us from turning it into merely a constraint. There is an experience of the transcendent in language. The relationship between experience and language is more complex, with an emphasis on the dialectics of encounter.

It is critically important to recognize the term 'experience' here. Experience, for Steiner, is encounter and response. Encounters, if offered and received in freedom, are a coming-up-against a real presence, to *being*. Language, in its infinite context does set the initial boundary for any encounter, but it always functions as more than simply restraint.

> All good art and literature begin in immanence. But they do not stop there. Which is to say, very plainly, that it is the enterprise and privilege of the aesthetic to quicken into lit presence the continuum between

23. Steiner, *Real Presences*, 139-140.
24. *Ibid.*, 140.
25. *Ibid.*, 163.
26. *Ibid.*, 155.
27. *Ibid.*, 163.

temporality and eternity, between matter and spirit, between man and 'the other'.[28]

Language is a catalyst for transcending both the work and the personal subjectivity to encounter real presence – to being – to being-in-relation-to. Transcendence, for Steiner, is the movement beyond the self, or anything constructed by the self, toward that which is truly other. "This essay argues a wager on transcendence. It argues that there is in the art-act and its reception, that there is in the experience of meaningful form, a presumption of presence."[29]

The relation of language to experience ultimately leads to theology because for Steiner the guarantee of a correspondence between 'word' and 'world' ultimately is God. This guarantee of correspondence between language and external reality is inspired by Descartes and Kant.[30] Steiner will continue this 'verification transcendence' as he terms it, with a wager on meaning in language. God, consequently, is necessary to reinsure sense – the presumption of meaningfulness in our encounter, our recollection of the 'other' through intelligible form.[31]

4. A Critical Evaluation

Language predicates, nominates and adjectivally qualifies our understanding of reality. It does not create reality, though it does contain the

28. Steiner, *Real Presences*, 227.

29. *Ibid.*, 214. Steiner's affirmation and "wager on transcendence" to insure the meaning of meaning is a deliberate contradiction to the deconstructive program. "Real Presences," is a direct play on real absence – the core of the deconstructive critique.

30. "Descartes wagers on the unprovable assumption that God has not devised a phenomenal universe such as to deceive human reason or such as to make impossible the recurrent application of natural laws. ... Kant postulates a fundamental disposition of accord between the fabric of human understanding and our perception of things." *Ibid.*, 213. Reference to Descartes' *Third Meditation* is mentioned on pp. 91 and 138. The claims of deconstruction are compared to the "answerability in any Cartesian or Kantian way," which is further elucidated on 215. Further elaboration on the Cartesian and Kantian sense of Steiner's wager on transcendence can be found in *Real Presences*, "No Passion Spent," 31, 33-35.

31. "It is a theology, explicit or suppressed, masked or avowed, substantive or imaged, which underwrites the presumption of creativity, of signification in our encounters with text, with music, with art. The meaning of meaning is a transcendent postulate. To read the poem responsibly ('respondingly'), to be answerable to form, is to wager on a reinsurance of sense. It is to wager on a relationship – tragic, turbulent, incommensurable, even sardonic – between word and world, but on a relationship precisely bounded by that which reinsures it." *Ibid.*, 216.

possibility of communicating meaning. Language embodies the correspondence, the meaning between the subject and the linguistic reference. For Steiner, meaning and reference can be intertextual, but reference can also be ontological. Though historically bound, language for
Steiner can transcend time and space to read and communicate such
ontological reality, such meaning to others. What was possible through
language, when the foundation of communication was a correspondence between 'word and world', was presumed self-evident. In the
everyday of common sense it still is. Steiner argues three theses that
serve to counter arguments of contemporary postmodernism. First, language cannot be comprehended by and then confined to a single 'theory'. Theory and language as understood by postmodernism embodies
an error of categories, one in which an applied science methodology has
been misappropriated for inquiry into an area (i.e., religious experience,
religion) that lacks quantification. Second, such an understanding of
language neglects the aboriginal nature of human 'experience' as self-
transcendent. To understand either language or 'experience', a mutuality
in the relation between them and not a priority in conditioning must be
emphasized. Finally, what appears to be a rejection of a common
humanity by postmodernism in general is an affirmation of a particular
kind of common humanity – one in which 'word and world' fail to
cohere due to the brokenness of the self. 'Experience', as a limited level
of knowing, is simply made universal.[32]

Steiner's understanding of the polyvalence of human experience can
contribute substantially to a sacramental theology emerging from
human experience, i.e., a sacramental reflection on human experience as
self-transcendent. While Steiner is helpful in addressing some errors in
postmodern philosophical anthropology, problems arise with his position on 'verification transcendence', i.e., God as guarantor. To make
such an approach to God fundamental is ultimately insufficient for a

---

32. Steiner, *Real Presences*, 104. The categories of "felt being," those located outside
language, are critical for humanity – and this realm transcends language. This is quite
different from the deterministic and finite language theories the early Wittgenstein is
cited to support. Language for Wittgenstein is very limited, *but what is, is not confined
to language*. Thus, although Wittgenstein severely limits how one ascertains or ascribes
"meaning" to language, one cannot simply assert that he "wanted his supposition to be
extended to its nihilistic finality." Ultimately, Steiner does view Wittgenstein as at least
contributing to the deconstruction of language. For more on Steiner's interpretation of
Wittgenstein, see George Steiner, "Retreat from the Word," *Language and Silence: Essays
of Language, Literature and the Inhuman* (New York: Atheneum, 1967) 12-35.

Christian theology.[33] God as the guarantor of a correspondence of language to external reality instantiates a theological functionalism reminiscent of Descartes and Kant.[34]

An approach to God that harnesses God to a system of thought as insurance for certitude – moral, epistemological, linguistic – is fraught with problems of its own. James Collins, in *God in Modern Philosophy*, comments on such a theological functionalism.

> The functionalist notion of using the conception of God to develop or shore up one's philosophical system has exercised a profound and steady attraction over the modern rationalists. As the analysis of pre-Kantian philosophy shows in classical outline, God must be invoked in a functional role as soon as one takes a certain view of philosophy itself. This role is required for the theory of God when philosophy is treated primarily as a deductive system aiming at a complete body of truths, obtained in an *a priori* and purely intellectual fashion. Such a view of philosophy provides an emergency answer to the disturbing challenge of the skeptics. God must then be called in to guarantee the objectivity of ideal constructs, the continuity of deduction, the comprehensiveness of the results, and their necessary generation of human happiness.[35]

The consequences of such a functional theology are problematic for Christian theology, for they "tend[s] to compromise the transcendence and freedom of this guarantor-God..."[36] God may insure epistemological certitude for Descartes and Kant, and linguistic certitude for Steiner, but this alone is insufficient for Christian, and especially, sacramental theology. The guarantor-God supports a secular mode of reasoning by expanding God's power and perfection "into primary deductive principles in

---

33. Steiner employs this term to describe his own approach and states that "'verification transcendence' marks every essential aspect of human existence. It qualifies our conceptualizations, our intellections of our coming into life, of the primary elements of our psychic identity and instruments, of the phenomenology of Eros and death," Steiner, *Real Presences*, 214.

34. This is to disagree with P. Phillips when he minimizes the influence of Descartes. "What Steiner is claiming here is inevitably opaque, yet I suggest that he is not to be thought of as arguing for a kind of psychological, or emotive, account of the possibility, genuine or otherwise, of an experience of transcendence. Steiner, like Heidegger, is claiming something about the nature of language. This is a wager on sense. We must not be misled here or elsewhere, by the reference to Descartes. Steiner's wager is something very different", P. Phillips, "George Steiner's Wager on Transcendence," *The Heythrop Journal* 39 (1998) 158-169. Steiner himself makes the claim throughout both *Real Presences* and "Real Presences," that such a wager is almost identical with both Descartes and Kant: God functions as the guarantor, of certitude about the world in Descartes, about the coherence of the ethical enterprise in Kant.

35. James Collins, *God in Modern Philosophy* (Chicago: Pregnery, 1959) 378-379.

36. *Ibid.*, 379.

philosophy" thereby subordinating God "to the demands of a rationalist system and hence given a functionalist treatment."[37] This can result in a vague pantheistic monism that can rationally, though not necessarily, undergird and reinsure meaning in language – a wager is after all, only a wager, not an affirmation.[38] This approach of course leads to the following inevitable question by Steiner: "How can 'the totally Other' act on us, let alone give any signal of its utterly inaccessible existence?"[39]

It is in answer to such a contemporary question that Christian theology must respond – and if such a response, such a theology, is to give an honest account of itself, it must emerge from the lived reality of God as personal and historical, i.e., as realized in relation to humanity in history. While Steiner responds significantly to some of the linguistic and anthropological challenges of postmodern theology, the guarantor-God is insufficient for grounding a sacramental theology. For such a response to the contemporary problematic in theology, it is now necessary to turn to an explicitly Christian systematic theologian.

5. Karl Rahner

It would be too simplistic to assert that Karl Rahner's theology resolves all the points of contention outlined thus far – to do so would trivialize the very real problems suggested by the postmodern critique today. But one might inquire how Rahner consciously or not responds to the issues outlined previously. One possible reason for the failure of contemporary Catholic theology to deal decisively with the postmodern critique can be understood by a lack of what Rahner deemed the most critical component of theology. "… theological statements are not formulated in such a way that the human can see how what is meant by them is connected with his understanding of himself, as witnessed to in his own experience."[40] Rahner's theology attempts to do just that.

> … the task of theology must precisely be to appeal in all the various conceptual forms in which it is objectified, to this basic experience of grace, to bring man again and again to a fresh recognition of that fact that all this immense sum of distinct statements of the Christian faith basically

37. Collins, *God in Modern Philosophy*, 379.
38. This is confirmed in recent autobiographical reflections, see Steiner, *Errata; An Examined Life* (New Haven/London: Yale University Press, 1997) 185.
39. *Ibid.*, 186.
40. Karl Rahner, "Theology and Anthropology," *Theological Investigations*, Vol. IX (New York: The Seabury Press, 1972) 40.

speaking expresses nothing else than an immense truth, even though one that has been explicated throughout all the levels of man's being: the truth, namely, that the absolute mystery that is, that permeates all things, upholds all things, and endures eternally, has bestowed itself as itself in an act of forgiving love upon man, and is experienced in faith in that ineffable experience of grace as the ultimate freedom of man.[41]

Steiner has provided solid justification for rejecting the postmodern understanding of experience and language – at least in its extreme manifestations. But as noted, the theological consequences of "verification transcendence" are unacceptable for a sacramental theological response.

A Christian response to the issues in theological method that center upon experience, language and the character of theology are essential to any sacramental theology, and can be formulated from the perspective of one "who is a Christian and wants to be a Christian."[42] And if the theologian is to respond, and respond adequately, she or he must do so in terms of the problem itself, i.e., where the problem leads the theologian must venture – into competing and contradictory understandings of language, of experience, of conceptions of human existence that seriously challenge an intellectually defensible faith.[43] This is especially true for Rahner, because it is the contemporary *situation* that "provides current theology with its starting-point."[44]

A dialogue between postmodernism and sacramental theology can be constructively advanced through an appropriation of Rahner's foundational theology, i.e., by entering into *the mutuality* of three dialectical moments that comprises his method and confirms his affirmation of a unity between philosophy and theology in a single reflection "upon the concrete whole of human self-realization of a Christian."[45] This unity of

41. Karl Rahner, "Reflections on Methodology in Theology," *Theological Investigations*, Vol. XI (New York: The Seabury Press, 1974) 110. See also, *Foundations of Christian Faith: An Introduction to the Idea of Christianity* (New York: Crossroad, 1990) 12.

42. Rahner, *Foundations*, 1.

43. *Ibid.*, 7-8. "Theology is a theology that can be genuinely preached only to the extent that it succeeds in establishing contact with the total secular self-understanding which man has in a particular epoch, succeeds in engaging in conversation with it, in catching onto it, and in allowing itself to be enriched by it in its language and even more so in the very matter of theology itself."

44. Rahner, "Reflections on Methodology," 70. In addition to being an excellent resource for the method of transcendental theology employed by Rahner, the first ten pages give Rahner's view of what it means to do theology in the contemporary world, especially over and against what it has meant to do theology previously (74).

45. Rahner, *Foundations*, 10. One cannot emphasize the mutuality, the perichoresis, of the three moments enough. For the purpose of individual consideration these moments are separated, but their essence is in relation to each other.

philosophy and theology is critical to a foundational level of inquiry that "summons man before the real truth of his being. It summons him before the truth in which he remains inescapably caught, although this prison is ultimately the infinite expanse of the incomprehensible mystery of God."[46]

There is first a reflection upon human experience – "upon man as the universal question which he is for himself, and hence we must philosophize in the most proper sense."[47] Second, one must take up (among others) history and language – "the transcendental and the historical conditions which make revelation possible must be reflected upon..."[48] Finally, reflection upon Christian doctrine and its informing relation to experience must be taken up – "the fundamental assertion of Christianity as the answer to the question that man is, and hence we must do theology."[49] These three moments, this triad – "mutually condition one another and therefore form a unity, a unity that is of course differentiated" – they can also respond directly to the topics constitutive of the contemporary problematic.[50]

But why is it necessary to begin a response to postmodernity from fundamental theology? Such a theology "reflects on the human condition for the possibility of a sacramental mediation of salvation; e.g., on the significance and efficacy of symbolic action."[51] A systematic reflection upon human experience is necessary, for it is the contradictory conceptions of the possibilities within human experience that constitutes the problem. If human experience can finally be understood as grounded by and drawn toward *holy mystery*, not understood in the sense of a 'placeholder,' not so distant as to force a '*sacrificium intellectus*,'[52] and not as something senseless and unintelligible – but as infinitely intelligible and immanent – then the human being can be understood as irrevocably

---

46. For this reason, both philosophy and theology are considered together. Rahner, *Foundations*, 24-25.

47. *Ibid.*, 11.

48. Rahner develops an extensive and detailed history of salvation and revelation – topics much too vast for this article. What will be argued is Rahner's understanding of language, and the relationship of language to "original experience." While this insufficiently captures what Rahner intends with the second moment of his method, it presents what is necessary for the current task.

49. Rahner, *Foundations*, 11.

50. *Ibid.*

51. Günter Koch, "Sacramental Theology," *Handbook of Catholic Theology*, ed. Wolfgang Beinert and Francis Schussler Fiorenza (New York: Crossroad, 1995) 615.

52. Rahner, *Foundations*, 12. For Rahner's comments on a common misunderstanding of mystery in the contemporary world see, "Reflections on Methodology," 101.

oriented toward absolute mystery. Only when the sacramentality of human existence that grounds Rahner's theology is articulated can there be a legitimate response to the postmodern critique.

Reflection upon human experience necessarily moves into the second topic. The relationship of 'experience' to language, to reflection, or as Rahner designates it, to its 'objectification', is of critical importance. Thus, in the introduction to *Foundations*, he states:

> It is precisely this permanent and insurmountable difference between the original Christian actualization of existence and reflection upon it which will occupy us throughout. The insight into this difference is a key insight which represents a necessary presupposition for an introduction to the idea of Christianity.[53]

This "original actualization" immediately enters into the domain of language upon reflection. It shapes language and is shaped by language. Ultimately such mutuality allows for a deeper understanding of both the objectification of 'original experience' as well as its own originality. This relationship of experience and language directly influences a corresponding understanding of the nature and function of doctrine and theology as constructive or descriptive. A progressive reflection upon Christian existence, mediated by language and culminating in doctrine reveals, incrimentally, a greater depth to such original actualization through the very language used to express it and the doctrine used to preserve and nourish it.

This understanding of doctrine as both expressive and constructive emerges for an understanding of sacramental theology that serves and preserves good dogmatic theology. Sacramental theology originating from the unity of foundational and dogmatic theology will contain all three differentiated moments – a reflection on Christian actualization of existence as self-transcendent, language as both descriptive and constructive, and doctrine as informative of the 'original actualization'.

For Rahner, there is a tension between original experience and language – between an 'experience' (of longing, for example) and its objectification in concepts – it is thus dialectical. First, there is a movement from original 'experience' out through actualization to its objectification. "The original self-presence of the subject in the actual realization of his existence strives to translate itself more and more into the conceptual, into the objectified, into language, into communication with

53. Rahner, *Foundations*, 2.

another." But the opposite is also true: "One who has been formed by a common language, and educated and indoctrinated from without, experiences clearly perhaps only very slowly what he has been talking about for a long time."[54] Both angles are mutually informing, and while there is a priority given to original experience it is, *de facto,* dependent upon language for its reflection and communication. "To that extent reflection, conceptualization and language have a *necessary* orientation to that original knowledge, to that original experience in which what is meant and the experience of what is meant are still one."[55]

Note that the tension is fluid and not static between an original experience and its objectification through actualization, conceptualization and reflection. Speech expresses non-thematic experience – non-thematic experience, in turn, gives intelligibility to the language used to express it. For example, "It is possible for someone to have authentic experiences of love, and express these experiences in erroneous ways." Conversely, "It is possible to give a very accurate and correct description of an experience, and to have never had such an experience before."[56] For this reason, "Experience as such and subsequent reflection upon this experience, in which its content is conceptually objectified *are never absolutely separate* one from the other."[57] It is the mutual relationship between an original experience and its objectification that is stressed, though there is undoubtedly a priority given to experience.[58]

With a metaphysical anthropology suggesting an aboriginal human self-transcendence and an understanding of language necessary for such experience, we can now explore doctrine as kerygmatic.

---

54. Rahner, *Foundations,* 16. It seems that from this particular text, original actualization is made manifest first in conceptualization (*Begrifflichkeit*) then in language (*die Sprache*) then in communication (*die Mitteilung*) and finally in a theoretical knowledge (*theoretische Wissen*) that points back to the original actualization. *But it must be kept constantly in mind that this movement is not static but fluid, and in tension with the opposite direction as well.*
55. Rahner, *Foundations,* 16-17 (emphasis added).
56. Rahner, "The Experience of God Today," 151.
57. *Ibid.* (emphasis added).
58. *Ibid.* "It is true that such basic experiences are prior to any conceptual objectification or interpretation of them, and are in principle independent of these processes." And again, "The actual experience of love is indeed absolutely basic and absolutely indispensable. But despite this fact the experience itself as such can in itself be accepted more profoundly, more purely, and with greater freedom when we achieve a knowledge of its true nature and its implications at the explicitly conscious level" (152).

6. Dogmatic Language as Kerygmatic

For Rahner, "... all theology is 'kerygmatic'.[59] Otherwise it is merely speculative philosophy of religion."[60] This is so because the exercise of faith, the actual existential acceptance of faith "opens up ... a whole view of reality, even though it seems that the profane theoretician of religion can know and say just as much or as little about Christianity as the believing theologian."[61] A dogmatic statement is a statement of faith not only because of its object, but because of the subjective act of believing – and in being this, it can effect three critical functions. First, it "participates in its own way in the expressed profession and praise of the message Christ has given us about himself and which leads us to him – in the expression of that message listened to and accepted." Second, it "leads towards the historical event of salvation" by accomplishing the first. Finally, it embodies an existential and not just theoretical relationship to "the historical event of salvation" and in so doing is "*ex fide ad fidem*" even in its theoretical character.[62]

But it is necessary to acknowledge that though the reality referred to is infinite and incomprehensible – the terminology at our disposal is finite and limited.[63] Dogmatic statements are, therefore, historical, limited, and open both to further unfolding and new terminology as necessary to mediate the truths of faith to particular historical situations. This tension and difference between the reality signified and the terms used to signify reveals another important function of the dogmatic statement – to lead one beyond the concepts to the reality signified.

> The dogmatic statement – like the kerygmatic one – is basically possessed of an element which (in the case of intramundane categorical statements) is not identical with the represented conceptual content. Without injuring its own meaning, *the represented conceptual content is in*

---

59. For an extensive discussion on this element of a dogmatic statement, see Karl Rahner and Karl Lehmann, *Kerygma and Dogma* (New York: Herder and Herder, 1969). Rahner and Lehmann designate kerygma as "an apostolic kerygma, complete and perfect, and as the "fundamental" kerygma it constitutes the criterion of all further kerygmatic utterance; but it is at the same time a *continuing and actualizing process and event*" (15, emphasis mine).

60. Karl Rahner, "Nature of Theology," in *Encyclopedia of Theology: The Concise Sacramentum Mundi*, ed. Karl Rahner (New York: Crossroad, 1975) 1689.

61. Rahner, "What is a Dogmatic Statement?," 50.

62. *Ibid.* The manifestation of faith that doctrine serves is not just an individual faith, but a communal manifestation of faith, i.e., the faith of the Church.

63. Rahner summarizes the two-fold nature of what he designates as the highest theological designation – dogma in "Dogma," *Sacramentum Mundi*, 352.

*this case merely the means of experiencing a being referred beyond itself and
everything imaginable. ...* We do not refer here to the concept of transcendence or the concept of grace, but to these realities themselves.[64]

A kerygmatic statement can be what it must be only if it does not
reduce its reference to the finite and manageable. Rather, through the
finite and manageable, it should affirm and reconfirm the permanent
mystery and the permanent incomprehensibility to that which it refers.
The terminology, the signs, the language of dogmatic statements ought
to "silently refer the believing person beyond themselves into the impenetrable light of God himself."[65] Note the self-transcendence of language
employed for doctrine. "... theological discourse does not only speak
about the mystery but that it only speaks properly if it is also a kind of
instruction showing us how to come into the presence of the mystery
itself."[66] The reality signified and the means to signify such reality are
different. Thus, it is erroneous to believe that "one has already arrived at
the reality in theological dogmatic discourse when one possesses its
conceptual term."[67]

The discussion of concepts, language, terminology, etc. has occurred
in the context of a faith statement and a faith act oriented toward an
object of faith. Such faith is existentially relevant, i.e., it informs the
whole of a subject's reality and the possibilities for all aspects of such
reality. But such reflection in faith upon the truths of the faith should
not be confused with or made identical to the 'Word of revelation' or the
"original statement of faith," though it may well be empowered by both.

> The difference between the original kerygma and a dogmatic statement,
> therefore, does not lie in the fact that in the former there is as it were the
> pure Word of God alone and in the latter only human reflection. If this
> were the case, then there could be indeed merely non-binding theologi-
> cal discourse talking round about this Word of God, but not a statement
> of faith which though different from the original Word of God, as
> announced originally, receives its real binding presence in the course of
> history. There could only be a history of theology in this case and not a
> history of dogmas. The fact that the latter exists can be explained only
> because the original statement of faith already includes that moment of
> genuine human reflection which makes it legitimate and necessary and
> which continues to be effective and to unfold itself in later theology.[68]

64. Rahner, "What is a Dogmatic Statement," 58-59 (emphasis added).
65. *Ibid.*, 59.
66. *Ibid.*, 60.
67. *Ibid.*
68. *Ibid.*, 61.

The kerygmatic element must always be in theology. Kerygma is the proclamation of Jesus Christ, accepted, appropriated and continually active and effective in communicating itself as the salvific word.[69] It is a meeting between believer and believed that empowers "those who are convinced of and filled by this word of the Lord to speak in turn in the same way, that that their mission is summed up in the words: 'He who hears you hears me' (Lk 10:16)."[70]

> Thus kerygma, in its fullest sense, is the actual and historically determined proclamation of the word of God in the Church by the proclaimer, authorized by God, who bears witness. This word, spoken by the proclaimer in the power of the Spirit and in faith, hope, and charity, *brings into being and makes present what is proclaimed* (the promise of God to man) as an evangelical message of salvation and as a committing and judging power; it does this in such a way, moreover, that salvation history, both beginning and end, becomes present "now" in Jesus Christ, and that this word, which has become an event in what is said and heard, can be received by the listener in faith and love.[71]

It is for this reason that theology is essentially "practical" not because it disdains the theoretical, but because "it is orientated to the acts of hope and of love, which contain an element of knowledge which is unattainable outside them."[72] Once again the principle of intersubjectivity is critical here, for it is not sufficient for something to be simply 'known', it must be realized in one existence as well.

The nature of dogmatic theology as intersubjective requires more than simply the subjective impulse of a theologian, and for this reason it is necessarily ecclesiastical, social and historical.[73] Theology as essentially intersubjective in the dimensions of Church, society and history has God in God's self for its formal object, i.e., as that under which all things are considered in theology both in terms of their beginning and end in God. But Rahner insists that this stipulation extend beyond the meaning it has been given traditionally. There is no possibility or purpose for considering God in God's self as somehow separate from history, rather, God's saving action in history allows one some entrance

---

69. This definition is an attempted summary of the critical points on this topic made by Eberhard Simons in the article "Kerygma," *Sacramentum Mundi*, 797-800.

70. *Ibid.*, 797-798.

71. Rahner and Lehmann, *Kerygma and Dogma*, 18 (italics mine).

72. Rahner, "The Nature of Theology," 1689.

73. Says Rahner, "Theology is necessarily ecclesiastical otherwise it ceases to itself and becomes the prey of the wayward subjective of the individual, which is today less fitted than ever to the cohesive force of a community," *ibid.*

into the nature of God.[74] Thus, the formal object of theology is God in God's self-communication, i.e., as active and salvific in human history.[75]

God communicating God's self as the formal object of theology offers advantages for sacramental theology, "since the formal object and the subjective principle of theology (God as the uncreated grace of faith) would clearly be the same."[76] It is for this reason that there is an essential unity between theology and anthropology. It is not enough to simply communicate a knowledge about God. Dogmatic theology, via sacramental theology, must articulate how the God who communicates Himself is accepted in faith by the human who is already oriented to God.

Conclusion

The unity between Rahner's foundational theology and his dogmatic theology can be understood through his sacramentology because in every tractate in theology one is finally dealing with God in His self-communication to us. This hope and this love manifest in the community through the kerygmatic promise of God's very self to that community is grounds for a sacramentality that has the living presence of Jesus Christ as a constitutive element of those whom we identify as Church. As a well-known American theologian states:

> Grace is always present. What is needed is someone to notice it. Sacraments are those persons, places, things and events which cause you and me to notice the grace. It allows you to see into its depth, to see the grace in which its existence is rooted, to acknowledge and celebrate God's absolute love for all that exists.[77]

Sacramentality in a postmodern context is really only possible in a community where the living presence of Jesus Christ, through the members of such a community "bring into being and make present that which is proclaimed."

---

74. Once again this is necessarily so given the principle of intersubjectivity for Rahner's dogmatic theology. Elsewhere he states, "A theological object's significance for salvation (which is a necessary factor in any theological object) can only be investigated by inquiring at the same time as to man's *saving receptivity* for this object," Rahner, "Theology and Anthropology," 35.

75. Rahner, "The Nature of Theology," 1690.

76. *Ibid.*

77. Michael Himes, *Doing the Truth in Love* (New York: Paulist Press, 1995) 108.

Schillebeeckx, God and Postmodernity

Dennis Rochford

> "Never before in history has God's presence in the world been so intimate and so tangibly real as now, in our own time, yet we do nothing but proclaim his absence..."[1]

1. Introduction

This paper draws together the thinking of Edward Schillebeeckx and the contemporary interest in postmodernity around the theme of stories about the human relationship with God and salvation. What is at stake here is the adequacy of Schillebeeckx's theological approach given the postmodern rejection of the system of panoramic legitimating grand narratives which finds resonance in the glitzy technological developments at the end of the millennium.

Throughout his work and until recently Schillebeeckx maintained a plea for a theological discourse that points to the divine presence within a secular world. God exists in all creation. Here the salvation of humankind can be experienced, always as an offer of grace from God. "God's testimony of himself is experienced *in ourselves*. We experience grace where we experience our humanity, and where we experience our humanity, we also concretely experience grace, because we are confronted in our freedom with grace – God, that is, with the divine saving will which is actively concerned with us."[2] This is nothing but "God's call in a human form that is intimately involved with this world."[3] Reality is always a 'graced' offer of human salvation. It is experienced through the created world. This reality is known through the notion of *implicit intuition* or the *non-conceptual* aspect of intellection following Schillebeeckx's mentor, Dominic Marie De Petter, in his interpretation of the Thomist intellectual tradition.

---

1. Edward Schillebeeckx, *World and Church* (London: Sheed and Ward, 1971, ¹1966) 78.
2. Edward Schillebeeckx, "The Non-Conceptual Intellectual Dimension in Our Knowledge of God According to Aquinas," *Revelation and Theology*, 2 (London: Sheed and Ward, 1967) 67.
3. *Ibid.*, 73.

More recently Schillebeeckx continued to point to a "… source and ground, inspiration and orientation which transcends all secularity – whom believers call the living God, the one who is not susceptible to any secularization."[4] And, he adds, "God is the reality to which at all events believers point by means of the images which are put at their disposal by the history of human religious experience."[5] In another publication by Francesco Strazzari, *Sono un teologo felice*, Schillebeeckx reflects on the themes of the Christian theological narrative such as creation, eschatology and ethics.[6] This time he highlights the negative contrast (anticipation) experience. In a kind of holy 'indignation', he continues to recall God's manifestation in the world. For Christians, this fundamental, contrasting experience and its implied rejection of injustice, as well as its open perspective on 'something better' become the place where history is unfolding 'as God's gift', although through men and other earthly factors."[7] With this affirmation, understood either positively or negatively, God's salvation to humankind is announced, stemming from the mystical relationship of humankind with God. The project of human fulfillment is directly linked with God's plan for the future of humankind. This is summarized as a narrative of optimism and hope:

> The biblical account summarizes the entire story of continued creation in a magnificent manner: "man created by God is called to become God's image." What we have here is the image of Himself that God has placed in the world and its history: the human being, that is, woman and man. Wherever human beings live and act, it should be clear to all that God reigns, that God's kingdom is unfolding, that is, that peace and justice will prevail among human beings and among nations, in a healthy and harmonious manner, in such a way that the universe will be at peace with the living God, heart and source of the history of salvation.[8]

What is striking in this understanding of the Christian narrative is Schillebeeckx's emphasis on the unique or particular *language* of Christian faith used. It is the strange and normative language of the Bible.

---

4. Edward Schillebeeckx, *Church: The Human Story of God* (New York: Crossroad, 1989) 234.

5. *Ibid.*, 73.

6. Cf. Jan Grootaers, "Schillebeeckx, een gelukkige teoloog," *De Standaard*, 22 April 1994.

7. Edward Schillebeeckx, *Conférence de presse* (Rome, 26 May 1993), Nijmegen Archives.

8. *Ibid.*, 7.

Thus it remains relatively 'undisturbed' by the hermeneutical methods, that Schillebeeckx indicated he was adopting from the 1960s, that engage different historical and cultural horizons in the production of new meanings for Christian faith. Ironically, the narrative, via the per-durance of its language, guarantees the on-going life of Christian universal claims to meaning. Thus the content of theological terminology and the existential import of Schillebeeck's understanding of the relationship with God is both *narratively grounded* and *hermeneutically preserved*. His strategy will become clearer in further sections of this paper.

However, the advent of a postmodern plurality of identity challenges the continuous and ongoing plausibility of Schillebeeckx's reference to a religious narrativity rooted in the hermeneutically valorized Christian tradition. The changed culture poses a serious question for the adequacy of his theological hermeneutics to engage the new cultural climate of pluralism and ambiguity characteristic of postmodernity.

2. Publications on the Sacraments

Narratives about God's presence in a secular world are an important part of the theological agenda of Edward Schillebeeckx. These first took shape during the period 1947-1957 when he was asked to teach dogmatic theology in Leuven at the *studium generale* of the Dominicans. In addition to courses in Creation, Christology and Eschatology, he taught Sacramentology. In 1952 Schillebeeckx published an edited version of the first part of his doctoral dissertation which he called *De Sacramentele Heilseconomie*.[9] This was more a compendium of traditional catholic sacramental theology which begins by situating sacraments within the Thomistic scheme of faith.[10] It further elaborates the historical, especially patristic and medieval sources of sacramentology but with little biblical exegesis.[11] This long, technical and seminal tome was primarily a text book for seminarians but it did tackle the contemporary issue of how people experience their encounter with God through Christ.

---

9. Edward Schillebeeckx, *De Sacramentele Heilseconomie: Theologische bezinning op S. Thomas' Sacramentenleer in het licht van de traditie en van de hedendaagse sacra-mentsproblematiek* (Antwerp: 't Groeit/Bilthoven: H. Nelissen, 1952).

10. *Ibid.*, 1-18.

11. See Philip Kennedy, *Deus Humanissimus: The Knowability of God in the Theology of Edward Schillebeeckx* (Freiburg: Universitätsverlag, 1993).

In a second derivative text, *Christ the Sacrament of the Encounter with God*, Schillebeeckx developed the notion of the sacramental experience of the divine where he elaborates the living core of Christianity as the intimate meeting between God and the human person through the encounter with Christ in the sacraments.[12] Sacramental presence is thus worked out narratively or in Thomistic categories. In other words, Christian stories about creation frame the divine initiative in meeting people through Christ, the exclusive avenue to God.

3. Hermeneutical Strategies

Schillebeeckx's later hermeneutical concerns attempted to retrieve and promote the relevance of these narratives about human salvation. Especially during the 1960s Schillebeeckx produced important books specific to Christology that highlighted the story of the human-divine relationship in terms of participation and gratuitousness and later on that of anticipation, from the experience of human misery, and mediated immediacy, through the mystical experience of God.[13] These developments were intended to situate the divine encounter in the experiences of contemporary people. And what cannot be named positively as meaningful is revealed *via* a negative contrast experience. That is, in critical resistance to that which is not humanly meaningful. Thus, the negative experience of misery and the positive experience of God's presence link the Christian narrative with both positive and negative experiences of meaning.

Two elements developed this epistemological framework. First, the hermeneutical developments announced in the 1960s that signal a distancing from the theoretical metaphysics of Dominic Marie De Petter towards an 'indirect' formulation of the still universal claims of Christian faith. This insertion of the negative contrast experience provides a non-expressible experience of meaning through which the universal meaning of the Christian narrative can be maintained. Second, the use of linguistic analysis values the logical structures and paradigms within the Christian narrative as normative. They are given a normativity which preserves the successive re-interpretations of the Christian story

12. Edward Schillebeeckx, *Christ the Sacrament of the Encounter With God* (London: Sheed and Ward, 1963).
13. Anton Houtepen, "Edward Schillebeeckx Lezing 1998: Op zoek naar de levende God," *Nieuws* (Stichting Edward Schillebeeckx, 15, 1998) 1.

by applying an objective logic and structural pattern. Together these two hermeneutical tools formed a methodological strategy for 'surfacing' the divine presence through the Christian narrative of human salvation from God.

4. Significance of Paul Ricoeur

In light of the recent publication by Paul Ricoeur, *Soi-même comme un autre*, concerning narrative and identity, Schillebeeckx's early enthusiastic interest in Ricoeur is significant.[14] The first became clear in 1968 when Schillebeeckx gave a tribute to Ricoeur on the occasion of his Doctorate, *honoris causa*, from the Catholic University of Nijmegen. Ted Schoof had previously made the observation that Ricoeur's hermeneutics influenced Schillebeeckx.[15]

Schillebeeckx elaborated several reasons for Ricoeur being honoured by theology and not some other discipline. Ricoeur was an opponent of the absurd and a prophet of the meaningful.[16] He advanced the idea that there is an abundance of meaning over nonsense in human life.[17] He observed: "Your firm conviction is that human existence is the laboratory of philosophy; but you are also convinced, as a Christian, that this human existence must be seen in the light of the Resurrection and of the 'New Creation' in Christ and that Christian faith concerns this very same human existence."[18] Ricoeur had elsewhere made reference to the ambiguity of life that philosophy would never exhaust.[19] However, Schillebeeckx appropriated this experience into the Christian eschatological discourse of faith:

> This faith in the abundance of eschatological meaning in our life, drives you into a constant search for meaning throughout history and its ambi-

---

14. Cf. Paul Ricoeur, *Soi-même comme un autre* (Paris: Éditions du Seuil, 1990). Translated as: *Oneself as Another,* trans. K. Blamey (Chicago: University of Chicago Press, 1992).

15. Cf. Edward Schillebeeckx, "Le philosophe Paul Ricoeur, docteur en théologie," *Christianisme social* 78 (1968) 639-645.

16. Cf. Paul Ricoeur, "Sciences humaines et conditionnement de la foi," *Recherches et Débats* 52 (1965) 141; "Prévision économique et choix éthique," *Esprit* 34 (1966) 189; *De l'interprétation* (Paris: Seuil, 1965) 507; *Histoire et vérité* (Paris: Seuil, 1964) 122.

17. Cf. Paul Ricoeur, "Approche philosophique de concept de liberté intérieure," *L'herméneutique de la liberté religieuse,* ed. Enrico Castelli (Paris: Aubier-Montaigne, 1968) 223.

18. Schillebeeckx, "Le philosophe Paul Ricoeur," 641.

19. Paul Ricoeur, *L'homme faillible* (Paris: Aubier, 1960) 24 and 34.

guities. This is precisely the reason why you are constantly in quest of signs of overabundance of grace ... on the world's vast stage.[20]

In this respect, Ricoeur's work analysed human experience in light of Christian faith but without confusing the autonomous philosophical and theological methodologies. This was exactly the same project that Schillebeeckx aspired to in his theological reflection on human history as a history of salvation.

Second, Ricoeur picked up on the notion of historical situation that is dear to Schillebeeckx and made a plea for the context in which Christian faith finds its home. Though not uncritical of both modernity and secularization, he remains optimistic that, even against such a background, Christian evangelization and the relationship with God can be maintained. Schillebeeckx expresses this very confidently: "... against the background of the process of secularization – in which you perceive, siding with the process of rationality, the loss of meaning, you remain convinced, faithful to your 'philosophy of hope', that the very idea that there may be a time unfit for evangelization is itself blasphemous."[21]

By the end of the 1960s Schillebeeckx himself was convinced that the Christian narrative, despite a concern for modernity and secularization, enjoyed a permanent relevance within Western cultures. Through his hermeneutical methods, both positive but mainly negative contrast experience, the Christian tradition appeared beyond the historical and cultural changes taking place and pointed to a 'religious depth' in excess of prevailing interpretations of experience. This becomes clearer through the examination of his work on the Eucharist in 1967.[22]

5. Eucharist

What is at stake in this book is again the divine presence compared to which 'transubstantiation' is, in the context of the Council of Trent, only a medieval intellectual expression. On the one hand, this divine reality of Christ's presence is grasped by faith; by knowing what God intends things to be and by what is actually given to us by God. On the other hand, according to Schillebeeckx, this is too 'extrinsic'. He favours

---

20. Schillebeeckx, "Le philosophe Paul Ricoeur," 642.
21. *Ibid.*, 643; Paul Ricoeur, "Prévision économique," *Esprit* 34 (1966) 188.
22. Edward Schillebeeckx, *The Eucharist* (New York: Sheed and Ward, 1968).

the interpretation of the eucharistic change as the 'divine constitution' of reality itself. In other words, reality receives what it is from the 'divine source of reality'. Then there is a sacrament which is 'determined' by its source and another sacrament which is 'inherently' a sacrament or formally its own goodness by which it is thus named.[23] This announces a difference in density of faith between what is received from God and what is 'ontologically' already present in reality, though still from the divine source of reality. That is, Schillebeeckx invests reality with an ultimate level of meaning received from God that is only ever partially grasped in experience.

Schillebeeckx's commitment to reality as religious ontology points to his on-going view that sacramental presence is a *datum*, a given, that hermeneutically re-surfaces in different cultural contexts. A theology of revelation shows the capacity to surface the Christian narrative in any number of circumstances under the impulse of changing experiences.[24] The secular culture is never devoid of grace, a source of reality that is not of this world – the grace that only God can give! New contexts and a new world of ideas create new interpretations. But critical to the future of the Christian narrative and to Schillebeeckx's hermeneutics of retrieval of the tradition of meaning and religious depth, in changing historical and social situations, is challenged by postmodernity with its insistence that the grand narratives of meaning and truth are over. It is to this discussion that we now turn more explicitly.

6. Christian Narrative in Postmodernity

The critique of grand narratives bears on the question of Edward Schillebeeckx's hermeneutics of Christian faith. What Schillebeeckx's narrative of human salvation does is tell a religious story of the past and then map this onto the future as a grand narrative, albeit in an anticipatory mode. The difficulty is, in terms of the postmodern condition of fragmentation, lost-identity and even bricolage, is that these grand

---

23. Schillebeeckx, *The Eucharist*, 78 n. 85.

24. *Ibid.*, 82: "According to the Catholic view of revelation and thus of the whole order of salvation, grace itself comes to us in a historical, visible form, on the horizontal level of human history (and, included in this, on the level of the cosmos or the corporeal world) and not simply vertically, like rain falling from heaven. What comes to us from heaven – grace – in fact comes to us *from the world*, from human history with its secular environment."

narratives *never tell particular stories*. And a second issue is that in order
to go on believing in a meaningful history almost requires that one necessarily go on believing in grand narratives. Or alternatively, believing in
a distopia, when at the end of the millenium everything will implode.
In either case, optimistically or not, all such stories are grand narratives
of a kind. These themes are taken up in a topical way by Don DeLillo.

Don DeLillo's novel *White Noise* contains a number of conversations
about truth and meaning in postmodernity.[25] The characters in *White
Noise* inhabit a world of shopping malls, of tabloids and of environ-
mental disasters. They eat fast-food from styrofoam containers in neon-
lit parking lots; they accumulate scraps of trivia from around the world;
they argue with each other about the workings of the technology that
surrounds them but which they barely comprehend; they generally try
their best to cope in a world that seems to be too complex and to be
changing too fast to give any answers to their deepest questions and
fears: How should I live? Why do I have to die? The bubble of television and the computer screen provides the backdrop to people's most
intimate moments. In short, they live in a postmodern world.[26]

This implies a cultural context that has ruptured with the past, bringing a sense of speeding-up and the loss of a fixed sense of absolute truth
about anything.[27] Nevertheless, maintaining a fascination for the rich
world of appearance, including greater access to the Internet and the
variable and multiple pieces of information characteristic of the technological changes at the end of the millenium. However, do these
postmodern ideas bring liberation and salvation in the trans-historical
narrative forms hermeneutically re-surfaced by Schillebeeckx? And what
is the status of narrative in postmodernity?

Postmodernity poses a challenge to authority and received wisdom,
whether religious, political or social. This is in line with the tradition of
general skepticism and anti-foundationalism in Western thought. Skepticism, in this sense, means challenging received wisdom, including
religious wisdom, that is embedded and coded in institutions and their
narratives. In other words, being skeptical and doubtful about the

---

25. Don DeLillo, *White Noise* (New York: Viking, 1985).

26. The term Postmodern, along with its variants: Postmodernism, Postmodernity,
the Postmodern condition, is used with increasing frequency as we approach the end of
the 20th century. It remains ambiguous. It could be a catch-all description of contemporary culture; and end-of-the-millennium escape clause for meaning and thinking.

27. Cf. "The Postmodern Grand-Narrative," *Encounter*, 10 October 1999 (Australian
Broadcasting Commission, Melbourne).

kind of ideas that have existed in traditional religious narratives. Jean-Francoise Lyotard has named this incredulity towards grand narratives or meta-narratives, that have dominated Christian faith in the West, as the 'Postmodern Condition'.

7. Hermeneutical Response to Postmodern Challenge

Schillebeeckx has tried to cope with concerns about the loss of the grand narratives and their legitimating function. They are used as legitimating devices in order to give authority to certain ways of understanding, acting and planning within a social group. This is, of course, an ethical issue surrounding stories of human meaning that Schillebeeckx has addressed in his hermeneutical 'correction'. He places emphasis on stories of human suffering and the plea for the desired but as yet incomplete *humanum*. But this only remains within the parameters of a 'modern' world of universal values and legitimation. Postmodernity has not only broken with the universal value system but with all forms of 'presence' in the sense of 'self-grounding' identity. This is what David Tracy calls "the unreality of the notion of presence in modernity's concept of present time" and "the unreality of the modern subject's self-understanding as grounded in itself."[28] The image of the *Internet* is sometimes invoked for the postmodern experience. It provides a capacity to access culture almost anywhere in the world in a non-hierarchical open-ended way. Truth is strictly open-ended, contingent on the way that the user shapes what the world is going to be like for them.

What postmodernity does to a narrative, religious or other, is to undermine the very idea of progress, or control of the future, on the basis of what one now understands about the past or the present. A narrative in postmodernity breaks from the past, the tradition, and any idea that you can control the future. Why this destruction? Simply because it was considered that those 'past' traditions no longer work. In a sense, like the counter-reformation, the modern religious narrative, which Schillebeeckx still believes in, tries to bring back the ornaments, symbolism, metaphors, colour and rhetoric of the past and present. But there is a new sensibility in culture. The building-blocks of a saving narrative are no longer popularly 'of the people' and their new-found taste for pluralism.

28. David Tracy, "On Naming the Present," *On Naming the Present: God, Hermeneutics and Church* (New York: Orbis, 1994) 15.

This is not only the rejection of a religious narrative. The whole domain of contemporary art and culture has become a matter of personal taste, something that can be either rejected or enjoyed. Furthermore, postmodernity signals the rejection of modern philosophy as well. This has consequences for questions of truth and ethics. Its chief target, the Enlightenment, which ushered in such a solid belief in reason and science, and insinuated that the individual and society would be 'emancipated' from superstition and irrationality, also proved to be false in the light of history. At the very least, postmodernity intends to humble the 'great truths'. It rejects dogmatic, non self-critical claims to possess truth *via* a privileged avenue, including that of any one religion.

8. Conclusion

Given the postmodern condition, what is left of the relationship with God and the sense of the presence of the divine in the world, that Edward Schillebeeckx so enthusiastically points towards? More particularly, where does plurality leave us, without recourse to an absolute universal foundation in religious truth? How can the Christian tradition actively maintain its truth in society if it recognises itself as just one voice among many? These are currently questions in dispute. On the one hand, in a pluralistic age and postmodern environment, the Christian narrative can aim to actually avoid a language which is only accessible to believers, in favour of a fuller participation in the public forum where arguments based on utility can become more readily comprehensible to all parties. On the other hand, this becomes much more complex when it is pointed out that the Christian church does have a particular story of human life and destiny, also about what is good and true, and we are entitled like any group to present that story.

What cannot be ignored about postmodernity is the undoing of the authority of any grand narrative. This includes the Enlightenment 'discourses' about social emancipation. For some this is a sign of moral and political apathy. For others, it is the demise of overarching narratives of liberation, including Feminism and Marxism, to make way for new stories of self-identification and a fresh religious and political participation. It is possible for a new radical plural culture to grow stories of human liberation that are merely miniature and individual though this necessarily involves a new and destabilising conception of self and of belief. Men and women become ambiguous authors of their own destiny. This is a mixed situation because on the one hand, one is more and more the owner of one's destiny but, on the other hand, having less clarity about what that destiny entails. The freedom of postmodern narratives are a mixed blessing.

Either a nostalgic return or, with Schillebeeckx, a kind of retrieval of the tradition under the influence of a new hermeneutical rubric of anticipation, try to stem the tide of history. This implies a resistance to the postmodern and globalisation. But nostalgia and retrieval are also predicated by the grand-narrative. "It used to be like this and that's the way that we would like to keep it." But the postmodern is, perhaps, not so feral and fruitless. Postmodernity opens up possibilities and alternatives which are perhaps what we should be looking for in the religious search for divine presence. Looking for an alternative to the choice between nostalgia and retrieval or just passivity and complicity.

Postmodernity may not be the end of ethics, politics and hope, except perhaps for the kind based on universals and grand narratives. The question for Schillebeeckx is whether religious traditions can do without the kind of nostalgia mentioned? For the Christian story, and its sacramentology, emphasis has historically been placed on its hegemony. At the very least, what is clearly important for Schillebeeckx, namely, the necessity for the Church and for keeping the Catholic story alive, is not at all immediately obvious to postmoderns. Because Christianity has been the dominant tradition of Western culture, it stands vulnerable before the emergence of postmodernity. But does the new postmodern narrative of pluralism spell the destruction of the Christian tradition?

This question confronts the 'adequacy' of Schillebeeckx's hermeneutical re-surfacing of narrative meaning. It also implies making a judgement about the adequacy of the 'postmodern' characterization given to contemporary culture. If indeed, as I have argued, pluralism reigns and meanings are no longer either fixed or universal, then the Christian story can only ever be one of a number of available stories on the shelves of the postmodern supermarket.

Thus, to draw on the theme of sacramental presence, is to remember that the Christian narrative and its celebration can only ever be an 'in-house' affair as a commitment to particularity. For Christians it affirms a particular identity which, for all its forthrightness, must be a dialogue partner or at least a fellow-traveler with the pluri-form religious movements of today.

Schillebeeckx's contribution is widely valued as magisterial. He continues to attribute to experience a 'sacramental depth.' In this he risks underplaying the 'intrinsic' value of things in favour of their 'transcendent' origin. On that score one can pertinently ask whether this is in fact the way postmodern people, not only existentialists and secularists, actually experience the world. In other words, when and how does his theology come to terms with changing patterns of experience? An adjustment to postmodernity would certainly strengthen the themes of historical and cultural sensitivity. While at the same time it must forfeit some of the emphasis on hermeneutical re-surfacing and relish in the challenge of mapping the historical change to the notion of sacramentality itself in the newly emerging postmodern context. Schillebeeckx understands the Christian narrative of God's salvific presence in the world as, either positively or negatively, able to be critically translated throughout history and culture, despite ruptures and breaks.[29] He has argued that: "Every dogma must have an orientation towards the future and be open to the sphere of the future. This has consequences for our conception of dogma itself, since truth then becomes, for us now, something whose fullness belongs to the future; to the extent that its content is already realized, it discloses itself essentially as a *promise*."[30] Nonetheless, this does not preclude the on-going critical re-interpretation of the Christian narrative throughout these different historical and cultural contexts based on models and paradigms contemporary to the age.[31] This remains Schillebeeckx's hermeneutical task.

He has argued for an on-going cohesiveness to cultural history in which, at one level, the structure of the Judeo-Christian story remains intact, though, at another level, manifesting a certain plurality of interpretation and expression. In this he draws not only on the hermeneutical approaches already outlined but on the French *Annales School* of historiography.[32] He utilizes the basic schema of the French theorists of

29. Cf. Edward Schillebeeckx, "Breuken in christelijke dogma's," *Breuklijnen: Grenservaringen en zoektochten*, ed. Edward Schillebeeckx, Bas van Iersel, Ad Willems, Herman Wegman (Baarn: Nelissen, 1994) 15-49.

30. Edward Schillebeeckx, "Towards a Catholic Use of Hermeneutics," *God the Future of Man* (New York: Sheed and Ward, 1968) 36.

31. Cf. D. Thompson, "Schillebeeckx and the Development of Doctrine: Historical Periods, Postmodernity and the Translation of Experience" (Catholic Theological Society of America, June 10-13, 1999, unpublished) 19-20.

32. Cf. Johan Van Wyngaerden, "D. M. De Petter o.p. (1905-1971): Een inleiding tot zijn leven en denken" (Licentiaatsverhandeling in Godsdienstwetenschappen, Katholieke Universiteit Leuven, 1989) 2-4; Dennis Rochford, "The Appropriation of Hermeneutics in the Theological Works of Edward Schillebeeckx: An Historical Textual Evaluation of the Theological Project to Bridge Christian Faith with Modern Culture" (Ph.D. diss., Katholieke Universiteit Leuven, 1995) 1.1-1.4.

culture to give an account of how Christian faith can diachronically sustain its narrative and truth claims. He argues that three major 'conjunctures' have dominated theological history, namely, the patristic, medieval and modern. But he now admits that culture is confronting a move to the postmodern.[33]

Postmodern pluralism must pose serious problems for the narrative that Schillebeeckx takes for granted. Can he adjust his view of reality to correspond with the new cultural sensibility? Though appreciation of historical consciousness certainly allows for a variety of conceptual expressions of Christian faith, for him this multifaceted reality is finally one, even if viewed 'perspectivally'. In other words, beneath the surface of the different cultural experiential, that is, conjunctural manifestations, there is only one reality and God is at its center. Narrative unity is, therefore, always the theme of Schillebeeckx's hermeneutically valorized work. As it emerges in his theology, hermeneutics is always about the surfacing of meaning within the parameters of the unified Catholic world and its philosophical background.

The plurality and ambiguity of human salvation, the patent lack of universal meaning in human history and the thematized plurality manifest in atheistic philosophies is effectively robbed of its particular postmodern horizon of experience. Instead, conceptual crystallisations of God-images which no longer resonate at the cultural level of experience, continue to live in the Christian narrative as 'suspended' life-forms in the Christian horizon of explanation. In the dialogue with culture, which always marked Schillebeeckx's work, the 'surviving' Christian synthesis seems to traverse postmodernity in terms of a metaphysical 'possibility' that is given to being, while eschewing the lost grand narratives of postmodernity which have been replaced by particular self-determining and individual stories.

Schillebeeckx has valorized the experience-tradition in such a way that the interpretation of these human experiences, including their individual and collective biographies, no longer occurs primarily through a positive metaphysical discourse but through a negative anticipation of meaning. To do this he has posited the negative contrast experience as a human constant in the real history of human suffering. Out of this comes the protest of hope in a yet to be realized *humanum* which is our human destiny. Of course, whether this approach is finally able to bridge the gap between experience in postmodernity and Christian

---

33. Schillebeeckx, "Breuken in christelijke dogma's," 27-30.

tradition remains open. The measure of meaningfulness of the Christian narrative, within postmodernity, identified in the dialectical relationship between praxis and mysticism and the partial break-through of an eschatological final horizon of meaning, cannot be dismissed. Nonetheless, at least in postmodernity, where self-legitimation narratives leave behind the grand-narratives of personal identity and meaning, the sheer ambiguity of life cannot be by-passed with a closed depository belief-system, whether atheistic or theistic. History remains a mixture of meaning, nonsense and misery for which a theologically adequate narrative must find space and respect for pluralism.

A Protestant Theology of Sacramental Presence
How 'Postliberal' Is George Lindbeck's Theology in *The Nature of Doctrine*?

Desiree J. Berendsen

1. Introduction

If someone does not understand the language of faith you just repeat it over and over again till that person is used to it. According to Lindbeck the grammar of religion can only be learned by practice.[1] This is the first characteristic of Lindbeck's theory of religion; religious doctrines are the grammar of a religion.[2] In this paper I will defend the thesis that in combining a 'cultural-linguistic' theory of religion with an intra-textual theory of truth *ex auditu*, Lindbeck developed an orthodox Protestant theology of the Word. Lindbeck's truth theory makes his 'postliberal theory' an example of classical fideistic Protestantism in which the Word is used sacramentally.

I will proceed as follows: first I will describe Lindbeck's cultural-linguistic approach to religion and the Wittgensteinian rule-theory with which he combines it. Next I will describe and analyse Lindbeck's theory of intratextual truth. Once I have clarified Lindbeck's position, I shall proceed to argue why I see Lindbeck's truth theory as a Protestant theory of sacramental presence of the Word of God. Finally I argue that this is not postmodern (postliberal) at all; it can only be called postliberal in the sense of neo-orthodox.

---

1. George A. Lindbeck, *The Nature of Doctrine: Religion and Theology in a Postliberal Age* (Philadelphia PN: Westminster Press, 1984).

2. *The Nature of Doctrine*, 80-81. Cf. Wittgenstein, *Philosophische Untersuchungen*, no. 373: "Welche Art von Gegenstand etwas ist, sagt die Grammatik. (Theologie als Grammatik.)."

2. Description and Analysis of Lindbeck's Cultural-linguistic Approach and His Truth-theory

Lindbeck's theory of religion consists of two parts, a cultural-linguistic part combined with rule theory and his truth-theory. First: what is Lindbeck's cultural-linguistic approach and how does he use it in his theory of religion?

Cultural-linguistic Approach

Lindbeck develops his cultural-linguistic approach of religion in contrast with two others: one that emphasizes the cognitive aspects of religion and one that stresses the experiential-expressive dimension of religion. In cognitivism, church doctrines function as informative propositions or truth claims about objective realities. This is the position of traditional orthodoxies. The 'experiential-expressive' (liberal) approach interprets doctrines as noninformative and nondiscursive symbols of inner feelings, attitudes or existential orientations.[3] This kind of approach began with Schleiermacher. Lindbeck proposes an alternative: his cultural-linguistic approach in which church doctrines are seen as regulative. In this approach emphasis is placed on the respects in which religions resemble languages, together with their correlative forms of life, and are thus similar to cultures.[4] Church doctrines are viewed mostly with regard to the function of their use, not as expressive symbols (as in the experiential-expressive approach) or truth claims (as in the cognitive approach of religion). Doctrines are seen as communally authoritative rules of discourse, attitude and action.[5]

According to Lindbeck, religion as a doctrinal system is second order discourse. Religion can be seen as a cultural and linguistic framework that shapes the entirety of life and thought. To become religious, then, is to become skilled in the language, the symbol system of a given religion. To become skilled in a specific religious tradition is to interiorize a set of skills by practice and training.[6] Thus, Lindbeck concludes, religion need not be described as something universal arising from within the depths of individuals; it can be just as plausibly construed as a class name for a variegated set of cultural-linguistic systems that differentially

3. *The Nature of Doctrine*, 16.
4. *Ibid.*, 18.
5. *Ibid.*
6. *Ibid.*, 33-35.

shape and produce our most profound sentiments, attitudes, and aware-
nesses.[7] So, according to Lindbeck religion is not generic, but a cultural
system. This does not say anything about whether human beings are
religious *a priori* or not, this is another discussion which Lindbeck does
not enter into.

Intratextual Truth

In matters of truth, Lindbeck sees two dangers with respect to the
cultural-linguistic approach. One possible consequence of using doctrines as rules is relativism; when in a religious system doctrines are rules
it is difficult to claim the truth of one doctrine over another – and even
more difficult to say that one religious system is more true than another.
The reverse consequence is fideism; if the truth of a doctrine is purely
intratextual, the choice between religions is a matter of blind faith.[8]
Lindbeck tries to avoid these dangers by developing his intratextual view
of truth *ex auditu*.[9] In this section I will analyse Lindbeck's intratextual
view on truth. The *ex auditu* element will be part of the next section.

According to Lindbeck, the liberal view of truth is extratextual. In
the liberal approach to religion the religious meaning is located outside the text, either in the objective realities to which it refers or in the
experiences it symbolizes, whereas for cultural-linguists the meaning is
immanent.[10] Intratextuality means that the scriptural world is able to
absorb the universe rather than the other way around. It is the text

---

7. *The Nature of Doctrine*, 40.
8. *Ibid.*, 128.
9. Lindbeck is much criticized on this point of combining the cultural-linguistic
method with a theory of truth. For example David F. Ford, "The Best Apologetics is
Good Systematics," *Anglican Theological Review* 67 (1985) 249: "… Lindbeck makes a
strong case for seeing it [the trinity, DB] as regulative, but his comments make too great
a distinction between seeing it as rule and seeing it as ontological proposition. The one-
sidedness of this lies in its suggested downgrading of the knowledge content in Christian worship and life, and the displacement of the ontological truth question into a
practical question…," and p. 250: "I have critized him for transcending the relativistic
limitations of the cultural-linguistic approach in one-sidedly practical terms." Lee C.
Barrett, "Theology as Grammar: Regulative Principles or Paradigms and Practices,"
Modern Theology 4 (1988) 171: "… no sharp distinction can be made between doctrines
as second-order regulative principles and the first-order truth-claims, emotions, pas-
sions, and behavior which they govern. In order to have any meaning, a doctrine must
have some paradigmatic instantiations and guiding long-term interests and concerns. To
change the paradigm is to change the very meaning of the rule." Steven M. Emmanuel,
"Kierkegaard on Doctrine: A Post-modern Interpretation," *Religious Studies* 25 (1989)
374: "The main weakness of Lindbeck's exposition is that it does not tell us enough
about the relation between rules and truth."
10. *The Nature of Doctrine*, 114.

which – in Lindbeck's words – absorbs the world, rather than the world the text. An intratextual reading tries to derive the interpretive framework that designates the theologically controlling sense from the literary structure of the text itself.[11] It is thus not possible to explain the meaning of a text with elements from outside the text. The meaning of the text is inseparable from a specific discourse, because this is constitutive for the text. Meaning, language and truth are inseparably bound up in Lindbeck's intratextual view of truth. Apart from the intratextual meaning of religion, Lindbeck also distinguishes some levels of truth in religion. Intratextuality is about the whole of a religion, a religion can be understood intratextually. The levels of truth we are observing now are inner-religious, i.e. on the level of utterances in a religion.

In *The Nature of Doctrine* Lindbeck distinguishes ontological, categorial and intrasystematical truth.[12] Ontological truth is the traditional view of truth as correspondence with reality.[13] Categorial truth is the adequacy of certain categories to describe reality.[14] Categorial truth is a necessary but not sufficient condition for ontological truth.[15] In other words, categorial truth can become ontological truth. One cannot make either true or false statements about reality if one lacks the categories to describe it in the first place.[16]

Finally, a truth-claim is intrasystematically true when it coheres with the context. An intrasystematic utterance is meaningless when it is part of a system that does not refer to reality. Lindbeck uses his famous example of the crusader to illustrate this point of intrasystematic truth. For Lindbeck a statement can be true in one context and false in another, for example the crusader crying 'Christus Dominus' in the battle. This crusader is uttering a false statement in Lindbeck's eyes. The crusader's utterance could be intrasystematically true, because the sentence 'Christus est dominus' coheres with the Christian cultural-linguistic system. However, the utterance is false since the crusader's actions do not cohere with the practices the Christian religion defines as

---

11. *The Nature of Doctrine*, 117-120.
12. We cannot explore categorial truth here. On the differentiation of truth claims in Lindbeck see Bruce D. Marshall, "Aquinas as Postliberal Theologian," *The Thomist* 53 (1989) 353-402 and Bruce D. Marshall, "Absorbing the World," *Theology and Dialogue: Essays in Conversation with George Lindbeck* (Notre Dame, IN: University of Notre Dame Press, 1990) 69-102.
13. *The Nature of Doctrine*, 64.
14. *Ibid.*, 48.
15. Marshall, "Aquinas as Postliberal Theologian," 360.
16. *Ibid.*, 361.

appropriate to such an utterance. Lindbeck holds this statement to be false in this context; does that imply that this utterance is wrong in this context, or meaningless?[17] Intrasystematic truth too is a necessary, but not sufficient condition of ontological truth. Categorial and intrasystematic truth together are the necessary and sufficient conditions of ontological truth.[18]

Thus, we saw that a truth-claim is intrasystematically true when it coheres with the context, it is ontologically true when it corresponds with reality. We can only discuss the car's color if it is obvious which car we are talking about. The same is true for religion; a religious statement only contains an ontological truth-claim if it is uttered in a context of praise or prayer.[19] Religious doctrines, as second order discourse, do not contain any ontological truth; they can only be intrasystematically true. Just as grammar by itself affirms nothing either true or false regarding the world in which language is used, but only about language, so theology and doctrine, to the extent that they are second-order activities, assert nothing either true or false about God and his relation to creatures, but only speak about such assertions.[20]

---

17. Lindbeck has received a lot of critique on this point of entanglement of truth and meaning. Slater's critisism on this point is that Lindbeck "rules out of bounds the common assumption that all religious people are somehow responding to the *same* sense of cosmic 'transcendence' prompting their different modes of personal transformation" (60). Indeed this is exactly the point Lindbeck wants to make, there is no common denominator to be found in religious traditions. The problem Slater has with this point is that it is only possible to know what it is to be truly religious within the respective traditions. According to Slater the cultural linguistic approach "commits us to agreeing that truth only arises where meaning is established and meaning depends on use in context" (61). This, according to Slater, is counterintuitive. Peter Slater, "Lindbeck, Hick and the Nature of Religious Truth," *Studies in Religion/Sciences Religieuses* 24 (1995) 59-75. Richards comments are in the same strain when he says that when the crusader's cry is false it "would seem to make it difficult for someone to be a hypocrite, since this term usually designates someone who assents to the truth of a certain belief, but then contradicts that belief with some action" (43). According to Richards, "Lindbeck often confuses truth with verification, justification, or *certainty*" (44). Jay W. Richards, "Truth and Meaning in George Lindbeck's *The Nature of Doctrine*," *Religious Studies* 33 (1997) 33-53.
From a very different angle, D. Z. Philips is likewise arguing that Lindbeck is confusing two grammars, when he wants to hold on some ontological truth next to his intra-systematic truth. "Lindbeck reverts to the tempting charm of the cognitivist theory and speaks as though a truth concerning God has to do with the relation between the grammatical rule and a reality independent of itself" (146). And: "... for him [Lindbeck, DB] first-order propositions make claims about extra-linguistic realities. Once again, this involves the confusion of grammars" (148). D. Z. Philips, "Lindbeck's Audience," *Modern Theology* 4 (1988) 133-154.
18. Marshall, "Aquinas as Postliberal Theologian," 366.
19. *The Nature of Doctrine*, 68.
20. *Ibid.*, 69.

Here the connection of the two levels of truth distinguished becomes problematic. The intrasystematic question can only be whether the rules are coherent with the context; the ontological question, however, is whether or not the statement corresponds with reality. For Lindbeck, intrasystematic truth is a necessary but not sufficient condition for ontological truth. Ontologically nothing can be said about the truth of religious doctrines, they can only be intrasystematically true. As a cultural-linguist Lindbeck could drop the idea of ontological truth, however, because of his fear to become relativist he also wants to say something about the ontological truth of religious doctrines.

3. Lindbeck's Theory of Truth Seen as a (Protestant) Theory of the Sacramental Presence of the Word of God

Now, I will develop the thesis that we can see Lindbeck's theory of an 'intratextual truth *ex auditu*' as a Protestant theory of sacramental presence. The Word of God, in this view, is sacramentally present in our world. In developing this thesis, I shall first explain what I mean by sacramental presence and then go on to examine the place of the Word of God in Protestant theology.

Sacramental Presence

By sacramental presence we mean the presence of something transcendent in the world. Because in Christian theology this transcendence is considered as eternal, sacramental presence has the character of the existence of eternity in time. Yet this seems an impossibility. In theology and philosophy people have given much thought to this problem of eternity in time. The Catholic theology of the Eucharist is a good example of the result of attempts to connect the eternal otherworldly with this temporal world. The Eucharist in the Roman Catholic mass is the moment in which the incarnation of Christ is present in the world again. It is not just remembrance of the last supper, it is not even repetition of this last supper of Christ with his disciples, it is the making present of Christ incarnate in the actual moment each and every time the mass is celebrated.

Word of God in Protestant Theology

The function of the Word of God in Protestant theology can be seen as analogous to that of the Eucharist in Roman Catholic theology.

Much more than Catholic theology, Protestant theology is a verbal tradition. The *sola scriptura* can be seen as the paradigm for this tradition.
No papal hierarchy, no saints, no images of saints and crucifixes, no
mass. Just the Word. Perhaps the most important protestant theologian in this century, Karl Barth, distinguishes three ways in which the
Word of God comes into the world. These are: Scripture, the preaching of the gospel in the church and Jesus Christ.[21] The Bible and the
preaching of the gospel are the Word of God which God uses to reveal
Jesus Christ. Thus, the Word of God is always an occurrence: the coming of Christ on earth. It is important to note that for Barth this
occurrence can never be grasped by human beings. If the Word of God
is always an occurrence, the coming of Christ on earth, then that
occurence can be seen as sacramental presence. The eternal Word
becomes present in our temporary world, the transcendent Christ
comes into the world.[22]

Protestant theology of the Word can become fideistic if we define
fideism as refraining from any point of contact (*Anknüpfungspunkt*) for
revelation in human reality, refraining from any human activity with
respect to divine grace. For a fideist the basis of theology is in divine
revelation or the gift of faith.[23] In this respect Barth and other theological positivists can be seen as fideistic, because Barth's fundamental thesis
is that the Word itself creates its point of contact with human reality.
A more fundamental kind of fideism is 'relativist fideism' as Tilley terms

21. Cf. section titles in Karl Barth, *Die Kirchliche Dogmatik* (München, 1932):
KD I/1 §4 "Das Wort Gottes in seiner dreifachen Gestalt." The subsections have
as theme respectively the "verkündigte, geschriebene und geoffenbarte Wort
Gottes."

22. Barth here uses Kierkegaard's notion of 'simultaneity'. Cf. Ronald F. Thiemann
"Response to George Lindbeck," *Theology Today* 43 (1986) 381: "For Barth, all knowledge of God has a *"sacramental" quality*, because we come to know God through a creaturely medium which is not God, an external reality chosen as the vehicle for revelation,
namely the humanity of Jesus. In choosing the humanity of Jesus, God has provided
sacramental and thus *indirect* access. ... Jesus Christ as God incarnate is God's sacramental presence among humankind, but even that *sacramental presence cannot be known
directly*, for God is known in Jesus Christ only through the witness of the biblical narrative" (emphasis mine, DB).

23. See for this definition and further differentiation in fideism, Terrence W. Tilley
"Incommensurability, Intratextuality, and Fideism," *Modern Theology* 5 (1989) 88. In
Denzinger the thesis against fideism reads: "Si quis dixerit, revelationem divinam exter-
nis signis credibilem fieri non posse, ideoque sola interna cuiusque experientia aut inspi-
ratione privata homines ad fidem moveri debere: anathema sit" (3033). Thus, fideism is
faith through inner experience and personal inspiration alone, because revelation cannot
become believable by external signs.

it. Relativist fideists claim that their own views can be understood only relative to their own commitments, and their opponents' views only relative to their opponents' commitments. If the two groups do not share commitments, there can be no understanding between them, whereas people with differing basic commitments are isolated from the possibility of true conversation and real disagreement.[24] Truth claims made by the first kind of fideists are universal, whereas the second are not.

Lindbeck's Truth Theory as ...

To what extent can we see Lindbeck as a representative of the Barthian fideistic tradition?[25] First of all one should note that Lindbeck's starting point is in ecumenical debate. His cultural-linguistic theory of religion is developed in order to provide a framework for the ecumenical dialogue. At the same time he wants to have a means to say that one tradition is better, more true, than another.[26] It is in this context that he develops his theory of truth *ex auditu*.[27] The *ex auditu* element of his truth-theory connects Lindbeck's intratextual theory of truth with

24. Tilley, "Incommensurability, Intratexturality, and Fideism," 89.
25. Apart from the question whether or not Barth can be read as a 'postmodern theologian' as some hold – e.g. Isolde Andrews, *Deconstructing Barth: A Study of the Complementary Methods in Karl Barth and Jacques Derrida* (New York: Peter Lang, 1996); Leendert M. Karelse, *Dwalen: Over Mark C. Taylor en Karl Barth* (Zoetermeer: Boekencentrum, 1999); Graham Ward, *Barth, Derrida and the Language of Theology* (Cambridge: University Press, 1995), to name but a few. On the other hand, of course, there are people who do not see Barth as postmodern at all. George Hunsinger, for example, sees Lindbeck more as a Thomist than a Barthian because he can be read as "offering a version of the idea that grace perfects but does not destroy nature" (49). "Is it not finally determined by God in such a way that cultural-linguistic considerations, however valid they may be on their own plane, cannot be either decisive or exhaustive?" (47). I appreciate Hunsinger's point that Lindbeck has a strong role for human agency in causing a theological utterance to be either true or false. My own view, however, is that Lindbeck disqualifies the possibility of human agency that he ascribes in his cultural-linguistic approach of religion in his theory of truth *ex auditu*. According to this theory someone is saved if at the moment of dying he or she opts for Christ (cf. *The Nature of Doctrine*, 57-59). George Hunsinger, "Truth as Self-Involving: Barth and Lindbeck on the Cognitive and Performative Aspects of Truth in Theological Discourse," *Journal of the American Academy of Religion* 61 (1993) 41-54.
26. "It is not the business of a nontheological theory of religion to argue for or against the superiority of any one faith, but it does have the job, if it is to be religiously useful, of allowing the possibility of such a superiority. It must not, in other words, exclude the claims religions make about themselves, and it must supply some interpretation of what these claims mean. If it cannot do this, it is at most of interest to purely scholarly students of religion and cannot be used by theologians and others who are religiously concerned." *The Nature of Doctrine*, 46.
27. Lindbeck refers to Paul here (Rom 10:17).

his cultural-linguistic approach of religion. The *ex auditu* is the way for Lindbeck to say that the Christian tradition is the best. Because, according to Lindbeck, saving faith cannot be wholly anonymous (Rahner) it must in some measure be explicit. This is why Lindbeck proposes the *fides ex auditu*. Non-Christians can share in the future salvation if they have *fides ex auditu*, which means that the ultimate decision about salvation is made at the very moment of dying. The moment you die, every human being is ultimately and expressly confronted by the gospel, by the crucified and risen Lord. It is only then that the final decision is made for or against Christ.[28]

As well as his intra-textual (pragmatic) view on truth Lindbeck proposes this prospective theory of truth *ex auditu*. It implies that in order to reach salvation the explicit confession of Christ as Lord is required. This is why Lindbeck's theory can be called 'an eschatologically qualified universalism'.[29] Through the backdoor of salvation Christianity becomes the one and only for Lindbeck. Of course Lindbeck does not want to say that only Christians are saved. Then the problem is how to reconcile the intrasystematic Christian *solo Christo*-truth with the salvation of non-Christians. Lindbeck proposes his prospective theory of truth ex auditu to solve this dilemma.

Maybe it is impossible to have your cake and eat it, which is what Lindbeck seems to want in combining his cultural-linguistic approach of religion – in which theology is a second order discourse with no possible truth-claims[30] – with his intratextual theory of truth *ex auditu*.[31] Lindbeck combines a realist theory of truth with a pragmatist view of rules in his cultural-linguistic theory. To put it in another way: Lindbeck wants to maintain some notion of ontological truth alongside his intra-systematic truth.[32] As a cultural-linguist he cannot decide anything

28. *The Nature of Doctrine*, 59.

29. The notion of 'eschatologically qualified universalim' is from Kenneth Surin, "'Many Religions and the One True Faith': An Examination of Lindbeck's Chapter 3," *Modern Theology* 4 (1988) 196.

30. *The Nature of Doctrine*, 69.

31. Timothy P. Jackson argues in this line too when he states that Lindbeck's opponents – the cognitivists and the experiential expressivists – are but a species of the larger opposition that defines the liberal dilemma: that between realism and pragmatism. Lindbeck wants to overcome this liberal dilemma in his postliberal account, but he fails to do so. Timothy P. Jackson, "Against Grammar," *Religious Studies Review* 11 (1985) 240.

32. Because of this I see Lindbeck as a Barthian rather than a Thomist (against for example B. D. Marshall). Lindbeck is – in my eyes – a Barthian because he wants to have means to say that one tradition as a whole is ontologically true (even more, brings salvation). He should have been Thomistic in this respect when that means were found in human nature, this is not the case. Lindbeck maintains an ontological truth, i.e. truth

about the truth of religious traditions; theology is 'just' second order discourse, the grammar for the first order, celebration, liturgy and religious language. Again, a cultural-linguist cannot decide about the truth of this. Moreover, there are no criteria within an intrasystematically defined conceptual scheme to determine whether a rule has been followed correctly. Rules never provide the criteria for their correct application.[33] Yet Lindbeck wants to have a criterium with which he can decide about the truth of traditions.

In combining pragmatist with realist elements in his truth theory, Lindbeck tries to connect things that cannot be connected. The mere fact that Lindbeck needs an ontological criterium for truth shows that he is not a pragmatist. For a pragmatist, intrasystematic truth is the only possible way of speaking about truth; language is not a vehicle for representing reality but a medium in which we live.[34] Combined with his intrasystematic notion of truth Lindbeck proposes a prospective truth *ex auditu*; with this proposal he gives the game away and reveals himself to be realist.[35] This realism and the rejection of alternatives to scriptural intratextuality justifies the charge of fideism against George Lindbeck.[36]

4. Is Lindbeck's Theology Postmodern?

Finally I want to pose the question whether Lindbeck's theology is postmodern. Lindbeck calls his approach postliberal, because he assumes that his theology postdates the experiential-expressive approach which is the mark of liberal method.[37] Is his 'post' in postliberal then merely

of correspondence, in combination with the universal truth claim that the Christ is the only saviour and the notion '*ex auditu*' which implies that the truth of Christ being saviour can only be heard and not justified otherwise.

33. Barret, "Theology as Grammar," 162, 168.

34. Jackson, "Against Grammar," 243.

35. Fergusson, who also holds that Lindbeck confuses truth and use (see footnote 9): "While this cultural-linguistic model would for some strengthen the hand of non-cognitivist theories of religion for Lindbeck it remains compatible with theological realism" (195). David Fergusson, "Meaning, Truth and Realism," *Religious Studies* 26 (1990) 183-198.

36. Tilley, "Incommensurability, Intratexturality, and Fideism," 101. This is against B. D. Marshall's "Aquinas as Postliberal Theologian," where he sees Lindbeck as a Thomist and Thomas not at all as a fideist. I still hold that Lindbeck is a fideist. Although he maintains ontological truth, this is not a truth outside the system, a truth that can be justified from outside. I see Lindbeck as a fideist because of his combination of ontological truth with a universal truth-claim that cannot be justified separately from the system.

37. *The Nature of Doctrine*, 135, note 1.

temporal? Indeed, the temporal element is apparent; Lindbeck tries to develop a theological method that supersedes the liberal method. But of course the 'post' also implies something concerning content. One main characteristic of modernity is that texts are primarily seen as objects of study. Historical-critical research on the Bible is typical for modernity. In all kinds of areas of research, however, this is changing. What is going on can be called the textualization of reality.[38] It has become commonplace to see reality as a text, or to see the world as language in which we live. One consequence of this for a classical text is that it is studied as a whole again, the analytic historical-critical methods are no longer the predominant ones. Moreover, it has become possible to read one's own life within a text again. The text is not just an object of study. This is what Lindbeck says he does: is this a reason to call him postmodern?

Two main characteristics of postmodernity are its refraining from traditional ontology and its emphasis on the importance of difference. Both in American neo-pragmatism (Dewey, Rorty) and in French deconstructionism (Derrida, Lyotard) there is a tendency to try to overcome traditional ontology. If one refrains from ontology, it becomes difficult to determine the truth in a given situation, let alone truth in general. If we live in language, if our lives are texts, then it is difficult to find a fixed point from which truth can be derived. What is true is what works, or truth will reveal itself. It is impossible to determine a priori what is true.

This is precisely why Lindbeck can be called post-neo-orthodox, or maybe postliberal, if we see it just in temporal terms, but not postmodern.[39] In his article "The Church's Mission to a Postmodern Culture,"

38. This expression is used by Lindbeck on p. 50 in "The Church's Mission to a Postmodern Culture," *Postmodern Theology: Christian Faith in a Pluralist World,* ed. Frederick B. Burnham (San Francisco, CA: Harper & Row, 1989) chapter 3.

39. Nancy Murphy, however, does see Lindbeck as a postmodern theologian for three reasons. First because "His own theory of religious language correlates with the postmodern emphasis on use in discourse by the community as the crucial clue to the meaning of its language." Secondly because he sees truth as coherence and thirdly because of his emphasis on praxis over tradition. "Thus Lindbeck's theology, departing decisively from all three of the modern axes described above, is through and through postmodern" (206-207). The modern axes are: representation, foundationalism, individualism. The postmodern opponents are: expressivism, scepticism and collectivism. See Nancy Murphy, "Distinguishing Modern and Postmodern Theologies," *Modern Theology* 5 (1989) 191-214. I do not agree with Murphy, because Lindbeck maintains a (universal) ontological truth alongside his intratextual truth and because he wants to have means to say that one tradition is better than another. Murphy revised her article in a chapter of *Anglo-American Postmodernity: Philosophical Perspectives on Science, Religion and Ethics* (Boulder, CO: Westview, 1997). Postmodernism is defined slightly different here, but Lindbeck is still seen as a postmodern by Murphy.

it becomes apparent that Lindbeck really longs for past times. He wants us to live in the medieval biblical world again. In this 'post-neo-orthodox' world, people live in the biblical language game, imagination is shaped by biblical images and symbols. By consequence, the Word is present sacramentally in the world. Because Lindbeck knows that this 'cultural linguistic framework', this 'language game', is the best and because he uses his theory of truth *ex auditu* to furnish the truth of this framework, I think it is appropriate to see Lindbeck as an orthodox Protestant theologian rather than a postliberal or postmodern thinker. Perhaps Barth, despite himself, was more postmodern than Lindbeck in his dialectical effort never to say anything purely positive about God in human terms.

If, in theology, we accept the postmodern criticism of ontological truth, I would like to try to develop a more 'postmodern' theology[40] that might depart from a cultural linguistic approach, but that abandons the orthodox Protestant residue of ontological truth that has to be accepted in order to reach salvation. One main point that I derive from postmodern thinking, in any case, is that there can be no direct access to transcendence; human beings cannot have direct knowledge of God. Although Lindbeck acknowledges that theological discourse is a second order discourse and that it does not give any direct knowledge, on the level of faith the knowledge that is gained *ex auditu* is direct and immediate. We should keep in mind that our knowledge is always indirect and mediated. Of course Lindbeck acknowledges this, but I think he does not take all the implications into account in *The Nature of Doctrine*. Knowledge of God can be mediated by a text, so a text can become sacramental. At the same time a text can always be interpreted

---

I agree with Tilley who does not see Lindbeck as postmodern; cf. p. 105 where he says: "A 'pure' intratextualism like Lindbeck's presumes easy access to a privileged framework which is already given. The identification of that final commensurating framework as 'the' Christian Scripture generates fideism." A privileged framework of any kind and postmodernism are incommensurable. Sheila G. Davaney too thinks that Lindbeck moves towards a postmodern agenda, but has not yet arrived there. One reason she mentions is "Lindbeck's concentration on the doctrinal core as an apparently unchanging given," but most importantly "the lack of political analysis in their [Lindbeck and Kaufman's] positions" (200). Sheila G. Davaney, "Options in Post-Modern Theology," *Dialogue* 26 (1987) 196-200.

40. In the strain of the thinking of Graham Ward. Cf. Ward, *Barth, Derrida and the Language of Theology*, "Textuality itself incarnates theology's realism; it is a realism in which God's passing resonates in a language which has learnt how not to say" (251). And the very last sentences of this book: "The postmodern critique of logocentrism actually generates theological investigation; an investigation particularly into the nature of incarnation. What the consequences of these observations are must now become the basis or *a postmodern theology of the Word*" (256) (emphasis mine).

in several ways: God is not himself present in the text, we can only recognize a trace of the divine while reading or hearing. On this basis of
not-knowing and non-presence, a postmodern theology, perhaps even a
postmodern theology of sacramental presence could be developed.*

* I am grateful to Mrs. Sherwood-Smith for her corrections in the English text.

The Possibility of Encountering God in Postmodernity: A Return to Apophatic Theology

Paul J. Levesque

From the popular press to academic conferences, the loss of a sense of transcendence in the Christian liturgy and sacraments is lamented. Solutions advanced for its recovery are ever abundant, from the restoration of the Tridentine liturgy to the complete secularization of the sacramental life. Yet, the loss of transcendence in Christian ritual is only a symptom of a broader phenomenon. The loss of transcendence in liturgy and sacraments is a result of the wider loss of transcendence in religion in general, which is a direct result of the larger loss of transcendence in postmodern Western culture.

We live in a world where the very possibility of a transcendent dimension has no meaning for our culture. The postmodern problematic is not simply the loss of belief in God, but the loss of the very *possibility* of such a belief. What is at stake is not how we envision God, but if God can be envisioned at all.[1] Paradoxically, where religion once provided the integrating concept of transcendence for culture through its understanding of God, now religion itself falls victim to the disintegration of this same cultural synthesis. This same loss of transcendence has caused the inability of postmodern persons to grasp religious symbols, since religious symbols require a transcendent referent. The necessary result of the whole development of Western culture is present-day atheism.

After briefly reviewing the historical shifts in the manner in which transcendence is conceived, this paper will identify possibilities to regain a sense of transcendence within the postmodern condition. It will be suggested that the most viable response to our current situation is a return to the apophatic mystical tradition. In the absence of cultural support, there is no choice but to turn to the inner darkness. This will lead to some brief reflections upon a final question: What ramifications

---

1. See Louis Dupré, "The Religious Crisis of Our Culture," *The Crisis of Culture,* ed. Anna-Teresa Tymieniecka; Analecta Husserliana, 5 (Dordrecht: D. Reidel, 1976) 214.

does this lack of cultural support and total reliance on negative theology
have for our understanding of the sacraments?

1. Presuppositions: The Postmodern Condition

*Postmodernity is Characterized by a Loss of a Sense of Transcendence in the
Very Fabric of Culture*

The epoch we now call ancient begins with the acceptance of *physis*
(nature) as the all comprehensive, creative principle; Thales being the
first Greek thinker known to make this proclamation.[2] However, already
with Plato and Aristotle limits begin to be placed upon the meaning of
physis which requires it to be coupled with additional terms for it to
equal nature as all encompassing. For example, among other constraints,
Plato denies that nature can function as the ultimate norm of conduct.[3]
Aristotle's definition of nature limits it to a principle of motion in those
beings capable of self-induced motion and rest.[4] While nature is direct-
ing these organic processes to their projected end, the term *kosmos* is
introduced to account for "the ordered totality of being that co-ordinates
those processes as well as the laws that rule them."[5] *Kosmos* encompasses
transcendent, human and cosmic dimensions and is coupled with *physis*
to express nature in its entirety. Nature remains a unified whole but now
is seen as possessing three dimensions: the cosmic, human and transcendent elements in an inseparable totality.

The next step in the Western understanding of nature is the complete
separation of transcendence from the cosmic and human dimensions of
reality; this action takes place in the medieval period. This step is qual-
itatively different from the move begun with Plato and Aristotle to add
concepts in order to safeguard nature's comprehensive character. Now,
instead of protecting the inclusivity of nature, this new shift severs the
integrity of nature by ripping the element of transcendence out of
nature and relegating it to a separate realm. In a nutshell, human beings
and Mother Nature become subservient to Almighty Father God.

---

2. In this section on the postmodern condition we will follow Louis Dupré, *Passage
to Modernity: An Essay in the Hermeneutics of Nature and Culture* (New Haven: Yale University Press, 1993).
  3. See Plato, *The Laws*, Book 10.
  4. See Aristotle, *Physics*, 2.1, 192[b].
  5. Dupré, *Passage to Modernity*, 17.

One instrumental factor in the separation of the divine from nature was the particular causal relation attributed between God and creation. Christian thinkers of the Middle Ages were challenged to reconcile the tension of nature's divine sufficiency and the acts of a transcendent God. Aquinas succeeded in explaining the Christian perception of the relation between God and creation through a synthesis with Aristotelian efficient causality, but he also had to balance this concept with Platonic participation.

When this Aristotelian framework was abandoned, the synthesis between God as cause of creation and human action deteriorated. This resulted in the nominalist theologies of the fourteenth and fifteenth centuries advancing the idea of an unrestricted divine power to an extreme never before witnessed. The relation between Creator and creature becomes barely intelligible; the actions of creatures appeared to be in a completely separate sphere which has no relation to God's power. Thus, by the end of the Middle Ages, nominalism had effectively banished God from creation. The transcendent had been successfully removed from nature and transferred to a "supernatural" domain.

Concomitant with the first split, there is a second tearing of meaning from nature which signals the dawn of modernity. With God removed into another realm separate from nature, the human subject becomes the sole meaning-giving agent. Humankind is exalted to a position as the sole master of nature. Devoid of its transcendent and human elements, nature is reduced to signifying only the cosmos. Reason is no longer immanent in the cosmos which is now respected only as an object; instead, the human subject is the exclusive source of reason imposed upon reality. Far from becoming deified, the human subject itself loses all meaning as it is reduced to a mere function of the process of objectification. Since the real contains no meaning of its own, the only place for stability and encounter with transcendent meaning is the lived experience of one's own subjectivity.

Leads to a Loss of a Sense of Transcendence in Religion in General

If the postmodern situation is thus characterized by a loss of a sense of transcendence in the very fabric of culture, then this has an immediate impact upon religion. Its primary effect is that the believer has in a very real way become a-theistic insofar as God plays no role in everyday concerns: "The most crucial issue in the modern problematic ... [is]

whether the idea of God has any meaning left."[6] The atheism of our culture is the abolition of true transcendence.

Historically, in the eighteenth century the idea of God by and large ceased to be an integral concern for the intellectualized mind set.[7] Rationalist deism can be characterized as 'latent atheism'. This progressed into the belligerent atheism of the nineteenth century. With the twentieth century this anti-theism has been replaced by a radical disposal of the very idea of God. In the nineteenth century, the atheist continued to determine a vision of life through a negative relationship to faith in God, whereas in the twentieth century, belief in God is not even a negative or polemical concern. Modern atheism is itself a religious phenomenon. With God relegated to a sphere outside of nature and the human subject having so fully objectified the world and having become the only creator of meaning and value, even spiritual phenomena are under its control.

Leads to a Loss of a Sense of Transcendence in Sacraments and Liturgy in Particular

With religious faith in general having undergone such a radical shift in meaning, it comes as no surprise that postmodern culture's inability to support a transcendent dimension of reality has severely affected the power of religious symbols. As religious ritual in general has been severely discounted by the postmodern situation, so too sacraments as a specific type of ritual have been reduced in significance. In fact, the effect upon sacraments has perhaps been even more devastating, since with sacraments the ritual action is effective and actually realizes the transcendent presence it signifies.

A sacrament as efficacious ritual action in which the word directs the immanent act toward a transcendent reality is no longer supported by the current cultural view. The removal of the transcendent to a realm separate from nature has resulted in the inability of postmodern persons to be receptive to any sacramentology. Secularism proposes the extreme position whereby sacraments are limited to the meaning of their earthly words and gestures. Without a transcendent referent, the natural symbols of bread, wine, water and oil will have only a limited effect today.

---

6. Louis Dupré, "Spiritual Life in a Secular Age," *Daedalus* III (Winter 1982) 30; reprinted with slight modifications in Louis Dupré, *Religious Mystery and Rational Reflection* (Grand Rapids: Eerdmans, 1998) 131-143.

7. See Dupré, "Spiritual Life," 21.

Sacramental words and gestures are not accorded symbolic meaning in their very essence; the intrinsic connection with the divine is denied. Instead, the sacramental character is viewed as being added onto ordinary actions and objects. Secularism has taken the further step of removing any transcendent addition, thus leaving only the worldly meaning. This can be understood as a radical anthropological approach to the sacraments at the expense of their transcendent meaning. The overall view of nature reduced to signifying only a cosmic dimension has desacralized our understanding of the world and sacraments along with it.

The larger loss of the sense of transcendence in nature is to blame for the loss of a sense of transcendence in sacraments. Of course, there are people in contemporary culture who are able to reestablish sacramental depth. Yet, as the solution below will discuss, such individuals do so rarely by *perceiving* the source of sacralization in the symbolic reality itself, but in *deciding* to hold objects and events as symbolic of transcendence.[8] Still, in choosing to accept a transcendent dimension in sacraments or in any other area of religion, all foundations have been removed except those established through a personal spiritual life.

The opposite extreme is also a possible outcome of the fracturing of nature: sacraments can turn into magic. If God exists in another dimension completely separated from the world, then any divine presence produced in and through human actions and words must be purely of a supernatural origin. The priest becomes the shaman who has special access to the divine sphere. However, accepting such a magical interpretation of sacraments would undermine the human subject's role as sole source of meaning and value. The need to look for answers from the theurgist neither reunites the fractured elements of nature nor considers the secularized notion of human autonomy.

Thus, the question arises as to what possibilities remain open to recovering a sense of transcendence.

2. Possibilities to Regain a Sense of Transcendence

Re-establishing the Past: Fundamentalism

One general solution which is proposed from various quarters – probably due to its clarity and simplicity – is to return to the visible rock of

8. See Dupré, "Spiritual Life," 24.

past ages. This is illustrated from exhortations to renounce technology,[9] to popular arguments to restore the Tridentine liturgy. However, a return to earlier, safer or less complicated structures will not address the needs of the contemporary situation.

> Those who, by updating past thoughts, hoped to neutralize such baneful features of modern thought as the opposition between subject and object or the loss of a transcendent component underestimated the radical nature of the modern revolution. Its problems cannot be treated as errors to be corrected by a simple return to an earlier truth. That truth is no longer available; it has vanished forever.[10]

A tide of fundamentalism is rising. The goal is to reestablish objective certainty by denying historical change. Those who choose this path close themselves to the values and beliefs of their own culture.

Others, without any desire to turn back the clock, attempt to isolate the secular from their deeper existence. Instead of providing a successful solution, this "schizoid attitude is bound to become untenable before long"[11] because there is no incorporation or reconciliation of personal beliefs with those of one's culture. Even before personally turning to one's deeper beliefs one must first acknowledge the loss of transcendence. "This is particularly painful to the believer who tends to hide his head in the sand of a past spiritual tradition in order to avoid the sight of his own atheism."[12] This does not provide hope for the future but an isolationism from the present by attempting a retreat to an irretrievable past. It is cultural suicide.

Re-interpreting Transcendence: The Death of Sacraments

Another solution to regain a sense of transcendence is offered by secular approaches to theology and other disciplines. Through a variety of methods these advocate that transcendence is present in the secular view itself.

Sometimes the response of secular theologians is to eliminate the notion of transcendence altogether as meaningless,[13] but usually they

9. See e.g., Jerry Mander, *In the Absence of the Sacred: The Failure of Technology and the Survival of the Indian Nations* (San Francisco: Sierra Club Books, 1991) 411-426 and the bibliography he provides.

10. Dupré, *Passage to Modernity*, 6-7. Also see Louis Dupré, "The Modern Idea of Culture: Its Opposition to its Classical and Christian Origins," *Archivio di Filosofia* 53 (1985) 483.

11. Dupré, "Spiritual Life," 23.

12. Louis Dupré, *Transcendent Selfhood* (New York: Seabury, 1976) 17.

13. See Paul van Buren, *The Secular Meaning of the Gospel* (London: SCM Press, 1963).

endeavor to reinterpret it in order to make it worthwhile. Bonhoeffer is commonly considered the initiator of this-worldly theology in allowing secularity to be considered a Christian category. His goal was not to eliminate God but to take God away from a supernatural realm that had lost its meaning. Genuine types of transcendence accept the life God gives and is not a foundation for escape.[14] From a Catholic theological perspective, Teilhard de Chardin also furnished a forceful inspiration for world directed theology. Often misinterpreted as advocating the embrace of the world at the complete neglect of any quest for the transcendent, he actually was a defendant of transcendence while constantly seeking to reconcile it with an immanence that required a new place in religion and philosophy. He did not deny transcendence but reformulated an understanding of it. The vital question was whether the higher, long dreamed of life of union and consummation sought Above should be pursued Ahead in the prolongation of the forces of evolution – or perhaps both.[15]

However, it is doubtful that a true religiosity can survive such a radical secular interpretation – nonetheless Christianity – since transcendence cannot be jettisoned and still maintain the authentic religious symbolization necessary to its expression. Some tried to solve this problem by suggesting that transcendence was never abandoned in the midst of their talk of the here-and-now. For example, Edward Farley, Kenneth Hamilton, and David Cairns drew on the resources of their day to demonstrate that the motif of transcendence had not disappeared.[16] More prominent secular approaches such as John A. T. Robinson and Harvey Cox suggested transcendence could be relocated, rephrased, or remythologized.[17] Both Robinson and Cox fail to elucidate what such a transcendence which can be reconciled with a radical this-worldly Christianity would look like.[18]

14. See Dietrich Bonhoeffer, *Letters and Papers From Prison* (London: SCM Press, 1971). Also see Martin E. Marty & Dean G. Peerman, "Introduction: The Recovery of Transcendence," *New Theology, Vol. 7,* ed. Martin E. Marty and Dean G. Peerman (New York: Macmillan, 1970) 14-15.

15. See Pierre Teilhard de Chardin, *The Future of Man* (London: Collins, 1964).

16. See Edward Farley, *The Transcendence of God: A Study in Contemporary Philosophical Theology* (Philadelphia: Westminster Press), 1960; Kenneth Hamilton, *Revolt Against Heaven: An Enquiry Into Anti-Supernaturalism* (Grand Rapids: Eerdmans, 1965); and David Cairns, *God Up There? A Study in Divine Transcendence* (Philadelphia: Westminster Press, 1967).

17. See John A. T. Robinson, *Honest to God* (Philadelphia: Westminster Press, 1963); Harvey Cox, *The Secular City* (New York: Macmillan, ²1966); id., *Religion in the Secular City: Toward a Postmodern Theology* (New York: Simon & Schuster, 1984).

18. See Louis Dupré, "Meditations on Secular Theology," *The Christian Century* 85 (November 1968) 1470.

.

Thomas Altizer is another who denies any need for a transcendent dimension. He adopts a more radical attitude and explicates a mythology without transcendence. He interprets the Incarnation as meaning that the divine has become completely identical with the human.[19] By contrast, Gordon Kaufman argues for the existence of a transcendent dimension even when mythology is abandoned.[20]

Return to the Apophatic Mystical Tradition

There is a third alternative which is clearly presented in the writings of Louis Dupré and James Wiseman. For the modern believer, and as well as the unbeliever and those disillusioned with Christianity, both recommend the apophatic mystics for direction.

The key for the contemporary solution is the recovery of the inner life. This inward turn must not be perceived as a total withdrawal from society; it always returns to reinterpret and reground culture. This inner life prompted by the complete absence of transcendence in secular culture places it in the tradition of negative theology. There is an intimate affinity established between the modern believer and the mystics of former generations.

The goal of the spiritual life has always been – in one form or another – to move ever closer to being the image of God.[21] This is accomplished, for example, by recognizing in love the Logos – which is the divine image of God and dwells in one's soul, making one the image of God (Origen, c. 185 – c. 253)[22] – or by purifying oneself from all creatures and unruly

---

19. See Thomas J. J. Altizer, *The Gospel of Christian Atheism* (Philadelphia: Westminster Press, 1966).

20. See Gordon D. Kaufman, "On the Meaning of 'God': Transcendence Without Mythology," *Harvard Theological Review* 59 (1966) 105-132; reprinted in *New Theology, Vol. 4*, ed. Martin E. Marty and Dean G. Peerman (New York: Macmillan, 1967) 69-98; also reprinted in *Transcendence*, ed. Herbert W. Richardson and Donald R. Cutler (Boston: Beacon Press, 1969) 114-142.

21. Louis Dupré, *Light from Light: An Anthology of Christian Mysticism* (New York: Paulist Press, 1998) 10-11 offers an outline of the history of image mysticism: "The Christian theology of the image, implicit in the New Testament, and first speculatively developed by Origen, survived uninterruptedly in the East. It re-emerged in the twelfth century Cistercian schools of the West. After the mystical schools of the Rhineland and Flanders it faded away in the fifteenth century, only to reappear with renewed vigor in the twentieth century (Merton, Teilhard de Chardin)."

22. For Origen the soul separates itself from the world in its confusion and wickedness, and recognizes the transitoriness of the world. Suffering through many types of trials, the soul receives consolation and visions for strength against future trials. See Origen, *Commentary on the Song of Songs* 2, 171 in *Origen: The Song of Songs: Commentary and Homilies* tr. R. P. Lawson; Ancient Christian Writers, 26 (Westminster, MD: The Newman Press, 1957). The next step is union of the soul with the Logos. He

affections in order for the image of the divine nature to be seen in one's own beauty as a union of love (Gregory of Nyssa, *c.* 335-394),[23] or by "living toward the Image" as the center of one's existence (Jan van Ruusbroec, 1293-1381)[24]. How does the mystic articulate this union with God? The answer is found in mysticism's intimate bond with negative theology.

> Negative theology means far more than that we find no adequate names for God. It means, on a practical-spiritual level, that there exists no failproof method for reaching God, and hence that my only hope lies in the humble awareness of my inadequacy[25].

We can look to Gregory of Nyssa for whom a dark cloud of unknowing surrounds the God of whom the soul is nevertheless an image[26]. Also, we can turn to the sixth century Pseudo-Dionysius who had a profound influence upon Christianity's understanding and employment of apophatic mysticism (first in the East and later in the West). Characteristic of his thought is an extreme Platonism along with a negative theology which is coupled with image mysticism. In the opening lines of his *Mystical Theology*, he prays to the Trinity to:

> Guide us to that topmost height of mystic lore which exceedeth light and more than exceedeth knowledge, where the simple, absolute, and unchangeable mysteries of heavenly Truth lie hidden in the dazzling obscurity of the secret Silence, outshining all brilliance with the intensity of their darkness[27].

explains this union through the image of Christ being born in the heart and growing in the soul, see *Commentary on the Song of Songs*, prol. 85. But most especially he uses the imagery of a mystical marriage, see *Commentary on the Song of Songs*, I, 4, see Johannes Quasten, *Patrology. 2: The Ante-Nicene Literature After Irenaeus* (Utrecht: Spectrum, 1950) 94-100. Note that in the version translated by Jerome, the Church is the bride of Christ, while in the version translated by Rufinus, the individual soul is the bride. See Quasten, *Patrology,* 2:50; 3:266.

23. See Gregory of Nyssa, *Sermon on the Beatitudes*, 6, in *Gregory of Nyssa, The Lord's Prayer. The Beatudes,* trans. Hilda C. Graef; Ancient Christian Writers, 18 (Westminster, MD: Newman, 1954) 85-175. On the union of the soul and God as a mystical marriage, see e.g., id., *In Canticum hom.,* 1, in *Gregorii Nysseni In Canticum Canticorum,* ed. Hermannus Langerbeck; Gregorii Nysseni Opera, 6 (Leiden: Brill, 1960).

24. See Jan van Ruusbroec, "The Spiritual Espousals," English and Latin translation with Middle Dutch original, ed. J. Alaerts, intro. Paul Mommaers, trans. H. Rolfson; Corpus Christianorum: Continuatio Mediaevalis, 103 (Turnhout: Brepols/Tielt: Lannoo, 1988).

25. Louis Dupré, *The Deeper Life: An Introduction to Christian Mysticism* (New York: Crossroad, 1981) 44-45.

26. See Gregory of Nyssa, *In Canticum hom.*, 23. Also see, e.g., Louis Dupré, "Negative Theology and Affirmation of the Finite," *Experience, Reason, and God,* ed. Eugene Thomas Long; Studies in Philosophy and the History of Philosophy, 8 (Washington, D.C.: The Catholic University of America Press, 1980) 153.

27. Pseudo-Dionysius, "Mystical Theology," *The Fire and the Cloud: An Anthology of Catholic Spirituality,* ed. D. Fleming (New York: Paulist Press, 1978) 56-57.

Inspired by the writings of Pseudo-Dionysius, there is a revival of
Neoplatonic mysticism in the Rhineland in the fourteenth century.
The most original and daring of these authors being Johannes Eckhart
(*c.* 1260-1327/8). He united negative theology and image mysticism[28]
and combined the thought of Pseudo-Dionysius with Thomistic terms
to which he instilled new meanings. Meister Eckhart explains that God
"is a transcending nothingness [about which] St. Augustine says: 'The
best that one can say about God is for one to keep silent out of the
wisdom of one's inward riches.' So be silent, and do not chatter about
God; for when you do chatter about him, you are telling lies and sin-
ning."[29] It is doubtful that much, if anything, ultimately can be said
positively of God in Eckhart.

With the Flemish mystic Jan van Ruusbroec we reach a profound
expression of the contemplative's journey through darkness.[30] When he
was a parish priest in Brussels, before he withdrew to a hermitage in
Groenendaal outside the city, he had already completed his masterpiece,
The Spiritual Espousals, along with four other mystical works. He is in
agreement with negative theology insofar as God does exist in darkness
and absolute oneness. He writes that the inner person must lose "himself in a modelessness and in a darkness in which all contemplatives
wander around in enjoyment and can no longer find themselves in a
creaturely mode."[31] Yet, Ruusbroec experiences this *via negativa* as leading to a second movement of light. He continues,

> In the abyss of this darkness in which the loving spirit has died to itself,
> there begin the revelation of God and eternal life. For in this darkness
> there shines and is born an incomprehensible light which is the Son of
> God, in whom one contemplates eternal life. And in this light one
> becomes seeing.[32]

28. See Louis Dupré, "Mysticism," *The Encyclopedia of Religion*, Vol. 10, ed. Mircea
Eliade (New York: Macmillan, 1987) 253: "Johannes Eckhart, possibly the most powerful mystical theologian of the Christian Middle Ages, synthesized the Greek and Augus-
tinian theories of the image with a daring negative theology in one grandiose system.
His mystical vision became the basis of an entire theology and, indeed, of a metaphysics
of being."

29. Johannes Eckhart, "German Sermons 83," in *Meister Eckhart: The Essential Sermons, Commentaries, Treatises, and Defense*, trans. Edmund Colledge (New York: Paulist,
1981) 207. Quoted in James A. Wiseman, "Mystical Literature and Modern Unbelief,"
Christian Spirituality and the Culture of Modernity: The Thought of Louis Dupré, ed. Peter
J. Casarella and George P. Schner (Grand Rapids: Eerdmans, 1998) 183.

30. Evelyn Underhill calls Ruusbroec "one of the greatest perhaps the very greatest of
the mystics of the Church," Evelyn Underhill, *Mysticism* (London: Methusen, [12]1930) 148.

31. Ruusbroec, "The Spiritual Espousals," 3.1, c53-55.

32. *Ibid.*, 3.1, c55-59.

Present day atheism and the response of an inward turn should be understood in light of this apophatic mystical tradition. In the complete silence of secular culture regarding the transcendent, one encounters the same darkness and negative knowledge of God as did the mystics of the past. As the mystics started their spiritual journey from within, so do modern believers, but not because believers today are disposed in the same manner. Instead, in the absence of cultural support there is no choice but to turn within. "The mystics start their spiritual journey from within, and that is the only place where the believer *must* begin, whether he wants to or not."[33] As the modern believer begins this self-ward passage the same absence that exists outward is encountered within. It is only by recognizing one's own loss of the very idea of God that there is hope for recovering transcendence.

Without a cultural foundation, ambiguity and an openness to a multiplicity of interpretations are the new hallmarks of experience. "An identical experience justifies the believer's faith as well as the unbeliever's unbelief."[34] Doubt regarding the correct interpretation of an experience is removed only by a subsequent decision of full commitment. "Religious men and women will continue to attribute a 'sacred' quality to persons, objects, and events closely connected with their relation to the transcendent. But they will do so because they *hold* them sacred, not because they *perceive* them as sacred."[35] The sacred possess a totally private character when it is still experienced today.[36] Thus, the religious person now *chooses* those doctrines and symbolic expressions that he or she finds meaningful for himself or herself, while in the past ecclesiastical institutions, verbal revelation, and culture determined the inner experience. Consequently, religion is now often considered as possessing a certain eclectic nature, or even an arbitrary appearance by those who judge by past objective standards. Those "who opted for a religious dimension in their lives will use institutions and symbols to the extent of their *personal* needs."[37] People today often turn to less formalized structures that are more in keeping with their own inward spirituality than to pre-established forms from a previous cultural era.

33. Dupré, "Spiritual Life," 25.
34. *Ibid.*, 24.
35. *Ibid.*, 24.
36. See Dupré, *Transcendent Selfhood*, p. 24.
37. Dupré, "Spiritual Life," 24. Here Dupré also notes that a significant result of the tailoring of religion to personal needs has been an unprecedented rise in the acceptance of religious pluralism – a pluralism which even helped the modern secular crisis along, but only after the subjective individual took precedence over objective institutions.

However, the recovery of the inner life of the self is not simply an individual enterprise. In fact, insofar as it is a personal quest it is not at all individualistic. Mysticism in itself demands that any inward experience must have a further outward expression. Returning to the thought of Ruusbroec, it is clear that contemplation is not simply rest. There is a balance between the interior life of divine rest and a moving out with the divine persons in works of charity.[38]

> For no one can enter into rest above activity unless he has first yearningly and actively loved. Therefore, the grace of God and our active love must precede and follow, that is, they must be practiced before and afterwards … And this is why no one who is master of himself and can surrender himself to love shall be idle.[39]

The inward experience of transcendence must be actualized in outward action.

Thus, any attempt to recover transcendence has become an existential choice in contemporary times. Without outward support or a clearly defined experience of the sacred, one must turn inward to the darkness of a personal spiritual journey. Many mystics of the past have made this quest based on some desire, but now the postmodern seeker is required to do so because there is no other alternative. While the path is the same and the modern contemplative is a kindred spirit with the mystics of the past, it is a mistake to assume that the ancient masters and monasteries possess all the solutions to the modern plight. "The doctrines, life-styles, and methods of a previous age were conceived within the reach of a direct experience of the sacred. This has for the most part ceased to exist."[40] Yet, the contemporary journey to recover transcendence must follow the one group of people who have achieved such an inward union with the transcendent – the mystics.

3. Product: The Hidden Presence of God in and through the Sacraments

Now I would like to offer some reflections upon a final question: What ramifications does this lack of cultural support and total reliance

---

38. This is the core of Ruusbroec's complex notion of the a common life. See Jan van Ruusbroec, "The Sparkling Stone," English and Latin translation with Middle Dutch original, ed. G. de Baere, Th. Mertens & H. Noë, intro. Th. Mertens & P. Mommaers, trans. A. Lefevere; Corpus Christianorum: Continuatio Mediaevalis, 110 (Turnhout: Brepols/Tielt: Lannoo, 1991) E780.

39. Ruusbroec, "The Spiritual Espousals," 3.1, b1922-1928.

40. Dupré, "Spiritual Life," 31.

on negative theology have for our understanding of the sacraments? I will briefly summarize my thoughts under three headings: sacramental encounter, sacramental expression and sacramental effect.

Sacramental Encounter

Who or what is it that we are left with to encounter in the sacraments? We are confronted with the challenge to uncover the hidden presence of God in and through eucharistic bread and wine, baptismal water, and oil for the sick. It is not an encounter which compels us to our knees before a clear image of a divine reality. Rather, it is an experience of mystery which summons forth hope and expectation – hope that there is some larger reality connected to our words and actions, expectation for a more complete vision. We encounter outward signs and hope for them to be real symbols. Is this not perhaps more in tune with the experience of the early church than that of the medieval period?

The epiphany we receive from the sacraments attempts to overcome darkness and uncertainty; but at best the light is gray, because the transcendent – if there is a transcendent – remains hidden in the words and actions. Marginal Catholics come to the church for marriage and to have their children baptized not because they have deep faith, but because it is a shot-in-the-dark hope that somehow the transcendent will be present. Perhaps what we can expect to encounter at best is the God proposed by Richard Elliott Friedman. He proposes a cosmic God, a God that is not necessarily personal. When we are reduced to space dust we may simply be part of a cosmic nonpersonal God.[41]

Sacramental Expressions

Secondly, how should we expect our sacramental rituals to be expressed in the postmodern age? We have already moved from an exclusive rigidity to acknowledging an inclusive unity in diversity; but is this enough for the postmodern world? If the postmodern believer realizes the inability of any words and actions to represent the transcendent in a positive light, then all words and actions are changeable and transitory. In reaching some experience of transcendence, the individual

---

41. See Richard Elliott Friedman, *The Disappearance of God: A Divine Mystery* (Boston: Little Brown, 1995); reprinted as *The Hidden Face of God* (San Francisco: Harper Collins, 1997).

believer will seek out others who articulate their experience in a similar fashion. Because the individual's experience will be multiplex, adaptable and ambiguous, so too any religious group to which he or she belongs will vary according to history, culture, and any number of versatile characteristics of its members. If there is to be unity, it will be expressed through subgroups and associations connected in a network whose hallmark is heterogeneity. Beyond unity in diversity, it is time to seriously consider plurality as not only viable but necessary.

Hand in hand with the issue of how the ritual is to be enacted is the question of who is welcome for it. In his own time and place Paul the Apostle to the Gentiles recognized: "There is no longer Jew or Greek, there is no longer slave or free, there is no longer male and female; for all of you are one in Christ Jesus" (Galatians 3:28 NRSV). I do not believe that it would be an improper hermeneutic to read today, something like, there is no citizen or illegal immigrant, married or divorced, gay or straight. The ritual expression of the sacraments should be as plural as those who gather for their enactment and all should be welcome.

Sacramental Effect

Finally, the effect or fruit of the sacraments can no longer include a direct encounter with the transcendent. The effect of searching for the hidden presence of God is to attain a sense of transcendence which demands this-worldly action. The effect is our concern for social justice and love of the other, not because I am worried about my salvation – or even because I am concerned for the other-worldly salvation of the other – but because the sacramental ritual has expressed to me that here and now we are connected and we have social responsibilities (which must not be overshadowed by our personal rights).

James Wiseman reminds us that in facing her death, Thérèse of Lisieux "was left only with the terrible fear that heaven was a mirage and that death was not the gateway to eternal life but rather a grinning mockery."[42] She writes that she heard death saying to her: "You are dreaming about the light, about a fatherland embalmed in the sweetest perfumes; … Advance, advance; rejoice in death, which will give you not what you hope for but a night still more profound, the night of nothingness,"[43] Wiseman suggests:

---

42. Wiseman, "Mystical Literature," 186.
43. Thérèse of Lisieux, Story of a Soul: The Autobiography of St. Thérèse of Lisieux, trans. John Clarke (Washington, D.C.: Institute of Carmelite Studies, ²1976) 213.

> How she dealt with this trial helps illustrate the nature of genuine mysticism in the original Christian sense of the term ... [namely,] 'to be fully convinced that Christ is living in us, and especially *to act accordingly*'. ... No longer having the joy of faith, she did everything she could at least to carry out its works, above all those flowing from the 'new commandment' of Jesus: that we not merely love others as ourselves but as Jesus loved us.[44]

And here perhaps is the key for the postmodern believer, and especially the unbeliever and those disillusioned with Christianity: "the God who cannot be comprehended and who might seem altogether absent can nevertheless be attained through love – and this emphatically includes the love of other human beings."[45]

In our postmodern loss of faith – and lack of a need for it – we turn to silence. It is a silence which compels us to act *as if* we believed. In our blind grasping for transcendence we touch another person – perhaps this is our salvation.

---

44. Wiseman, "Mystical Literature," 186, quoting L. Bouyer, *Mysterion: Du mystère à la mystique* (Paris: O.E.I.L., 1986) 348 (Wiseman's emphasis).

45. *Ibid.*, 187.

PART THREE

TODAY'S IMPERATIVE:
UNCOVERING THE TRANSFORMATIVE POWER OF
SACRAMENT IN A POSTMODERN AGE

Making Us Make Ourselves
Double Agency and Its Christological Context in the Thought of Austin Farrer

Patrick Terrell Gray

1. Introduction

Can an infinite God act in a finite creation? If so, where do we see the evidence of God's action? It is questions like these that continue to occupy the attention of theologians as well as many of those in the scientific realm. One such notable theologian who saw the importance of these questions was Austin Farrer, former Warden of Keble College, Oxford, holding this position from 1960 until his death in 1968. For Farrer, science did not invalidate theology, but actually affirmed the necessity for theological thinking, particularly in the area of biological evolution. Likewise, theology needed to listen to what science had to say concerning the nature of the world: "The highest spiritual achievements attainable *within this world* are still activities of bodily creatures; and so there is nothing in the world which, on some side of it, the science of physics does not touch."[1]

One topic in which Farrer's thought has continued to elicit debate is in his development of the concept of double agency, which serves as a point of departure for much of the contemporary science/religion discussion, both pro and con. The critics of double agency, though, fail to keep in mind its christological context when discussing its foibles,[2] thereby missing Farrer's ultimate concern – Jesus Christ as the interpretive clue to this profound mystery. For Farrer, it is, in a sense, the antiphonal call-and-response of the finite and the infinite that gives double agency the form it needs, summed up in the person of Jesus Christ.

---

1. Austin Farrer, *God Is Not Dead* (New York: Morehouse-Barlow, 1966) 19.

2. John Polkinghorne condemningly writes, "Although Farrer wrote so extensively and so entrancingly about his notion of double agency, I find it an unintelligible kind of theological doublespeak." John C. Polkinghorne, *The Faith of a Physicist: Reflections of a Bottom-Up Thinker* (Minneapolis: Fortress Press, 1994) 81-82.

2. Double Agency in the Thought of Austin Farrer

According to Farrer, the discussion concerning God's action in the world will inevitably arise for the theologian, since she "is bound to find a course between anthropomorphism and ineffability."[3] This quotation aptly describes the course of Farrer's own work, particularly in his later books. In his quest, however, Farrer was not interested in *how* God connects to God's creation, but rather, as Brian Hebblethwaite writes, "what God can do in and through his creatures, without forcing them or faking the natural story."[4] This is what the concept of double agency entails: a thorough understanding of what divine action means for creation, and humanity in particular.

We must stress at the outset, however, that double agency is not an apologetic for miracles.[5] Farrer insists that God can operate otherwise than in the gaps of natural agencies. In fact, God is in and through the natural agencies themselves, so that there are always two agents in every action. Double agency, then, is an attempt to understand that God makes the world make itself.

God Is a God of Particular Action

"We can think about nothing – that is, about no (supposed) reality – about which we can do nothing but think."[6] It is this empirical principle that for Farrer ends any talk of a deistic God who is not involved in creation, since we as creatures have no Archimedean point by which we could determine if God simply set the world in motion or not.[7] Rather, the God who makes creation make itself is a God of action, who in no way is an object of static theoretical contemplation. In other words, we know God through God's actions. Farrer goes so far as to say that

---

3. Austin Farrer, *Faith and Speculation: An Essay in Philosophical Theology* (New York: University Press, 1967) 140.

4. Brian Hebblethwaite, "Providence and Divine Action," *Journal of Religious Studies* 14 (1978) 224.

5. On miracles, Farrer writes, "No one who believes in miracles wants to say that God *violates* the natural working of the created order by a dislocating interference. It is rather that he enhances, or extends, the action of his creatures; they are able to do what is analogous with what they can commonly do, but goes beyond it." Austin Farrer, *Saving Belief: A Discussion of Essentials* (New York: Morehouse-Barlow, 1965) 81-82.

6. Farrer, *Faith and Speculation*, 36.

7. *Ibid.*, 38.

"the idea of God summarises the history of his action; the soul's direct
touch upon God is not through any (self-luminous) idea of him."[8]

In fact, Farrer states that it is only God's *particular* action that can be
spoken of, for there is no such thing as an abstract action of God's, even
if we are unable to pinpoint God's active presence in every situation.
The lack of clarity does not nullify the fact that "there is more theology
to be dug out of a saint than out of a sandpit."[9] To only think of God's
actions in broad strokes, is, for Farrer, to miss God altogether.

Finding the Causal Joint: The Criticism of Peacocke and Polkinghorne

But where exactly is that 'causal joint' between God and creation
located? Farrer remains agnostic on this question.[10] Although he claims
we have a real commerce with the divine, "we do not touch God with
our fingers as we touch him with our 'souls'."[11] Farrer has been roundly
criticized for holding to this view. Arthur Peacocke writes that "advo-
cacy of this paradox [of double agency] comes perilously close to that
mere assertion of its truth … since Farrer on his own admission can give
no account of the 'causal joint' between the agency of the Creator and
… human action."[12] In other words, Peacocke argues that if you cannot
say *how*, you cannot say *that*.[13] John Polkinghorne makes a similar argument: "Austin Farrer's account of double agency is so emphatic about
the inscrutability of the divine side of it as to provide us with no help."[14]
For these two, asserting that something *is* does not have much cash
value. Polkinghorne goes so far as to call double agency "a fideistic eva-

---

8. Farrer, *Faith and Speculation,* 33. Elsewhere, Farrer writes, "Our thought of God is
the summary of a tale which narrates the actions of God." *Faith and Speculation,* 35.

9. *God Is Not Dead,* 17.

10. Farrer, *Saving Belief,* 39.

11. Farrer, *Faith and Speculation,* 80.

12. Arthur Peacocke, *Theology for a Scientific Age: Being and Becoming – Natural,
Divine and Human* (Minneapolis: Augsburg Fortress, 1993) 149.

13. Theologians who expound that God acts in the world, according to Peacocke,
"tend to resort to just assertion that there is such a link in the case of human action and
that the link in God's action is analogically similar. They make such assertions usually
without saying anything about human action itself, which illuminates *how* God might
be conceived of exercising his influence on events in the world." Peacocke, *Theology for
a Scientific Age,* 148.

14. John Polkinghorne, *Reason and Reality: The Relationship between Science and
Theology* (Philadelphia, PA: Trinity Press International, 1991) 46. Elsewhere, Polkinghorne writes, "[Double agency] is so mysterious a notion that it effectively removes
the question of God's action from discussion in ordinary human conversation." John
Polkinghorne, *Scientists as Theologians* (London: SPCK, 1996) 31.

sion of the problem."[15] From Polkinghorne's standpoint, the search for a causal joint between God and creation can never be given up, and Farrer stands guilty of acquiescing to agnosticism. The nature of human agency demands that we continue to search for the causal joint.[16]

Farrer, however, would ask of Peacocke and Polkinghorne for examples of what is explainable in the terms that they wish double agency to be responsible. Surely faith has just such an unexplainable character, but *that* we have it is undeniable.[17] For Farrer:

> We *believe* that God's way of acting is the infinitely higher analogue of our way, but we cannot *conceive* it otherwise than in terms of our own. God's agency must actually be such as to work omnipotently on, in, or through creaturely agencies without either forcing them or competing with them. But as soon as we try to conceive it in action, we degrade it to the creaturely level and place it in the field of interacting causalities. The result can only be (if we take it literally) monstrosity and confusion.[18]

Polkinghorne's insistent quest for the 'causal joint' in the name of religion would be misguided at best in Farrer's opinion, and no doubt idolatrous at worst. We are not capable of giving an exact account of the term 'persuasion' or 'influence' when used in conjunction with 'divine.'[19] Yet this search is what constitutes Polkinghorne's continued interest in various theories such as 'information input.'[20] Farrer, however, thinks such a move to be folly in the extreme, thinking that we can bring God and God's creatures together "by attaching our temporal conditions to [God's] existence."[21]

---

15. John Polkinghorne, *Belief in God in an Age of Science* (New Haven, CT: Yale University Press, 1998) 58. This is an unfair charge levelled against Farrer, however, since Polkinghorne uses the word 'fideistic' incorrectly to describe Farrer's unwillingness to delve into how God interacts with the world. 'Fideism' in *The Oxford Dictionary of the Christian Church* is defined as "A term applied to a variety of doctrines which hold in common belief in the incapacity of the intellect to attain to knowledge of divine matters and correspondingly put an excessive emphasis on faith ... Scholastic theologians regularly charged the Modernists with 'Fideism'" in their theories of knowledge." Frank L. Cross and E. A. Livingstone (ed.), "Fideism," *The Oxford Dictionary of the Christian Church* (Oxford: Oxford University Press, ³1997) 609. Farrer nowhere argues that the intellect cannot attain knowledge of divine matters. We need only look at Farrer's examination of the interplay between Reason and Revelation in his *The Glass of Vision* (Westminster: Dacre Press, 1948) 1-15, to see that Farrer is not a fideist in Polkinghorne's sense.

16. Polkinghorne, *Belief in God in an Age of Science,* 58-59.

17. Farrer describes doctrine as such, particularly the doctrine of the Trinity. See Farrer, *Saving Belief,* 66.

18. Farrer, *Faith and Speculation,* 62.

19. *Ibid.*

20. Polkinghorne, *Reason and Reality,* 45.

21. Farrer, *Faith and Speculation,* 165.

The Criticism from the Perspective of Theodicy

Perhaps the most damning criticism of double agency is from the perspective of theodicy. Ian Barbour and Polkinghorne both think the concept fails on this crucial point. How can evil be explained in the face of what Barbour calls such "divine determination?"[22] Farrer, though, is not oblivious to the problem of evil: "A good God created good sorts. The problem remains, why he should let them go so rotten,"[23] especially if God is so involved in creation, as the concept of double agency entails. Farrer does not think any answer will easily satisfy, because the answer offers no consolation to the sufferer, and generalities will never speak to the particular case.[24] Nonetheless, Farrer says as much as he thinks can be said, so as not to remain silent on this issue.[25]

Speaking of evil's existence is really a misnomer, according to Farrer, since evil is non-existence, or no-thing. If God created and maintains all things, then to be or to have existence is to be or exist as a good thing. But evil, writes Farrer, "is essentially the parasite of a good, whose existence it presupposes."[26] This may satisfy the philosophical distinction between God and evil, but it still does not broach the subject as to why God allows evil *to happen.* In answering this, we must always look to see what God has done about evil, what purpose God has revealed through it. According to Farrer, what we discover is that God deals with evil humanly, that is, in a human fashion. He writes, "When God removes evils in the human sort of way, it is commonly by the employment of human hands. [God's] own divine way is to make unthought-of goods out of permitted evils, and to triumph by new creation."[27]

Evil, then, can only have 'meaning' if put in an eschatological perspective. This is not to say that Farrer thinks evil should be passively endured. Quite the contrary, the life of faith is a life lived against such (no)things. Farrer concludes, "If we are speaking of the ills that are peculiar to [humanity], we can say nothing of God's purpose in regard

---

22. Ian G. Barbour, *Religion and Science: Historical and Contemporary Issues* (San Francisco: Harper SanFrancisco, ²1997), 312. Polkinghorne writes, "The ascription of all that happens to God's primary causality faces this difficulty [of evil and suffering] in a peculiarly acute form." Polkinghorne, *Scientists as Theologians,* 32.

23. Austin Farrer, *Love Almighty and Ills Unlimited* (New York: Doubleday, 1961) 31.

24. Farrer, *Saving Belief,* 57.

25. Farrer, *Love Almighty and Ills Unlimited,* 12.

26. *Ibid.,* 24.

27. Farrer, *Saving Belief,* 57.

to them which has not some reference to that one ultimate and revealed end."[28] It is to this ultimate and revealed end that we now turn.

3. Jesus Christ: The Interpretive Clue to Double Agency

As we have argued, the detractors of double agency tend to misunderstand Farrer's concept of double agency due to their insistence on finding the 'causal joint'. Ironically, their search for the connection between finite and infinite does not allow for the proper interplay these two concepts demand. Although not explicitly stated by Farrer, it would appear from his writings that the interpretive clue to double agency, that which allows for the interplay between finite and infinite, is Jesus Christ, both fully God and fully human, who, in a sense, recapitulates all the benefits and problems of double agency in his person.

For Farrer, the Incarnation of God in Christ shows us the ultimate potential of humanity, which in turn effects our vision of our fellow human beings, because once having seen "man in God, we know that we have seen man as he is; we can never again believe another picture of ourselves, our neighbours, or our destinies."[29] In fact, the very action of Jesus *is* divine action – "what God does about the salvation of the world."[30]

Jesus Christ, however, is not some sort of universal human. In fact, it is in the very particular nature of the Incarnation, Jesus the Jew from Palestine born of Mary, that the universal application becomes possible. In other words, Jesus Christ had to be truly human. As Farrer writes, "If God was to put on a coat of flesh, the coat was sure to be made of causal stuff. He could not be a man-in-general."[31] Christ was (and certainly to Farrer's mind, is) the person where the divine and the human mutually interpenetrate completely. We should keep in mind that divine and human are categories of being because they are categories of action, so Christ showed who he was, both divine and human, by his actions.[32]

It is Jesus Christ, then, who becomes the clearest and most difficult instance of "the relation between human history and its providential

28. Farrer, *Love Almighty and Ills Unlimited,* 146.
29. Farrer, *Saving Belief,* 26.
30. *Ibid.,* 74-75.
31. *Ibid.,* 69.
32. *Ibid.,* 75.

guidance."[33] Perhaps our thesis is therefore incorrect. If Christ is the most difficult instance of this relationship between finite and infinite, his introduction into the concept of double agency may only muddy the waters. Yet Farrer, as we have seen, is not deterred by paradox. He writes, "The relation between a Maker who makes things make themselves, and their own making of themselves, is paradoxical anyhow for our minds (not for God's, of course). The absolute instance of the paradox is the clearest, or most undeniable instance. It is also the most glaring, and therefore the most difficult."[34]

So why would Farrer insist on continuing in this christological vein, knowing full well that he was dealing with that which would be most scandalous to double agency? No doubt it has to do with what Farrer considers the task of theology – to delve into "the groundedness of created energies in the action of God."[35] And Farrer, although recognizing the paradoxical nature of what he explores, nonetheless understands that knowing God implies doing God's will, for that is where God will be found. Jesus as the Incarnation of God, then, becomes our supreme clue, "for he is the absolute instance of such groundedness. But if Jesus is the clue to all things, all things are the background to Jesus. A Christian's thought moves backwards and forwards, from the circumference in to the centre, from the centre out again to the circumference."[36]

Thus, double agency only makes sense (albeit paradoxical) in the light of the Incarnation of Jesus Christ. And as we allow the Incarnation to inform this mystery for us, we begin to see that all of God's works are illuminated by Christ in what Farrer calls a "graded sympathy."[37] Christ casts light on every fact, who, like the sun, "too bright to look upon, reveals his luminous power by the fresh colours he awakens in the wide garden of the world."[38]

Trinity and Church – Prolegomena to a Conclusion

Although Farrer thinks it is possible to understand double agency philosophically, his own line of argumentation makes it clear that theology is necessary to 'enflesh' the concept, thereby making it applicable to

---

33. Farrer, *Saving Belief,* 75.
34. *Ibid.,* 75-76.
35. *Ibid.,* 78.
36. *Ibid.*
37. *Ibid.,* 79.
38. *Ibid.*

humanity. Hence the importance of the Incarnation, where "Jesus is both more human and more fully himself than any man."[39] Such a doctrine, then, cannot be deemed by the onlooker as merely interesting. Rather, the Incarnation demands a response, a confrontation where a choice must be made.[40] It is this fact that commonly stands as a direct affront to our own understanding of what it is to be human. Farrer writes,

> Christ forces upon us conditions in our creaturely environment which challenge our voluntary response, and, when the response is unworthy, shows it up for what it is. So Christ bears upon mankind, and his crucifixion shows us what we are.[41]

If human action is still 'made' by God, as it were, a protest will arise that double agency fails on the teleological level – the end is already known to some degree, so why participate in God's will? Isn't my own lack of participation in God's will part of God's will after all? Although there is not space to develop it here fully, Farrer hints that this question is best answered ecclesially. For Farrer, there is no doubt that our participation with Christ is real, and that it occurs in the present. But the 'location' of the participation is in the Church, the very Body of Christ.[42] Farrer writes that "in this man [Jesus] … a new humanity is born; we have been living him out ever since."[43] In other words, the Church is the continued Incarnation of Jesus Christ. Thus, the divine action in Christ is the same divine action in us, and we learn God's will for us by becoming Christ himself in the Church.

Our incorporation into the life of Christ in his body of the Church, however, is not done on our own initiative, as if we did the work without God. Rather, incorporation into the mystical body of Christ is the work of the Holy Spirit, so that God makes us make ourselves *trinitarian-ly*. In other words, double agency in light of the Incarnation implies that God makes us make ourselves *by God, with God, and in God*. Here Farrer cites the early church's understanding of the interplay between God and world, where "acknowledgement of Holy Church was linked with acknowledgement of Holy Spirit."[44] Continued association with

---

39. Farrer, *Saving Belief,* 79.
40. Farrer, *Faith and Speculation,* 91.
41. Farrer, *Saving Belief,* 125.
42. Austin Farrer, "Very God and Very Man," *Interpretation and Belief,* ed. Charles C. Conti (London: SPCK, 1976) 128.
43. Farrer, *Faith and Speculation,* 92.
44. Farrer, *Saving Belief,* 131.

Christ in his Body the Church, then, opens us to the action of the Holy Spirit, who in turn brings us into conformity with Christ.

4. Conclusion

According to Farrer, there is a providential purpose when we are shaped into Christ's image, both for us *and* for God. Just as God needed Mary's womb to become incarnate, God needs the body of believers to become incarnate eschatologically, the place where God will appear on the Last Day.[45] Farrer would have us to believe, then, that when God makes us make ourselves, we are making him![46] But as we can gather from the tenor of Farrer's argument, he would not say that God *needs* us, but rather that God has *chosen* to need us. And, we, in turn, are given that same God-like ability to choose God or not.

---

45. Farrer, *Love Almighty and Ills Unlimited*, 115.
46. *Ibid.*, 116.

"This Is My Body" Which Is "For You" ...
Ethically Speaking

Michael Purcell

In this paper I would like to argue an ethical understanding of the Eucharist. In other words: when, in the narrative of institution, we speak of Christ giving his body "for you", and shedding his blood "for you," this "*for you*" is to be understood primarily in terms of the "*for-you*" of substitution and responsibility of which Levinas speaks. The eucharist can be understood as substitution as well as substance; it is about the substitution of the "one-for-the-other," where, following Levinas, the "*for*" is the turgescence, or welling-up, of the responsibility which the other-in-me provokes.

I want further to argue that this substitution of the one-for-the-other should not be taken as referring only, or even primarily, to the relationship between the elements of bread and wine and the Body and Blood of Christ, but rather to the incorporation of the individual into the ethical community of the Church which, as Rahner says, is not only *sacramentum* but the proper *res sacramenti* effected by the eucharist. In other words, the institution narrative finds its focal point not simply in the elements of bread and wine, but in the institution of an ethical inter-subjectivity which becomes the ongoing narrative of the Church. Such an argument will involve a consideration of the notion of transubstantiation – its reference, intention and scope.

To do this, I will use as a framework the "deduction ... of eucharistic persistence" which Jean-Luc Marion outlines in a few pages of *God without Being* where he addresses "The Gift of Presence" and "The Urgency of Contemplation," and develop, with Levinas and Rahner, some of the points raised and themes introduced there. Marion suggests a "deduction ... of the eucharistic persistence on the basis of the logic of charity (hence of the Cross)."[1] That deduction has three parts: the exteriority or alterity of the Eucharist; the transformative effect of the Eucharist; and, intimately linked to this, the ecclesial dimension of the Eucharist. These three ideas will guide this reflection.

---

1. Jean-Luc Marion, *God without Being,* trans. Thomas A. Carlton (Chicago: University of Chicago Press, 1995) 177.

There is a further oecumenical implication: much confusion and
disagreement on the nature of the Eucharist derives from confusion and
disagreement as to how this is to be expressed philosophically. Revisiting
the question of substance and transubstantiation, and developing an
ethical understanding of the nature of the Eucharist, might prove a
fruitful avenue for dialogue between different and disparate eucharistic
communities as we move towards a shared goal.

1. The Exteriority or Alterity of the Eucharistic Event

Marion writes:

> The Body and Blood persist in an otherness that goes as far as the species and
> the appearance of bread and wine – not to assure an (idolatrous and imperi-
> alist) permanence – but to continue to give themselves without return.[2]

Herein lies the question of what *gives* persistence, presence and permanence. Allied to this is the relation between species and the substance
which is taken to persist. There is also the question of time and permanence (as persistence in time),[3] which is the question of what *gives* time,
if not the gift given in the Eucharist. But this question of time also
opens on to the question of what *gives* a subject.

Marion opens up a whole sacramental theology as well as a theological
anthropology – which can be said to be an ecclesially or eucharistically
ordered consideration of the human person – by digging into the doctrine of transubstantiation. The value of the notion of transubstantiation is that it maintains the exteriority of the gift such that the eucharist
is not reducible to the work or action of an individual or a corporate
group. "Eucharistic presence persists ... beyond our conscious attention."[4] The failure of transignification and transfinalisation is that they
repatriate the significance and finality of the eucharist on the side of the
subject (whether individual or collective), whereas the eucharist
"requires of whoever approaches it a radical conceptual self-critique and
charges him with renewing his norms of thought."[5] Marion notes that,
in terms of transignification, the community that celebrates the Eucharist

---

2. Marion, *God without Being*, 177.
3. Emmanuel Levinas, in *Existence and Existents* (The Hague: Martinus Nijhoff,
1978) writes of existence being "a persistence in time" (75).
4. Marion, *God without Being*, 177.
5. *Ibid.*, 163.

discovers nothing other than itself. The "irreducible presence of Christ
... is displaced from the thing [bread and wine] to the community."[6]
In such an understanding, "the unanimity of the community is no
longer here a fruit of communion but, as collective consciousness of self,
its condition."[7] The community finds in the Eucharist its own reflection
or image, an image which, in truth, is an idolisation of itself. The community is the beginning and the end of the Eucharist, its significance
and its finality, while the Eucharist itself gives nothing. Further, the
irreducible gift which is the Eucharist is reduced to the present time.
"The (human and representational) present commands the future of
divine presence" in such a way that "presence disappears as soon as the
consciousness of the collective self defines itself."[8] The presence of
Christ is thus a moment of or function of the conscious self-presence of
the community. What I want to argue is that the present does not command the future, nor appropriate the past to itself. Rather, it is the past
and the future which give a present in which subjectivity and community arises. The question of Eucharistic persistence and presence, then, is
perhaps more about re-casting modern subjectivity in a more ethico-
theologically considered way than about re-configuring the Eucharist.

Nor are the elements of bread and wine to be dispensed with and
substituted by other material elements which are seemingly more perti-
nent to or relevant in the life of the celebrating community. The species
of bread and wine mark a boundary of otherness and are themselves
other with respect to the community. Not only are they significantly
implicated in a past which the community cannot command, but, in
philosophical terms, they are, in a sense, "real accidents" (accidentia
quaedam realia) which verge towards their own independent substantiality.[9] In terms of the Eucharist, bread and wine cannot mean simply
what I want them to mean, nor should any other elements be employed
to mean what the bread and wine used in the Eucharistic celebration
actually do mean (a meaning which is yet to be drawn out). The
Eucharist cannot be an action which does no more than refer us back to
ourselves, or simply reflects the particular cultural and social symbolic in
which we operate.[10] The intentionality, or direction, of such an action is

6. Marion, *God without Being*, 166.
7. *Ibid.*, 227 n. 11.
8. *Ibid.*, 167.
9. Comp. Jean-Luc Marion, *On Descartes' Metaphysical Prism* (Chicago: University
of Chicago Press, 1999) 191.
10. This is not to deny the need for the any particular Eucharist also to be culturally
situated and reflect the understandings and aspirations of a particular community. But

at odds with the absolute significance of the eucharist (and I use "absolute" in the sense in which Levinas employs the term). If one were to express it in ecclesiological terms, one would have to say (hermeneutical difficulties notwithstanding) that the ecclesial community of the Church is more a function or operation of the Eucharist rather than that the Eucharist is a function or operation of the Church. In short, Eucharist gives rise to Church, rather than Church giving rise to Eucharist. The Eucharist can never be *my* Eucharist. Nor ultimately could it ever be *our* Eucharist, where "*our*" is in opposition to "*your.*" The value of the doctrine of transubstantiation, according to Marion, is that this "thing"

> *exists*, in other words, poses itself outside the intermittencies of attention, and mediates the relation of consciousness to presence.[11]

The community becomes conscious not of itself but of a reality other than itself.

> What the consecrated host imposes, or rather permits, is the irreducible exteriority of the present that Christ makes us of himself in this thing that to him becomes sacramental body.[12]

The notion of *exteriority* is important here, for this is the guarantor and foundation of subjectivity. One can quote Levinas who offers *Totality and Infinity* "as a defence of subjectivity" on the basis of exteriority, or infinity.[13] Just as the emergence of the self as subject is enabled by a relationship with an other than the self (whom the self can neither command nor encompass), so it is with the relationship between the ecclesial community and the Eucharist. By the very fact of the reality and the meaning of the eucharist being in excess of that reality which we name Church, the Church finds itself in the position of being addressed by a past and a future which it cannot circumscribe, and so finds itself instituted in the present as a faltering attempt at faithful

---

the eucharist also is its own culture and its own history. These two have to be related sympathetically, but in a way which does not so reduce the event of the Eucharist that its meaning is solely dictated by the demand of the here and the now. If one were to attempt to articulate this relationship between "ecclesial community" and "Eucharist" in a Levinas-inspired language, one might suggest that the relationship is radically dissymmetrical, with a priority being given to the Eucharist rather the ecclesial community.

11. Marion, *God without Being*, 168.

12. *Ibid.*, 169.

13. Emmanuel Levinas, *Totality and Infinity: An Essay on Exteriority,* trans. Alphonso Lingis (The Hague: Martinus Nijhoff, 1979) 26.

response. The narrative that the ecclesial community becomes takes its origin or institution in the prior event of the institution narrative which, apart from the collective consciousness of a particular ecclesial community, has its own meaning and significance.

If one were to transpose this to the logic of the gift (which is the logic of charity of which Marion speaks), the key notion would be the exteriority and excess of the gift. The gift can neither be commanded nor manufactured, nor even confected. A gift conjured up on the basis of my willing or my need is no gift, but is simply something wishful and wish-fulfilled, and in its reception, I encounter only the lack that I already have. True gifts and proper giving (that is, a giving which is proper (*propre*) to itself) are radically exterior to my will, my intention, and command. In terms of intention and intentionality, the direction does not proceed from a constituting consciousness (whether individual or collective) but is, rather, reversed.[14] Consciousness (whether individual or collective) is not constituting but is constituted by the reception of the gift given in which the giver is inextricably implicated. Stephen Webb makes this point well when he speaks of the anteriority and exteriority of giving:

14. If one were to translate such a notion into the distinction between *ex opere operantis* and *ex opere operato*, one might well have to gravitate towards the latter. The Eucharist is not an *opus operantis*. Ultimately, the eucharist is not of my or our doing. It is some "thing" which is done is us. It happens *ex opere operato*, where the passive voice speaks not about the automatic summoning of eucharistic presence as a result of some *hocus-pocus*, but rather about the passivity and receptivity involved in Eucharistic presence (which is both provocative and revelatory of the eucharistic person and community). The doctrine of grace is implicated here. *I* cannot summon Eucharistic presence *ex opere operantis*. This can only be achieved by a certain deed being done (*ex opere operato*) which refers me back to an event, reality, and significance which predates me and is apart from me.

Professor Paul Moyaert's remarks in the final colloquium are also significant here. The point was made that, perhaps, in the ritual act, the enactment of that ritual is the moment when I am "at rights" with God; that a ritual has its own specific intentionality; and that perhaps a ritual is an act which could be done without meaning *on my part*. This not to say that ritual celebration is a meaningless act. Rather, the meaning is not in my gift. The reality (*res*) of the eucharist is not constituted by a meaning-bestowing act on the part of a constituting consciousness. The eucharist is *its own meaning*. It is, following Levinas, *kath'auto*. In short, "I" do not effect/confect eucharist; eucharist effects "me." In practical terms, whether as celebrant or participant in the eucharistic event, there are times when I can bring no meaning to this event, but, in the very doing of this action, I discover the meaning of what I am doing. Nor is this necessarily open to the Heideggerian criticism that such an action would be inauthentic (*uneigentlich*), and perhaps better not being done. The proper celebration of the Eucharist cannot be inauthentic, because it was never my own (*eigen*) in the first place. In short, sometimes things just have to be done because they have to be done – *but this also is not without significance.*

> I want to argue that authentic gifts are not an expression of personality
> or a capacity of personhood because they precede the individual and
> their momentum connects the individual to a larger whole. The gift is
> not controlled by the intention of the individual; the gift has its own
> amorphous and fluid energy, which moves along in unpredictable and
> even faceless directions.[15]

Webb further links God's gracious giving to the summoning of the
Church. God's act of excessive giving "inevitably takes shape in the lives
of the people who choose to respond to it, and this response is community."[16] Within the eucharistic logic of charity, "the primary response is
doxological (liturgy and ethics)."[17] Again,

> All gifts … create time. They also create space. The church can be
> defined as the place where excess meets excess, where, that is, the pro-
> portionate response to the disproportionate grace of God marks the site
> of the process (the continuing event) of the gift.[18]

The notion of the gift giving time is significant in terms of the
Eucharist. The Eucharist, as a past and continuing event, is outwith the
power or domain of the present. In fact, the eucharist, as gift, gives a present. It gives a eucharistic time (the model of all time), and makes possible the reality of the present – a "real presence" which is, from the first,
ethical. This, of course, is the point that was noted above in Marion: the
persistence of the Body and Blood under the species of bread and wine
does not so much assure permanence but the continuance of the gift.
What is made present in the eucharist is an ongoing ecclesial reality
which lives out its calling in a time which is, from the first, eucharistic.

---

15. Stephen Webb, *The Gifting God: A Trinitarian Ethics of Excess* (Oxford: Oxford
University Press, 1996) 128. Webb's insight, philosophically obscured in modernity, has
perhaps a pedigree which has never been fully obscured theologically. For example, it is
striking how Robert Southwell (1561?-1595), in his poem on *The Nativity of Christ*,
weaves together the various strands in the dynamic of the gift: the prevenience and self-
communication of God in the incarnation, the notion of gift begetting giving, as Webb
rightly draws attention to, and the notion that subjectivity is constituted as gift, that is
as other-oriented, or "for-you." Southwell wrote:
    Gift better than himself God doth not know;
    Gift better than his God no man can see.
    This gift doth here the giver given bestow;
    Gift to this gift let each receiver be.
    God is my gift, himself *he freely gave* me;
    God's gift am I, and none but God shall have me.
    (Italics added)
16. Webb, *The Gifting God*, 128.
17. *Ibid.*, 125.
18. *Ibid.*, 148.

Eucharistic Time

There is also what we might term the "temporality of the eucharist." Given the grounding of the eucharistic event in the alterity of the past, there is what we might term "eucharistic time." The eucharist is not only a present event. In fact, it is only temporally present insofar as it is situated within the logic of the "present"/gift. If, following Derrida, we grant that the "gift gives time," then the time in which I live – my chronological present – is a time which is given in terms of the eucharistic *kairos*. *Chronos* always unfolds within a *kairos*. It is a Eucharistic time – time relative to the Eucharist. Marion comments,

> The rigours of the gift must order the dimensions of the temporality where the present is made gift.[19]

Or, we might say, the giving of the gift given makes the present (with all the equivocation and play that the very word conjures up). The articulation of the particular temporality of the eucharist has a noble pedigree. One needs only to recall Aquinas' words,

> *O Sacrum convivium in quo Christus sumitur:*
> *Recolitur memoria passionis eius,*
> *Mens impletur gratia,*
> *et futurae gloriae nobis pignus datur.*

However, following Marion (and Levinas), one must alter this temporal order, making it other than it is presented (for, does not the eucharist displace the present time in order to make it the time of the gift/present?). Thus we would have to read,

> O Sacred Banquet in which Christ is our food:
> the memory of his passion is recalled,
> a pledge of future glory is given,
> *and* (so) our lives are filled with grace,

where this "and" is not simply a conjunction which associates the present with the past and the future, but also has the force of a concluding "so/therefore." The gift, then, orders time. The present/gift gives a present-time. It arises in a past covenant; it points to an eschatological future charged with hope and promise; and because of this, it establishes a present.

---

19. Marion, *God without Being*, 177.

For Marion, as we indicated, the exteriority of the past is important for it preserves the eucharistic gift from any idolising tendency which would reduce its significance or finality to an individual or collective constituting consciousness. The present celebration of the eucharist is referred to a past which exercises a certain judgement over the present and summons the present celebration to be responsible and faithful celebration. But, so too with the future orientation of the eucharist. The life, death and resurrection of Christ which establishes the new covenant inaugurates the kingdom of God, and thus provides a substantial anchor for that "pledge of future glory" (*pignus futurae gloriae*). That future is not an empty promise; it has already been established. It would an interesting endeavour to pursue Luce Irigaray's *positive* interpretation of Feuerbach's notion of religious projection in this regard.[20] The human task is to project a "divine horizon" which enables human becoming, not only individually but socially. The religious project(ion) is about developing a new symbolic which enables our original situation of ethical responsibility (as Levinas might say) to flourish and incarnate itself as justice. The present time of the eucharist is about anticipating and realising the justice of the kingdom of God, the practical elements of which find expression in Matthew's portrayal of the Last Judgement (Mt 25:31-36). The kingdom of God is a kingdom in which food is given to the hungry, water to the thirsty, clothing to the naked; it is a kingdom in which the stranger is made welcome, and the sick and the prisoner are visited. But, the projection of such a divine horizon which

    20. What I would want to argue theologically is that the religious projection which Feuerbach critiques, and which Irigaray appropriates with a positive interpretation is not simply a "wishful thinking", but is already pledge and promise of future glory (*pignus futurae gloriae*) on the basis of the continuing irruption of the "past" and "future" into the present. For example, how often has the statement "Christ has risen" been proclaimed, when the theological reality is that "Christ *is* risen"? This is not simply a syntactical, or semantic, or grammatical nicety which provides food (even canapes) for theological erudition. It raises questions of temporality and subjectivity which have often not been properly or rigorously problematised by philosophical modernity. "Theological" time (is there ultimately any other?) unfolds in the light of the resurrection. The present commands neither the past nor the future. Rather, past and future "give" or "offer" a present/subjectivity. Covenant is both memorial and pledge, and present/subjectivity emerges within that horizon.
    In terms of Irigaray's gendered perspective (which has both masculinist and feminist implications and potential), she acknowledges in *Sexes and Genealogies* (New York: Columbia University Press, 1993) that "in order to become," a horizon is needed, "otherwise, becoming remains partial and subject to the subject" (61). "As long as woman lacks a divine made in her image she cannot establish her subjectivity or achieve a goal of her own. She lacks an ideal that would be her goal or path in becoming" (63-64). For Irigaray, the term "God" "designates the horizon of fulfilment of a gender, not a

enables the flourishing of justice is not a vain or empty hope. It already has a content which has been realised in the life, death and resurrection of Christ. As Rahner puts it, Christ is, "the historically real and actual presence of the eschatologically victorious mercy of God."[21] The future has already been realised and continues to be realised whenever justice and mercy are done, a doing which gives a present. The new covenant has already been established. Thus, as with the past, the future has a certain exteriority with regard to the present. It is that which, along with the past, gives a present.

Let us continue briefly with this notion of the temporality of the eucharist, particularly in view of the inter-subjective character of time. Just as we can say with Derrida that it is the gift which gives time, so Levinas' notion that it is the other who gives time is also important. Time does not start from a "here and now" which is mine, and move into a future which I can make my own, and in which I can both project and realise my ownmost possibilities. I do not temporalise myself. Time, rather, unfolds from the other person. It is the other person who enables my temporalisation, and the time I inhabit is always (in) the time and (in) the gift of the other person.[22] Time is indeed "relative," but not to a subjectivity in terms of which time is constituted. Subjectivity arises in terms of a time which is other than its own making.

In short, the significance and finality of the Eucharist take their origin beyond the temporally present community which celebrates it. One might say that the Eucharistic memorial belongs to "an immemorial past" which signifies "starting from the responsibility 'for-the-other.'"[23] In this sense, it is Eucharist which is creative of the community, rather than the community which is creative of the Eucharist. Further, it is only to the extent that the eucharist has first summoned the community

---

transcendent entity that exists outside becoming" (63). Positively, it entails "positing new values that would essentially be divine" (67). Such ideas are a fertile and fruitful milieu for theology. Irigaray also notes that such a positive projection seeks "the horizon and the foundation needed to progress between past and future" An Ethics of Sexual Difference (London: Athlone Press, 1993) 69. In other words, a horizon which gives a present. Certainly, past and future are associated by the present. The difficulty with Irigaray is that the future is configured in terms of the present, but lacks what we might term a substantial grounding. One cannot simply start from the here and now and egress into past and future. Past and future constitute a present. But is this not eucharistic time?

21. Karl Rahner, The Church and Sacraments (London: Burns & Oates, 1963) 14.
22. Cf. Emmanuel Levinas, Time and the Other, trans. Richard A. Cohen (Pittsburgh: Duquesne University Press, 1987) 79.
23. Ibid., 113.

together that the community can be said to be expressive of the eucharist. Put otherwise, the community realises itself as Eucharist in the present on account of past gift and future promise.

The Eucharist and the Logic of the Cross

Marion makes a further point: the logic of charity, which is the logic of the gift, is also the logic of the Cross. We might say, then, that the Eucharist is a *crucial* endeavour, for it is the meeting point of God's action in Christ, and of the community which is the Church. What is significant is that, from the *crux* or *cross point* of that encounter (which is obviously Christo-centric), the movement is outwards or kenotic. What is crucial, or what gives the Cross, is a movement from the self, an intentionality towards an other than the self. This kenotic movement is not simply a negative evacuation of the self, but a positive displacement of the ego by the other *for*-whom I become responsible.[24] Further, this movement is a movement of response and responsibility. It does not takes its origin in an individual or collective constituting consciousness. The community which celebrates Eucharist finds itself drawn and directed away from itself towards God and towards others.

In this sense, Eucharist is liturgy *par excellence*. As *Sacrosanctum Concilium* puts it, the Eucharist is "source and summit."

> From the Liturgy, therefore, especially the Eucharist, grace is poured forth upon us as a fountain; and the sanctification of men in Christ and the glorification of God to which all other activities of the Church are connected, as towards their end, are achieved with maximum effectiveness (*Sacrosanctum Concilium*, 10).

What is of significance in the quote from *Sacrosanctum Concilium* is the direction of the action: in "the doing" of the Eucharist, or perhaps even more significantly, in the Eucharist "being done," the movement of grace is towards us. The paradox is one of the relation between activity

---

24. Philosophically speaking, this is perhaps the obstacle or scandal of the Cross, of which Paul speaks in 1 Cor 1:23: – "We are preaching a crucified Christ: to the Jews an obstacle they cannot get over, to the gentiles foolishness..." For a (Greek) philosophy which prizes, and takes its point of departure from, an ego-subject, the crossing over to a subject evoked by alterity is a stumbling block which it cannot get over. As Levinas comments in *Otherwise than Being*, "Here the subject is origin, initiative, freedom, present. To move oneself or have self-consciousness is in effect to refer oneself to oneself, to be an origin. Then a subject-origin which is also a subject of flesh and blood becomes problematic – Emmanuel Levinas, *Otherwise than Being* (The Hague: Martinus Nijhoff, 1981) 78 – for to be flesh and blood is to be vulnerable, passive, and essentially open to a more original alterity. Perhaps indeed (philosophical) salvation comes from the Jew.

and passivity. "Grace *is poured forth* upon us." Human sanctification and God's glorification *"are achieved."* Marion links this directedness and finality of the liturgy with the "for-you" structure of the eucharist, linking it to Christ's expiatory offering of himself on the cross. In the crucifixion Christ gives himself – in obedience to the will of the Father – "for-you." Thus, in the Last Supper narrative, we read "This is my body given for-you;" "This is my blood shed for-you" (Lk 22:20).

I would like to pursue this "for-you" structure of the eucharist further, for it has implications for our understanding of the structure of human subjectivity which is caught up in the Eucharist event, and is not only affected but also *effected* by participation in the event of the Eucharist. Some speakers have already spoken of the notion of transubstantiation in terms of its reference to those who participate in the Eucharist, indicating that the focal point is not so much the elements of bread and wine but rather the effect upon those who receive the bread and wine as Body and Blood and are thereby themselves a transubstantiation. For example, L. Hemming, using the framework of Aristotelian Physics, mentioned that the subject is the (unwilled) *locus* or *topos* of transubstantiation. Following Levinas, I would like to pursue this with the intention of developing an ethical understanding of eucharistic subjectivity. But first a word of caution: Levinas rejects any notion of a transubstantiation of the self. Explicitly, he writes,

> As substituting for another, as me, a man, I am not a transubstantiation, a changing from one substance into another, I do not shut myself up in another identity; I do not rest in a new avatar.[25]

Subjectivity, as substitution *for-you*, is not a transubstantiation of the self[26]. Levinas, of course, is rejecting the dominance of ontology and the ousiological language in which it is articulated. Yet, he immediately continues by asking,

> Must we pronounce the word expiation, and conceive the subjectivity of the subject, the otherwise than being, as an expiation?[27]

25. Levinas, *Otherwise than Being*, 14.
26. Levinas writes, in a section entitled *On the Way to Time* in *Existence and Existents* (85-96), of *cognition and the Ego as a Substance*. Since Descartes, "the substance par excellence is the subject" (86). Jean-Luc Marion also explores the egological deduction of substance in *On Descartes' Metaphysical Prism*.
27. Levinas, *Otherwise than Being*, 14. It has to be said that Levinas' criticism is perhaps not as considered as it should be. The very notion of transubstantiation marks a break with the ousiological tradition which Levinas criticises, since, in terms of the eucharist, the relationship between substance and accident is other than in Aristotle. Levinas's criticism is directed towards a substantial, non-relational, understanding of the

What I want to argue is that the structure of the eucharistic event is the model of who we are called to be. What is celebrated and realised in the Eucharist extends to those who participate, for they are summoned to become what the Eucharist is. The institution narrative of the Eucharist becomes the institution of my own narrative as a eucharistic person. The words of institution evoke eucharistic subjectivity.

The Liturgical Orientation of the Self

What can we say happens in the Eucharist, which is *liturgy* par excellence? What is its dynamic and its intentionality? Let us first of all note the Levinas employs the term "liturgy" in a philosophical sense. Liturgy

---

self. Substance is non-transcending. "The apparition of a substantive," he writes, is an "act without transcendence of taking position" (*Existence and Existents*, 82-83). The substantial self is "an invariable *substratum*" (*Existence and Existents*, 98), "an indestructible point, from which acts and thoughts emanate, without affecting it by their variations and their multiplicity" (*Existence and Existents*, 86). For Levinas, a substantial basis for subjectivity raises two questions: firstly, "can the multiplicity of accidents not fail to affect the identity of the substance?" (*Existence and Existents*); but also, the isolation of the subjectivity of the subject within its own substantiality places it outwith time, and renders time redundant not only within the economy of being, but also within the economy of salvation, and thus the further question, "How indeed could time arise in a solitary subject?" (*Existence and Existents*, 93)."

But, as we have argued, *with* Levinas, time arises as a result of past promise and future hope, for "the present is not the point of departure" (*Existence and Existents*, 99). "To have a time and a history is to have a future and a past. We do not have a present; it slips between our fingers" (*Existence and Existents*, 97). "This is the 'paradox of the present'" (*Existence and Existents*).

In terms of the self-enclosure of the subject as non-relational subject, Marion points out that the eucharistic doctrine of transubstantiation marks a breakdown of the ousiological framework which Aristotle advances, for, in transubstantiation the accidents perdure cut off, as it were, from that underlying *substratum* which would be required to sustain them. The accidents, as real accidents, perdure, being a less a function of substance than being there in their own right and according to their own manner. One is tempted to say that the real accidents are *kath 'auto*. Marion addresses this in *On Descartes' Metaphysical Prism*, where, quoting Descartes – "*quicquid etiam per quantumvis extraordinarium Dei potentiam potest esse sine subjecto, substantia est dicendum*" (*Responsiones VII*) – he makes the point that "accidents without *subjectum* would already count as substances" (154). Again, "... *docuit Ecclesia species panis et vini remanentes in Sacramento Eucharistiae esse accidentia quaedam realia, quae, sublata substantiacui inhaerebant, miraculose subsistant*" (191), quoting Descartes' correspondence with Arnauld. Marion further points out that "the physical explanation of the eucharistic transubstantiation cannot extend to the entire doctrine of substance" (*On Descartes' Metaphysical Prism*, 154), as Levinas would seem to think.

The ethical import of this, in terms of a Levinas-inspired approach to the Eucharist, is this: the eucharist evokes a new subjectivity, which we term ethical or eucharistic. Transubstantiation implicates those who receive the Eucharist and are called to become eucharistic reality. Although seemingly accidental within a substantial framework, this ethical accidentality is actually not strictly speaking accidental but assumes its own reality or substantiality (hence *real accidents*).

is a work which is "a movement of the Same towards the Other which never returns to the Same."[28] In other words, "The liturgical orientation of the work does not proceed from need."[29] It is a "heteronomous experience" which "demands a generosity on the part of the Same" but this is a generosity which is the result of a prior and absolute generosity, and thus it is not all pure loss.

Further, this liturgical orientation of the self is not simply a movement beyond oneself towards a divine other. It is a crucial movement towards the other person, a movement in which the self is constituted as "for-the-other." As Levinas comments,

> Such a work can be termed liturgy, not understood at this moment in its religious sense, even if a certain idea of God should show itself as a trace at the end of our analysis. On the other hand, as an action absolutely patient, liturgy does not range itself as a cult besides works of ethics. It is ethics itself.[30]

Now, Levinas describes Liturgy as *œuvre*.

> The Work (*Oeuvre*) thought radically is in effect a movement of the Same towards the Other which never returns to the Same.[31]

Liturgy is a work (*ergon*), but it is a work which is to be understood not primarily in terms of human travail (*travail*) and effort and achievement. Rather, liturgy is *œuvre*, and as *œuvre*, it involves a certain passivity on the part of the subject. In other words, liturgy is not a work of the subject. It is, as the very word indicates, a work of the people, an other's work. To go further, one might say that I can participate in the liturgy (the work of the people) because I have become (through the liturgy as the work of the people) a liturgical person. In other words, to the extent that liturgy affects me and, in being so affected, *effects* an ethical subject, we might also speak of the subject *as liturgy*. To be a subject is, as Levinas says, to undergo the other, to be the object of the other's approach. One must say again,

> Work (*œuvre*) thought radically is a movement of the Same towards the Other which never returns to the Same.

The "movement of the Same towards the Other" is a transcendence which takes its origin elsewhere than in the subject. In terms of the

28. Emmanuel Levinas, "La Trace de l'Autre," *En découvrant l'existence avec Husserl et Heidegger* (Paris: Vrin, 1988) 191.
29. *Ibid.*, 192.
30. *Ibid.*
31. *Ibid.*, 191.

Eucharist, the work involved in the eucharist is not some *travail* that we
do or intend, but is essentially an *œuvre* done in us which elicits from us
response and responsibility. Marion rightly quotes psalm 115: "What
return can I make to the Lord for his goodness to me? The cup of salvation I will raise ..." In this sense Stephen Webb is right when he
speaks of the excessive logic of the gift. The Trinitarian nature of giving
is excessive in that it multiplies giving. Divine giving encourages and
enables human giving.

Now, we have said that the inner structure of liturgy is essentially
"for-the-other" but that this structure is cruciform. Liturgy is a transcending movement towards the other who is God, a movement of
praise in which God is perfectly glorified. But liturgy also issues in the
responsible "for-you" of service of the other person. The synoptic narrative of the institution of the eucharist which is "for-you" becomes the
Johannine mandatum: I have given you an example that you should
imitate. One should note, as Levinas stresses, that these two movements
are inseparable. Transcendence is a movement "in which the distinction
between transcendence towards the other man and transcendence
towards God must not be made too quickly."[32]

In other words, the "for-you" structure of the Eucharist is realised
incarnationally. The eucharist, in which the glorification of God is
achieved, might be said, to use Levinas' words, to be realised "as correlative to the justice rendered unto men."[33] The crucial movement of the
eucharist is a movement beyond the self not only towards God but also
– and *in* the same time – a movement towards you and towards many,
a movement by which I become "for you and for many." Here is what
we might term the ecclesial significance of the eucharist.

2. The Transformative Effect of the Eucharist

A second main point to which Marion draws attention in his consideration of eucharistic persistence is the transformative effect of the
eucharist. The eucharist is given "only in order to feed."[34] It is given *ut
sumatur*. But what, he asks, does it mean "to feed"?

---

32. Emmanuel Levinas, "Philosophy and Awakening," *Entre Nous: Thinking-of-the-
Other* (New York: Columbia University Press, 1998) 87.
33. Levinas, *Totality and Infinity*, 78.
34. Marion, *God without Being*, 178.

Marion notes that our consumption of the Eucharist, rather than assimilating Christ to ourselves, assimilates us "by the sacramental body of Christ to his ecclesial body". Again, "the eucharistic present is deduced from the real edification of Christ's ecclesial body."[35] Paradoxically then, the intentionality of the consumption of the eucharist is not a movement towards me, but a movement away from myself towards the social and ecclesial reality of the Church. In short, the eucharist has an ethical intent. I become "for-you" as Christ himself in his giving offered himself with a giving which was "for you and for all," or, in Levinas' terms, for-the-other-person (*autrui*) and for-all-the-others (*les autres*). Thus, the eucharist is not simply the basis of responsibility for-the-other-person, but the basis of eschatological and realised justice for-the-others.

One might briefly raise here the paradox of viewing a consumptive model of the Eucharist as the basis for ethical activity. Levinas, in *Existence and Existents*, draws the distinction between the intentionality of eating and the intentionality of loving.[36] Now, the Eucharist is given *ut sumatur*. But, eating is an essentially destructive act. Some reality which is other than the self is appropriated by the self, and subjected to the most appalling masticatory violence, before being reduced, broken down and eventually assimilated into the self. The Other is reduced to the Same. Obviously, eucharistic eating cannot be conceived on this model. The notion of sacrifice and expiation has to be introduced, because the intentionality of eucharistic eating has to be more modelled on the intentionality of loving which does not proceed from the emptiness or lack of need within the Same and return their having fully realised its intention. Liturgy, like loving, is a movement of the Same which proceeds preveniently from the Other exciting in the Same a desire or insatiable hunger and thirst for the Other. In loving, we are constituted by the other as for-the-other. In eucharistic eating, then, the one who draws close is the one who in his own life, death and resurrection freely and willingly and vicariously offers himself for-the-other that we might become who he is, namely, for-the-other. Eucharistic eating, then, would not become the appropriation and assimilation of what is other, nor the reduction of the other to the same, but the *reception* of one who freely gives himself that *I* might live, that I might become a eucharistic person. Thus, Marion's stress on our assimilation by the

35. Marion, *God without Being*, 178.
36. Cf. Levinas, *Existence and Existents*, 42-44.

sacramental body into the ecclesial body. Eucharistic eating, to use Levinas' language, would be the displacement by the other-in-me of my self-centred subjectivity. And this presence of the other-in-me institutes me as a responsible ethical subjectivity who is "for-the-other," that is, who is "eucharistic." In this way, the eucharist not only effects ethical subjectivity but also reveals it. In the eucharist, we recognise ourselves as being who Christ Jesus is.

3. *Sacramentum et Res*

A final notion which Marion indicates is the distinction between *sacramentum* and *res*. It is, he says, presumed that the focus of the distinction concerns the elements of bread and wine and the body and blood of Christ. This is linked to the notion of our assimilation or incorporation into the ecclesial or mystical body of Christ, for this is the real effect of the Eucharist. We become part of an ethical community which is characterised by the "for-you" of service (which is the *realisation* of the Eucharist, or, we might say, the transubstantiation of the self). It is Church – this ecclesial body – which is *sacramentum et res*.

This, of course, is not simply Marion. Some four decades previously, Karl Rahner, in *The Church and Sacraments*, made a similar point: "*Sacramenta, significando efficiunt gratiam*" ("The sacraments, by signifying, effect grace").[37] The eucharistic present – the grace/gift of the present – is effected by signifying. But what is signified is our deeper incorporation into the ecclesial reality of the Church. The Church in Rahner's schema is the fundamental sacrament whose reality is effected in the eucharist:

> The Church is always and unchangeably the sign which brings with it always and inseparably what it signifies.[38]

The operation of grace in the eucharist is not to be conceived in terms of an efficient causality whereby we are either recipients of grace, or directed towards God. No, the point of reference is the ecclesial and ethical community of the Church. The sacraments intend the Church. With regard to the eucharist, what the sacrament effects is the individual's "participation in the physical body of Christ" which is itself *sacra-*

---

37. Rahner, *The Church and Sacraments*, 36.
38. *Ibid.*, 19.

mentum, and thereby "imparts the grace of Christ to us."[39] Eucharist, then, as *res et sacramentum*, is "the more profound incorporation into the unity of the Body of Christ," which is the Church[40]. So, too, with Baptism: incorporation into the Church is both *sacramentum et res*."[41] So too with reconciliation: "the *pax cum ecclesia* is the *sacramentum et res* of reconciliation with God."[42] For Rahner's theological anthropology, as for Levinas' ethical subjectivity, there can be no distinction between the movement towards God and the movement towards the other person. As embodied subjects, we find ourselves always and already in an inter-subjective situation, and the movement towards God coincides with the movement towards the-other person and all-the-others. Theologically speaking, we might say that, *crucially* in the flesh, we bear the imprint of the crucified one.[43]

Conclusion

The eucharist betrays an intentionality which presents to us the structure of our true humanity (who is Christ), for the Eucharist is the celebration of the "for-you" of Christ's sacrifice which is realised ethically and ecclesially in the "for-you" or our service of and responsibility "for-the-other." In the Eucharist, we are transformed by being incorporated into a community of others who summon us and enable us to become "for-the-other" as Christ himself in his life, death and resurrection was "for-the-other."

This transformation (which has been most aptly termed "transubstantiation") is primarily ethical. This is not to deny the ontological. Rather, it is to recognise the ecclesial dimension, which is the fulfilment of the Eucharist, and which for both Marion and Rahner, is both *sacramentum* and *res*.

---

39. Rahner, *The Church and Sacraments*, 83.
40. *Ibid.*
41. *Ibid.*
42. *Ibid.*, 94.
43. Cf. Gal 6:14.

Ethical Subjectivity as Sacramental Presence?
The Contribution of Emmanuel Levinas's Ethics
of Responsibility

Marie L. Baird

1. Introduction

In recent times, Christian spirituality has placed an important, although not exclusive, emphasis on the individual's personal relationship with a God typically encountered in the one-on-one context of devotional practices.[1] This sense of personal encounter has also informed sacramental participation.[2] Personal piety, in other words, has existed more recently as any number of such practices that stress the development of this personal relationship and sacramental participation has been regarded as the primary arena of one's graced encounter with God. A perusal of both academic and more popular texts will confirm that this emphasis still persists to a surprising degree in Christian spirituality, even in a postconciliar church.[3] The priority accorded to the development of a personal relationship with God that of necessity consigns the Other, and the community at large, to an important yet secondary status may seem to many people to be merely self-evident, natural, and hence indisputable. In a sacramental liturgical context, the practical outcome may be a parish that comes to resemble a worshipping aggregate of individuals. I believe that much current Christian spiritual praxis has yet to reflect adequately the more properly communal focus that post-Vatican II sacramental theology has appropriately espoused, in other words.[4]

1. See Michael Downey, *Understanding Christian Spirituality* (New York: Paulist, 1997) 105, where he asserts: "The common perception is still that spirituality is primarily concerned with the life of the soul, the interior life, one's prayer life, one's spiritual life, as a separate component of the Christian life. The tendency to equate the spiritual life with the interior life is particularly prevalent in our own day."

2. Downey, *Understanding Christian Spirituality*, 46.

3. See, for example, Daniel A. Helminiak, *The Human Core of Spirituality: Mind as Psyche and Spirit* (Albany, NY: SUNY, 1996); id., *Religion and the Human Sciences: An Approach via Spirituality* (Albany, NY: SUNY, 1998). The popular forum provides examples too numerous to mention.

4. This has been an issue for many American parishes, which often contain a very active core community. Such parishes also struggle, however, to engage the majority of their membership overall beyond the weekly liturgy.

It is worth asking whether Christian spirituality's more recent focus on personal experience in relation to God is a 'natural' occurrence exempt from critical scrutiny. To what extent may Christian spirituality continue to posit a self in relation to God without the mediation of the human Other? Is the absence of that human Other from the self-God encounter as benign as we might commonly suppose? These are two of the general questions that a postconciliar sacramental theology might already pose to a Christian spirituality that continues to emphasize the primacy of personal self transcendence in relation to a divine Other, but that does not sufficiently include the fact of interrelatedness with human Others as a vital, mediating component of this self-God encounter.

In addition to the communal orientation just alluded to, sacramental theology after Vatican II also offers several other foci to which Christian spirituality should pay attention: a "more egalitarian conception of human life, and a closer relation between sacraments and human activity" and hence a real "concern for the ethical dimension of the sacraments."[5] This ethical concern, a feature of postconciliar sacramental theology, needs to be more fully integrated into current Christian spirituality's self-understanding and praxis. Although there is no doubt that ethical action plays a significant role in Christian spirituality as it has been understood in the tradition overall, there is, however, a question about the status of the role of ethics in the current model.

This essay will argue, first of all, that given the primacy accorded to the individual's personal relationship with a God encountered in devotion and sacramental participation, ethical engagement occupies an important, yet secondary position in much contemporary spiritual practice. I will argue further that the relegation of ethical action to a status derivative of a prior, one-on-one relation to God should be reexamined as Christian spiritual practice in a postmodern context. Given this context, I am using the terms 'postmodern', 'postmodernity', and 'postmodernism' to refer to the rejection of the hegemony of rational systems of thought to the extent that they sacrifice the unique irreplaceability of the human Other to their totalizing visions, assumed to be universal and foundational.[6] Specifically, if the credibility of current Christian

---

5. Susan A. Ross, *Extravagant Affections: A Feminist Sacramental Theology* (New York: Continuum, 1998) 124.

6. For definitions of these terms that support my own usage as delineated, see Zygmunt Bauman, *Postmodern Ethics* (Oxford: Blackwell, 1993) 10-15; David Tracy, *On Naming the Present: God, Hermeneutics, and Church* (Concilium; Maryknoll/London: Orbis Books, 1994) 4.

spiritual practice is to be demonstrated compellingly in a postmodern context, a focus that reinforces more recent notions of sovereign, individual subjectivity in relation to God as the universally recognized foundation for Christian spirituality must be counterbalanced, if not replaced altogether, by a model of subjectivity that builds responsibility for the Other into its primary self-understanding. And if any claims of 'universality' may still be made, these claims stress "the universal significance of [the subject's] unsayable particularity."[7] In light of Emmanuel Levinas's ethics of responsibility, to be a subject in relation to God is to be always already answerable for the plight of the neighbor and the stranger who is always and everywhere ethically incommensurable, in other words.

Secondly, I will show how Levinas's ethics can be of service to a reconfigured understanding of the sacramentality of life through ethical responsibility for the other. The discussion will highlight Levinas's analysis of ethical substitution for the Other whose simultaneous transcendence and destitution call forth my ethical response. Here is a viable source of inspiration for a Christian spirituality that stresses a renewed valuation of the sacramentality of life that echoes the ethical thrust of postconciliar sacramental theology.

Finally, I will show that although Levinas may not be immune to the charge of foundationalism, his model of ethical subjectivity, particularly in its relation to God, remains sufficiently de-ontologized to contribute to a renewal of sacramentality in Christian spirituality that evades charges of idolatry. I will also discuss two implications of Levinas's ethics for a reconfigured Christian spirituality that stresses the sacramentality of life: the question of whether the ethical 'otherwise than being' is more properly taken up as a 'being otherwise' that can be empirically enacted and the question as to whether or not Levinas's God is a God to whom we can pray.

2. Why Human Subjectivity as Ethical Responsibility?

As stated at the outset, I seek to replace the primacy that Christian spirituality has recently given to the individual's personal relationship

---

7. Fabio Ciaramelli, "Levinas's Ethical Discourse: Between Individuation and Universality," *Re-Reading Levinas*, ed. Robert Bernasconi and S. Critchley (Bloomington, IN: Indiana University Press, 1991) 94.

with God as encountered in devotional and sacramental practice with
the primacy of ethical engagement. One might legitimately ask why.
Isn't ethical concern built into the very heart of the Gospel message (for
example Mt 25.31-46 and Lk 10.25-37)? Does Christianity not bear a
very long and venerable tradition of coming to the aid of the outcast
and the victim? Am I in fact not arguing against further reflection on
sacramental presence as a proper *locus theologicus*?

Yet should we not scrutinize, at least from an ethical perspective, the
modern turn to the primacy of rationality, with the attendant outcomes of bureaucratization and technologization? Should the Holocaust not continue to trouble us, with its implementation of bureau-
cratized and technologized genocide? Should we consider the
Holocaust to be an outcome of modernity? This question is indeed
contentious. Yet one cannot dismiss lightly Zygmunt Bauman's assertion that "the Holocaust was born and executed in our modern rational society, at the high stage of our civilization and at the peak of
human cultural achievement, and for this reason it is a problem of that
society, civilization and culture."[8] This is a very serious charge, with no
easy response. Bauman locates an important cause of the failure of
modernity in the primacy given to ontology over ethics.[9] More specifically, the primacy given to ontology in Levinas's sense of being as
'totality'[10] has lost from view the unique irreplaceability and vulnerability of the human Other.

Yet one may ask what the modern primacy of ontology over ethics
has to do with Christian spirituality's more recent focus on the individual's personal relationship with a God encountered in sacrament and
devotion? How does this 'trickle down' into the lives of ordinary people?
Such a focus presupposes a theological anthropology that is firmly
sourced in the assumed priority of ontology. Much of the more recent
literature of Christian spirituality is also sourced in theological anthropological models that stress ontology over ethics. As a result, both

8. Zygmunt Bauman, *Modernity and the Holocaust* (Ithaca, NY: Cornell University
Press, 1989) x.

9. One could also claim that Levinas built his entire philosophical project on the over-
throw of ontology as primary. For corroboration, see Bauman, *Postmodern Ethics*, 72.

10. The notion of being as 'totality' is a central theme of Levinas's entire philosophical project. Its classic discussion occurs in Emmanuel Levinas, *Totality and Infinity: An
Essay on Exteriority*, trans. Alphonso Lingis (Pittsburgh: Duquesne University Press,
1969). In general, 'totality' indicates the subjection of the uniquely irreplaceable Other
to conceptualized categories of being that obscure the fact of the Other's ethical incommensurability.

Christian spirituality as an academic discipline and Christian spiritual practice as informed by this more recent literature, both academic and popular, stress the primacy of an autonomous human being who seeks to transcend his or her 'mundane' self concern by encountering that horizon of ultimate being and meaning called God. I am an embodied spirit, or ensouled body, who seeks to transcend my personal horizon of being by means of sacramental and devotional encounter with the Triune God, in other words. Having received the spiritual sustenance such an encounter provides, I am then free to return to the world to engage in merciful and compassionate action, an ethical widening of my personal horizon that reflects the grace I have received. Philosophical concerns aside for a moment, some scholars in spirituality have noted that the primary concern with personal self-transcendence in relation to God risks becoming excessive in a way that borders on the narcissistic.[11] Such a state of affairs is in no way benign because it risks relegating the indigent and vulnerable Other to the status of relative invisibility. Or, equally troubling, it makes whatever aid I give to him or her to be a function of my own project of self-transcendence, whether or not I am consciously aware of that fact! The pernicious quality of this problem is only intensified when sacramental participation is also viewed as yet another function of this goal.

One of the more salutary outcomes of postmodern thought in general has been to introduce a new humility into scholarly thinking about human subjectivity. The free standing, autonomous subject with rational head held proudly upright has been metamorphosed into the one whose own possibilities of individuation presuppose a profoundly interdependent set of relations with the Other understood in primarily ethical terms.[12] That Other forever slips the bonds of thematizing consciousness, is not to be captured within the conceptual categories according to which he or she is routinely identified in the 'real time' of history. For Levinas, human subjectivity as taken up ethically escapes thematization altogether because such thematization presupposes ontologically driven conceptual categories that obscure the Other's ethical incommensurability. The Other's 'unsayable particularity' occurs here; his or her ethical incommensurability knows no basis for

---

11. See Downey, *Understanding Christian Spirituality*, 105-106.
12. For Levinas, the subject is constituted in ethical substitution for the other. See chapter 4, "Substitution," in Emmanuel Levinas, *Otherwise than Being or Beyond Essence*, trans. Alphonso Lingis (Pittsburgh: Duquesne University Press, 1997) 99-129.

comparison within conceptual categories of being and is therefore unavailable to any spoken language that, of necessity, functions according to such categories and indeed makes them possible. If one can speak of 'the universal significance' of this 'unsayable particularity' it is only in the sense that there is never an Other for whom ethical incommensurability does not hold. It is important to add, however, that these considerations are contextualized within Levinas's philosophical analyses of the ethical relationship, and have not yet entered the 'real time' of history. I will discuss this important qualification below, in considering the critique of Levinas centered around his claim that his philosophy analyzes the ethical relationship as an 'otherwise than being'.

This scholarly humility also extends to more recent discussions of how this decentered, radically interdependent subject can be morally responsible when he or she is desirous of the good yet uncertain about his or her own capacities to realize it. In other words, human subjectivity is characterized by ambivalence, unpredictability, and a very real sense that morality is 'incurably aporetic'.[13] What are both Christian spirituality and ethics to do with Bauman's conviction that ethics "substitutes the learnable knowledge of rules for the moral self constituted by responsibility. It places answerability to the legislators and guardians of the code where there had formerly been answerability to the Other and to moral self-conscience, the context in which moral stand is taken?"[14] How are Christian theologians to respond to his charge that morality is 'not universalizable' and hence without foundations, and to posit otherwise is to lead to "the incapacitation, even destruction, of the moral self?"[15] These are properly postmodern challenges.

How then can Christian spirituality reconfigure its own understanding of human subjectivity such that it factors the mediation of the human Other into the very heart of what it is to be human and God-oriented? How can sacramental participation come to express more adequately "an ethical horizon for Christian living?"[16] How can the thought of Emmanuel Levinas be helpful in responding to these questions?

13. Bauman, *Postmodern Ethics*, 11.
14. *Ibid.*
15. *Ibid.*, 12.
16. Downey, *Understanding Christian Spirituality*, 81.

3. Ethical Responsibility and Sacramentality:
Levinas's Contribution

I believe that Levinas's thought can accommodate the idea of sacramentality. However, if we may speak of the sacramentality of the ethical relationship, it is not a sacramentality that renders present a God 'capturable' within thematization. Neither is it a 'making present' that presupposes ethics' subordination to ontology. Indeed, there is serious question as to the availability of Levinas's ethics to translation in terms of empirical engagement in the world.

Yet we can also see that sacramentality and Levinas's ethics both presuppose a world and that God, either in God's 'real presence' or God's 'trace',[17] cannot be encountered apart from the world. The question arises immediately as to whether or not this world can be historicized. Certainly, Christian sacramental theology's central rootedness in the event of Jesus Christ presupposes the historical Jesus of Nazareth as well as the incarnated, crucified, and risen Christ. I am not so sure that Levinas's world is as easily historicized, a point to which I will return.

In Levinas's thought, ethical responsibility results in subsequent theological statements of faith after the temporally diachronous and conceptually incommensurable 'holiness'[18] of substitution for the other. Such 'holiness', or 'religion',[19] is the site of the interface I am proposing between Levinas's thought and sacramentality. To discover sacramentality in Levinas's thought, in other words, requires an analysis of the ethical substitution for the Other of his later work. For Michael Purcell: "to speak of the face as the trace of the other – beyond representation – is to speak of the sacramentality of the face."[20] The face never appears in

17. Levinas's notion of God's 'trace' designates a wholly transcendent God outside of both history and conceptuality, a God who is never present in the 'real time' of history and who therefore always already escapes conceptual thematization. See Emmanuel Levinas, "God and Philosophy," *Of God Who Comes to Mind*, trans. Bettina Bergo (Stanford: Stanford University Press, 1998) 64, 66, for his use of the term 'trace' in relation to God.

18. See Levinas's "Preface to the Second Edition," in *Of God Who Comes to Mind*, ix. It is, strictly speaking, inaccurate for me to situate theological reflection after ethical responsibility in a temporal sense. Levinas's ethics is diachronous to theological reflection, not prior to it. My analysis, as conceptualized, cannot step outside the bounds of an ontologized discourse but can only point in the direction of such a transgression.

19. See Levinas, *Totality and Infinity*, 80-81.

20. Michael Purcell, *Mystery and Method: The Other In Rahner and Levinas* (Milwaukee, WI: Marquette University Press, 1998) 262-263. See chapter 6, "The Sacramentality of the Face, Or, Sacramental Signification." My own focus on the sacramentality of ethical substitution is not intended as an implicit refutation of his emphasis on the sacramentality of the face, but rather presupposes it.

its phenomenality for Levinas; one does not move from the face of the Other to the Other him or herself because the Other's face is, properly speaking, never seen.[21] To see the face of the Other is always already to have objectified him or her within conceptualized categories of being, in other words. The face, rather, is that which leads the ethical subject outside of all conceptualization, calling forth a non-intentional 'Here I am!' from the ethical subject who has just emerged, through his or her own responsibility for the Other, into human subjectivity. This answer to the Other that calls me forth from the restless humming of being, prior to intentionality and radically 'enactive' of self, is the site of the sacramentality of the ethical relationship as I wish to pursue it in this essay. Without denying or otherwise rejecting either the sacramentality of the face or the ethical value of the sacraments, it is important to emphasize also the other term of Levinas's ethical relationship, the sacramentality of ethical substitution for the Other. It is another way, perhaps, of seeking to articulate an ethical sacramentality that attempts to remain as free of ontology as possible. In other words, what can sacramental reality possibly 'be' without an 'ontological res' that assures sacramental objectivity? My own interest lies in this particular question.

I am linking the event of ethical substitution for the Other with an ethical 'Saying' that Levinas also characterizes as 'testimony', 'witness', 'inspiration', and 'prophecy'.[22] As will become apparent, it is this linkage, as well as the notion of the 'trace', that opens ethical substitution up to the passage of God. The 'Saying' is the enactment of a sacramental Word.[23] For the purpose of discussion, however, the 'Saying' is 'first' the enactment of ethical substitution.

Ethical substitution also enacts a 'Saying' to the Other that precedes any thematized 'Said'. This 'Saying' is the extreme exposedness of an ethical subject without resources to protect itself, yet plenteously armed with resources – itself as resource – to shield the Other from harm: "It is a saying without words, but not with empty hands."[24] Levinas also

---

21. See Levinas, *Totality and Infinity*, 194.
22. See Levinas, "God and Philosophy," 74-76. The 'Saying' designates one's ethical responsibility for the other that is 'otherwise than' conceptual thematization. Such thematization occurs in the 'Said' of the language that structures thematizing consciousness. See also *Otherwise than Being*, 5-7.
23. See Purcell, *Mystery and Method*, 269: "But the notion of Word is at the heart of Sacrament." It is also the case, however, that any sacramentality of the ethical 'Saying' in Levinasian terms will not be tied to a eucharistic frame of reference. My essay will respect Levinas's refusal.
24. Levinas, "God and Philosophy," 74.

designates the ethical 'Saying' as a "pure witnessing that bears witness not to a previous experience but to the Infinite"[25] although not in any manner that would bring the Infinite forth into symbolic representation much less 'real presence.' This is not to reject, however, the sacramentality of a 'Saying'-as-witness if one accepts the sacramentality of the Suffering Servant and the prophetic stance of "subjection to an order prior to the understanding of the order."[26] May the sacramental Word not enact itself through ethical substitution? Although Purcell will point out that "Eucharist is a substitution, 'the normative structure of inter-subjectivity' ... which lies outside the ontological order and 'rests on appeal and obedience rather than causation and comprehension',"[27] it is important to assert that ethical substitution stands on its own in a thought that does not require Christianization in order to exhibit sacramentality.[28] It is for this reason that I would like to take a somewhat closer look at Levinas's characterizations of 'Saying' as witness, testimony, and prophecy.

For him, the prophets, and particularly the Suffering Servant, enact the ethical relation as an extreme passivity through which the 'passing'[29] of a God incommensurable to intentionality and temporality occurs as a 'trace'.[30] The Suffering Servant is therefore not a prefiguration of a divine Incarnation within history. God's trace will 'pass' through an ethical relation that enacts the very 'beyond', outside of time and unavailable to representation. This wholly transcendent God will remain obliquely near, yet absolutely unthematizable, in the ethical subject's obligation toward the Other.[31] For Levinas, the prophets and the Suffering Servant take up this very enactment of ethical subjectivity. The prophets, like all ethical subjects, also 'bear' the anarchic trace of God.[32]

25. Levinas, "God and Philosophy," 74.

26. *Ibid.*, 75.

27. Purcell, *Mystery and Method*, 286.

28. For a view that differs radically from mine, see John van den Hengel, "One for all Others: Levinas's Notion of Substitution and the Figure of Christ," *Église et Théologie* 30 (1999) 111-135.

29. Levinas describes 'passing' as "disturbing the present without allowing itself to be invested by the arche of consciousness" in *Otherwise than Being*, 100. God 'passes' obliquely, in other words, without giving God's self to the present time of thematization. Instead, God's 'passing' inclines me toward the Other.

30. Levinas's God is "transcendent to the point of absence, to the point of his possible confusion with the agitation of the there is (emphasis his)." See Levinas, "God and Philosophy," 69.

31. See Levinas, *Otherwise than Being*, 99-102.

32. *Ibid.*, 196. We can thus assert that the face of the Other is not alone in 'bearing' the trace of God.

By putting themselves entirely at the service of God, by uttering the
Here I am! that precedes any revelation, by putting themselves at the
mercy of a divine an-archy they could not possibly understand, the
prophets bear witness to a God they could never hope to adequately
represent. Prophecy, witness, and the giving of testimony are not representation; they are, rather, a pure undergoing for the sake of the Other
and an attestation to the infinity of the Other who cannot be totalized
thematically. If such an undergoing can be an expiation for an infinite
Other who bears the trace of God, then this undergoing is perhaps also
the bearer of a sacramentality akin to that of the Other's face. Is this
not an ethically-enacted site of the sacramentality of human life? Can
Christian spirituality not find here a counterbalance to its emphasis on
a *personal* self-transcendence in relation to God? Is it not time to
acknowledge my responsibility for the Other's wellbeing, as well as the
mediation of the Other's face, as spiritual practice with significant sacramental import?

4. De-Ontologized Spirituality, Responsibility, and Sacramentality?

I have argued in favor of the inclusion of ethical substitution for the
Other as a viable engagement of sacramentality that deserves a primary
place in Christian spirituality's current understanding of the encounter
with God. This is so particularly in light of postmodernity's emphasis
upon a subjectivity that is constituted by a profound interdependence
upon the Other for the emergence of personal selfhood. I have also called
upon Levinas's thought as working out a de-ontologized enactment of
ethical responsibility that, though universalizable, is only so in the unique,
irreplaceable particularity of the ethical subject's Here I am! that escapes
being. Or does it? Is Levinas's ethics as de-ontologized as I seem to have
been assuming? Is it without foundations? Or, to cite a concern common
among Levinas scholars using Levinas's own words: is 'otherwise than
being' more properly a 'being otherwise'? *If* it is possible to maintain the
integrity of the 'otherwise than being' claim, what is its status as a model
of ethical engagement in a historicized world of empirically available,
'hands-on' *experiences*? Isn't it here, after all, that Christian spiritual praxis
actually occurs? And finally, what is the status for Christian spirituality of
a God who passes in a 'trace', whose absolute exteriority defies thematization? Is this a God to whom we can pray? I will close my essay by entertaining these fascinating and complex questions.

The 'later' Levinas of *Otherwise than Being* and other writings insisted that his ethical analyses overthrew the primacy of ontology as first philosophy. The 'otherwise than being' of ethical substitution was precisely incommensurable to thematization and anachronous to the present time of its representation – all of this in a philosophical language that pushed its capacities for signifying 'otherwise than metaphysically' to their limits. He also insisted, therefore, that he proceeded methodologically in a way that sought the 'superlative' rather than the 'foundational':

> The transcendental method consists always in seeking the foundation. ...
> On the other hand, in my way of proceeding, which starts from the human ... there is another sort of justification of one idea by the other: to pass from one idea to its superlative, to the point of its emphasis.[33]

And so, to offer an example, he asserts that the superlative of passivity is 'the fission of oneself' that occurs when one's proximity to the Other eschews the conceptualization of such proximity in favor of a surrender to the point of substitution.[34] In this regard, it is perhaps helpful to invoke Richard Cohen's observation that ethics escapes ontology for Levinas not because ethics is or isn't onto-theological, a properly ontological judgment, but because ethics, as ethics,is better than being and is not enacted in ontological terms.[35] What are we to make of these claims?

The responses to these assertions are varied. I believe that Richard Cohen ratifies Levinas's claim as to the incommensurability of ethics and ontology and interprets 'otherwise than being' in terms of this incommensurability.[36] Interestingly, Zygmunt Bauman agrees that "ethically, morality is before being [like Cohen, in the sense of 'better']. But ontologically there is nothing before being, as ontologically also the 'before being' is another being."[37] He also seems to espouse the 'incommensurability' claim, in other words, while acknowledging ontology's claim to primacy from an ontological perspective. Robert Manning seems to agree with Bauman, noting that "Levinas's interpreting otherwise than Heidegger results, then, in his demand that the process of knowing and the quest for truth be directed by *the ethical sense or ori-*

---

33. Levinas, "Questions and Answers," *Of God Who Comes to Mind*, 88.
34. *Ibid.*, 89.
35. Richard A. Cohen, translator's introduction to *Ethics and Infinity*, by E. Levinas (Pittsburgh: Duquesne University Press, 1985) 8.
36. See Cohen, "Translator's Introduction," 1-15.
37. Bauman, *Postmodern Ethics*, 75.

entation in but beyond Being."[38] For these thinkers, 'otherwise than being' points to the ethical subject's location within being by virtue of his or her existence, yet beyond being by virtue of the 'superlative' passivity that undoes the primacy of his or her ontological subjectivity. Subjectivity then emerges as ethical when the Other fills the void of such passivity by commanding and imploring the ethical subject to be responsible and his or her Here I am! – better than being – enacts subjectivity through substitution. There are, however, other readings of Levinas's work that dispute entirely the 'otherwise than being' claim in favor of a 'being otherwise'. Their arguments are important to any scholar who would seek to bring Levinas's ethics into the sphere of historical, empirical engagement in the world.

James Olthuis explicitly champions a 'being otherwise' that provides ontological support to a subject who is then ethically engaged in relations of mutuality and shared concern.[39] Although I am in many ways sympathetic to his position, particularly from the standpoint of an ethically-enacted spirituality, I am suspicious that it may rest on a misreading of Levinas. For example, Olthuis rightly cautions that "when legitimate self-needs are denied, they have a way of coming back with a vengeance, often in disguised, underhanded, and dangerous ways."[40] Olthuis may be conflating Levinas's philosophical analysis of ethical subjectivity with the psychological concerns of a subject actually immersed in the throes of experience. Although Levinas does not deny the importance of psychological considerations in relation to ethical subjectivity, he does insist that his own analyses do not proceed from this point of reference.[41] At the level of spiritual praxis, however, Olthuis is perfectly correct to voice a properly psychological concern. Yet the 'otherwise than being' or 'being otherwise' question must be addressed on philosophical, not psychological, grounds.

Michael Purcell also emphasizes that "ethical existence – the relationship with the absolute exteriority of the other – is not an otherwise than being, but a being otherwise."[42] If we argue, following Cohen, Bauman, and

---

38. Robert Manning, *Interpreting Otherwise than Heidegger: Emmanuel Levinas's Ethics as First Philosophy* (Pittsburgh: Duquesne University Press, 1993) 9 (emphasis added).

39. See James Olthuis, "Ethical Asymmetry or the Symmetry of Mutuality?," *Knowing Other-wise: Philosophy at the Threshold of Spirituality*, ed. James Olthuis (New York: Forham University Press, 1997) 131-58.

40. *Ibid.*, 155.

41. See Levinas, "Questions and Answers," 91, 93.

42. Purcell, *Mystery and Method*, 320.

Manning, that ethical existence takes place within being but is better than being, and therefore beyond being because it is incommensurable with representation, Purcell will counter that being is wider than representational knowing – that representation does not exhaust being, in other words. He insists that "there is no need for Levinas to locate the good beyond being and, in so doing, evacuate being of all but its cognitive sense."[43] More importantly for Levinas's potential contribution to a Christian spirituality that is enriched by an ethically enacted sacramentality is Purcell's claim that "Levinas' stress on the other beyond being to whom the subject is always and already responsible may affirm the absolute uncompromisable value of the other, but it offers no way of linking responsibility with practical commitment to the other."[44] This is indeed a serious concern. He therefore proposes "a wider understanding of being which accommodates the good, and enables the good to be actualised."[45] His suggestion is obviously of enormous importance for my own project, although the final word on this issue has perhaps not yet been spoken.

John Caputo charges that Levinas's analysis of the face conjures forth a being otherwise that is 'being in its purest state' as a *hyperousia*.[46] Worse, Levinas's thought is 'recentered around the other'[47] in a way that becomes a new form of totalization. Also, it is impossible to posit an 'absolute otherness' as Levinas does because we would of necessity remain 'oblivious' to it.[48] Perhaps Caputo's most withering critique is his charge that the infinite infinity of Levinas's God teeters over into the anonymity of the *il y a*, a point to which I will return. Although such a God remains free of any charge of idolatry, this God may also remain free of any charge of 'divinity' as well.[49] For the moment, the problem that is attendant upon such potential confusion is that "Levinas would repeat the most classical of gestures … which is to cut through empirical experience and come up with a founding, foundational super-structure, a deep substratum or *a priori*, that somehow underlies – or arches over – familiar empirical experience."[50] Here then, would lie the charge of an

43. Purcell, *Mystery and Method*, 321.
44. *Ibid.*, 329.
45. *Ibid.*
46. John D. Caputo, *Against Ethics: Contributions to a Poetics of Obligation with Constant Reference to Deconstruction* (Bloomington, IN: Indiana University Press, 1993) 81.
47. *Ibid.*, 84.
48. *Ibid.*, 80.
49. I will take up this issue in my final comments.
50. John D. Caputo, "To the Point of a Possible Confusion: God and *il y a*," *Levinas: The Face of the Other: The Fifteenth Annual Symposium of the Simon Silverman Phenomenology Center* (Pittsburgh: Duquesne University Press, 1998) 20.

'ethico-theo-logical'[51] foundationalism that Levinas's own thought explicitly seeks to reject.

What can be said in the face of such charges? Jeffrey Dudiak's response to Caputo is to put forth an absolute otherness "*not with respect to her being,* but in that she presents herself as refusing the domination of the same, as refusing (ethically) to be nothing more than an extension of my (quasi)hermeneutical, transcendental forestructures."[52] The other is therefore other "as an ethical prohibition (that is at once a positive ethical command)."[53] Dudiak would seek to rescue Levinas from the charge of foundationalism that Caputo levels by proposing that the Other, as *kath'auto*, "is not dependent upon being placed in any prior context of meanings; indeed, it makes such contexts possible."[54] I would hesitate to assert, however, that even Dudiak would argue in favor of an 'otherwise than being' that escapes being altogether.

My own response is to argue in favor of an 'otherwise than being' that posits an existent subject, but one whose subjectivity emerges through ethical engagement that is irreducible to thematization. The subject is a 'being' whose subjectivity is enacted 'otherwise than ontologically' because, unlike Purcell, I am hesitant to include the good within a wider understanding of being. I do not see how a good whose goodness remains ontologically circumscribed – no matter how wide the range – escapes the threat of totalization and the potential for violence.[55] Of course there is an important sense in which the ethical subject is 'being otherwise' when viewed ontologically, yet this ontological perspective cannot capture, nor enclose conceptually, the subject's 'superlative' responsibility because the 'being otherwise' of such substitution cannot touch the 'otherwise than being' of its ethical value. I would probably side with Cohen, Bauman, Manning, and Dudiak in other words, not

51. John D. Caputo, *Demythologizing Heidegger* (Bloomington, IN: Indiana University Press, 1993) 200.

52. Jeffrey Dudiak, "Again Ethics: A Levinasian Reading of Caputo Reading Levinas," in *Knowing Other-wise*, 190 (emphasis added).

53. *Ibid.*, 191.

54. *Ibid.*, 199.

55. Caputo believes that "the encounter with the 'absolutely other' ... leaves one in a state of absolutely ineffable obedience, which is the structure of pure or absolute violence which makes the Nazi analogy possible." See *Against Ethics*, 145. I would suggest that the passivity of the ethical relation is not a structure of pure violence but rather a structure of pure goodness, as passivity is awakened by the other's transcendence and destitution. It is not awakened by just any command, in other words. It is awakened by the command, first of all, not to kill the Other and then by the command to take charge over the Other's extreme vulnerability.

least because I believe this position also opens the ethical relation to an
eventual dialogue with historicized experience. I will admit, however, to
a lingering sense that one cannot have it both ways in regard to this
issue, at least from Levinas's own perspective, and that he would regard
this position as a diminishment of his own.

If it is possible to posit an 'otherwise than being' that is an ethically
superlative subjectivity that occurs as a 'being otherwise' from an ontological perspective, how available is such ethical subjectivity to a real
world of actual experience? A pure 'otherwise than being' that escapes
ontology altogether also remains untouched by – and unable to touch –
history, a sad irony for an ethics of responsibility, yet an inevitable fate
for a formalized ethics that calls itself 'diachronic'. It is interesting in
this regard that although Levinas insists that the ethical relation is outside of thematization, he also comments that "an event of unlimited
responsibility for another ... certainly has a historic meaning, it bears
witness to our age and marks it."[56] And he also believes that "the *unlimited* responsibility for another, as an enucleation of oneself, could have a
translation into history's concreteness."[57] He illustrates this assertion
with an account of a discussion held with students concerned about a
crisis in South America, and characterizes them as 'hostages' to this crisis because of their 'utopia of conscience'.[58] It is here, perhaps, that Levinas would approve of the translation of the ethical 'otherwise than
being' into a historicized 'being otherwise'. This 'utopia of conscience' is
not analogous to the sensible, non-intentional consciousness that characterizes his analyses of ethical subjectivity but it does evoke *affective*
concern that transcends conceptual thematization. Perhaps this affective
concern that holds students hostage in fear for others' wellbeing is an
enfleshed, historical instance – an ontologized *exemplum* – of the ethical
consciousness that accompanies the de-ontologized structures of ethical
subjectivity. As a historicized instance, it is a degree of self-transcendence that achieves its fullest enactment when fear becomes embodied
as responsibility. Could this affective self-transcendence that issues forth
in ethical engagement not augment Christian spirituality's more traditional understanding of self-transcendence as described at the beginning
of my essay? Could this self-transcending ethical engagement not
encounter a God who 'passes' in the sacramentality of the Other's face,

56. Levinas, "Questions and Answers," 81.
57. *Ibid.* (emphasis his).
58. *Ibid.*, 81-82.

in agreement with Purcell? Could this loving engagement itself not body
forth a sacramentality that is an echoing of God's own saving action
within history? Yet we must ask, finally, whether Levinas's God is ever
engaged in history and therefore whether or not this is a God to whom
we can pray.

Who 'is' this God anyway? Caputo has charged that Levinas's God is
"the deep structure, *au fond du Tu*, in any personal address, that which,
escaping from any direct address, by that very withdrawal assigns me to
you."[59] This structure, this aridity 'escapes' history as a trace incommensurable to thematization and diachronous to lived time. Levinas himself
notes that

> God is not simply the 'first other' ... but other than the other, other oth-
> erwise, and other with an alterity prior to the alterity of the other, prior
> to the ethical obligation to the other and different from every neighbor,
> transcendent to the point of absence, to the point of his possible confu-
> sion with the agitation of the there is [*il y a*].[60]

A God 'possibly confused' with 'the anonymous and senseless rum-
bling of being' although Levinas will also assert that the *il y a* is not 'an
event of being'.[61] Clearly, Levinas's God is not conceptualizable. Levinas's God is thus 'safe' from idolatry but perhaps at the price of a transcendence beyond approachability, except through ethical responsibility
for the neighbor. I have found the God of Levinas's philosophical analyses to lie infinitely beyond the Jewish and Christian affirmation of a
God who relates meaningfully to humans within history, his invocation
of the prophets and Suffering Servant notwithstanding.

However, if one turns to Levinas's talmudic writings, a somewhat different picture emerges. There, Levinas follows the thought of Rabbi
Haim of Volozhin and distinguishes between two aspects of God: YHWH
who remains completely beyond the world and Elohim, the God who
holds the world in creation but is unable to do so without humans' ethical adherence to Torah:[62] "And so God reigns only by the intermediary
of an ethical order, an order in which one being is answerable
for another."[63] Herein lies his understanding of kenosis in Judaism.

59. Caputo, "To the Point of a Possible Confusion," 10.
60. Levinas, "God and Philosophy," 69.
61. Levinas, *Ethics and Infinity*, 52, 48-49.
62. See Emmanuel Levinas, "Judaism and Kenosis," *In The Time of the Nations*
(Bloomington, IN: Indiana University Press, 1994) 114-132. See also my article, "Divinity and the Other," *Église et Théologie* 30 (1999) 103.
63. Levinas, "Judaism and Kenosis," 126.

Interestingly, prayer enters into this thinking as a necessary aspect of Elohim's continued association with the world: "He needs prayer, just as he needs those who are faithful to the Torah, in order to be able to associate himself with the worlds, for their existence and elevation."[64] This prayer that helps to maintain Elohim's association is always for others, never for oneself. If we are to discover a God to whom we can pray in Levinas's thought, the arid God whose trace is deflected into the ethical relationship – outside of time and incommensurable to thematization – must be augmented by the Elohim dependent upon the ethical goodness of humans in time and thus in the faithful observance of Torah. Such faithful observance is, again, universalizable in the unique particularity of ethical responsibility for the Other, no matter what the fact of personal religious adherence or lack thereof.

I have no wish to argue against a Christian spirituality and sacramentality without faith. I do wish, however, to widen the focus of Christian spirituality to include a sacramentality of life in ethical responsibility for the Other as central to its own self-understanding. I believe that sacramental theology after Vatican II has issued this call to Christian spirituality and that it is a call from which Christian spirituality would benefit. It is a call from which we would all benefit at the close of this volatile century. I believe that Emmanuel Levinas is a valuable dialogue partner as Christian spirituality seeks, in a new millennium, to discover its own response to that call.

---

64. Levinas, "Judaism and Kenosis," 129.

The Re-enchantment of Reconciliation
Rereading the Sacrament of Reconciliation in Light of the Work of Levinas and Derrida

David J. Livingston

Reconciliation is a sacrament that offers the divine presence/absence of healing. The mystery, which lies at the heart of reconciliation, is the possibility of genuine healing within the knowledge that the brokenness may never be fully compensated. This paper applies the categories of responsibility and forgiveness proposed by Levinas and Derrida as a constructive hermeneutic for reassessing the value of reconciliation within the sacramental life of the church. Reconciliation, because it involves at its very core both the categories of responsibility and forgiveness-gift, becomes an impossible possibility. Levinas and Derrida have each shown that responsibility (Levinas) and forgiveness-gift (Derrida) are phenomenological aporias or mysteries because they are both possible and impossible. It will be the goal of this paper to claim that if the church will take seriously the insights of Levinas and Derrida it has the capacity to re-enchant the sacrament of reconciliation in a way which deepens, rather than eliminates, the mystery of the sacramental presence/absence of God, always claimed to be at the core of the sacraments.

In Edward Farley's book *Deep Symbols*, he claims that deep symbols have become atrophied in our postmodern context, but that they can be re-enchanted through the process of centering, sorting and re-embodying.[1] Each of these steps involves recognition of the nature of deep symbols as fragile and fallible. Deep symbols need re-enchantment because they are inherently corruptible. Farley does not mention the symbol of reconciliation in his text, but his method of re-enchantment offers an illuminating path toward the mystery of reconciliation. This phenomenological analysis is what Farley terms the centering process. It is the goal of this process to "grasp the god-term itself."[2] As Farley states,

---

1. Edward Farley, *Deep Symbols: Their Postmodern Effacement and Reclamation* (Valley Forge, PA: Trinity Press International, 1996).
2. Farley, *Deep Symbols*, 39.

> Rethinking the being of something is not just getting a succinct defini-
> tion, a formal essence. It is more the recovery of the origin in the sense
> of the situation and powers that bring forth the god-term[3].

The god-term, which we will attempt to bring forth in this paper, is
the deep symbol of reconciliation. After the centering process has been
accomplished, Farley speaks of the need to sort through the inadequate
interpretations of the symbol until we arrive at a re-embodied symbol
which can function as the guiding cognitive framework for an embodied sacramental expression.

It may appear inappropriate that I speak only of the symbol of reconciliation when this is a conference that attempts to address the sacraments in a postmodern context. We must then ask what is the connection between symbols and sacraments. Sacraments are often understood
as the guaranteed presence of grace and symbols are potential expressions of grace. It is this very claim to guaranteed presence that I wish to
challenge. This paper calls on the theological community to engage in a
redefinition of the sacraments, which is more in keeping with the early
church and our current postmodern sensibility. This new understanding
of the sacraments is one that recognizes that a sacrament is the impossible-possibility of the divine presence/absence reenacted within our
midst.

The definition of sacrament is dependent on the recognition of the
interplay between symbolic language and enacted grace. In the fifth century the phrase *lex orandi lex credendi,* came into use, this phrase forced
praxis to the fore and theory and dogma to a secondary position[4]. *Lex
orandi* highlights the importance that the early church placed on the
encounter, rather than on any definitive statement of doctrine. The
early writings of Tertullian and Augustine on the sacraments translate
the term mystery (*mysterion*) into the term sacrament (*sacramentum*).[5]
Mystery has remained at the core of sacramental theology, but has been
emphasized and de-emphasized at different stages of the Church's his-

---

3. Farley, *Deep Symbols,* 39.
4. This classical phrase is often translated "the law of praying is the law of believing,"
but we may wish to translate it as "the sacramental law is the law of believing." *Lex
orandi lex credendi* appears first in the Indiculus around 440. Cf. Frans Jozef van Beeck,
God Encountered. Volume 1: *Understanding the Christian Faith* (San Francisco: Harper
and Row, 1988) 225. Also Denzinger-Schönmetzer, *Enchiridion Symbolorum* (hereafter
DS), 246.
5. Joseph Martos, *Doors to the Sacred* (New York: Doubleday, 1982) 42-60; Francis
Schüssler Fiorenza and John P. Galvin (eds.), *Systematic Theology: Roman Catholic Perspectives,* vol. 2 (Minneapolis, MN: Fortress Press, 1991) 192-193.

tory. It is the contention of this paper that the postmodern context draws us back into a deep understanding of the mystery at the heart of all of the sacraments. I will argue below that the nature of encounter is one of mystery and always involves a presence/absence, never a pure presence. Therefore, as Regis Duffy has put it so well, "… the very nature of God's presence is such that sacrament is rooted in an experience of the mystery of God."[6] I would only wish to insert that the presence/absence of God is an experience of mystery, or that the nature of God as mystery implies a presence/absence and not only a presence.

Every sacrament both exceeds and is bound by the symbol, which it seeks to embody. Reconciliation is grounded in the mysteries of encounter, responsibility, and forgiveness. By encounter is meant the experience of being in relationship with the other in his or her concreteness and vulnerability. Responsibility may be understood as the recognition that one has a duty to the other. Forgiveness is the desire for right relation after violation has occurred. The possibility of violation and the desire for right relation is the phenomenological ground out of which the necessity for reconciliation arises. It is this praxis based foundation which is the first step toward an articulation of reconciliation and finally to its formality as a sacrament. The classical Thomistic model of reconciliation mimics this phenomenological approach by stating that reconciliation involves contrition, confession, satisfaction and absolution. Aquinas assumes that the first two steps, relation and violation, have already occurred.

We will then begin with an examination of the desire to reenter a relation once it has been violated. The sacrament of reconciliation is an attempt to ritualize the desire for renewed relationship. I have violated someone and I wish to enter into right relation with that person again. This is something that has been at the core of Christianity since its inception in the Jesus movement. Jesus called his friends to forgive. (Mt 6:15; 18:15-35) Reconciliation comes from the root *concilium*, which means community. Therefore reconciliation means to reenter a right relation to the community. After a violation, right relation requires both forgiveness and justice. Justice demands responsibility. In order to accomplish this in an ecclesial community, there is a need for multiple responsibilities. The responsibility the violator has to the violated, the responsibility the community has to the violated, the responsibility the community has to the violator and the responsibility the community,

6. Fiorenza, *Systematic Theology*, vol. 2, 186.

the victim, and the violator have to the divine mystery. The second step is equally complicated, for it involves the gift of forgiveness. Each of the relationships cited above must experience some form of forgiveness so that these relationships may be healed. Examining the relationships involved in reconciliation, it becomes clear that it is a matrix of relationships all of which require both responsibility to the other and forgiveness of the other. These relationships are not symmetrical, but asymmetrical in nature. That is to say, the responsibility the violator has to the victim is not comparable to the responsibility the victim has to the violator and the forgiveness, which the victim owes to the violator, is far different than the forgiveness which the violator may owe to the victim. Additionally, one would need to say with Levinas that all relationships of responsibility are asymmetrical relationships by their very nature. The phenomena of both responsibility and forgiveness call on the agent to be more responsible or more forgiving than the recipient. Levinas often quoted Dostoyevsky on this point, "We are all responsible for all, before all, and I more than all the rest."[7]

The fundamental problem is that both responsibility and forgiveness are impossible-possibilities. Both of these actions are experienced as possible and yet remain outside of our ability to accomplish. Here we must turn to Levinas and Derrida as means of uncovering the impossibility and possibility of both responsibility and forgiveness.[8] The sacrament of reconciliation is the demand for a recognition of rupture and a simultaneous demand for forgiveness. Each person in this matrix of relationships confronts a rupture, which can both be healed and can never be healed.

The tradition does not use this language in describing the sacrament, but the classical language describes the same phenomenon. The first moment of reconciliation, as understood by Aquinas, is the need for contrition, for recognizing the depth of the violation. It is not just feeling sorry for what I have done, but it is coming to hate the violation

---

7. Emmanuel Levinas, *Ethics and Infinity*, trans. Richard Cohen (Pittsburgh: Duquesne university press, 1985) 101.
8. For the sake of the shortness of this paper, I will skip over an argument demonstrating the character of encounter itself as aporetic. At the core of any encounter one faces a fundamental presence/absence of the other. It is at the heart of much of the work of recent phenomenology and deconstruction to demonstrate that the encounter with the other is an encounter with the mystery of the other. See Emmanuel Levinas, *Totality and Infinity: An Essay on Exteriority* (Pittsburgh: Duquesne University Press, 1969); Martin Buber, *I and Thou* (New York: Scribner, 1958); Martin Heidegger, *Being and Time* (New York: Harper and Row, 1962).

itself. Contrition is a sickness unto death, a sense of being overwhelmed by the reality of the pain I am capable of bringing forth through my actions. This moment is necessary and it is only possible in my I-ness. Only as an I, can I recognize that I am responsible. If I attempt to minimize my actions, deny that I did it, or blame my actions on someone else I have moved outside of contrition and so denied the possibility of responsibility.[9]

Contrition, confession, and satisfaction are all connected to the phenomenon of responsibility. We must now ask whether responsibility is possible. Levinas begins his meditations on responsibility by recalling Dostoyevsky's previously cited phrase from *The Brothers Karamazov*: "We are all responsible for all, before all, and I more than all the rest." Levinas restates this sentiment in his own terminology as follows,

> The infinity of responsibility denotes not its actual immensity, but a responsibility increasing in the measure that it is assumed; duties become greater in the measure that they are accomplished. The better I accomplish my duty the fewer rights I have; the more I am just the more guilty I am.[10]

It is the aporetic structure of responsibility that Levinas identifies. Keenan restates this idea,

> The more I am responsible, the more irresponsible I am, because (on the one hand) responsibility holds me accountable, and (on the other hand) responsibility discounts me (insofar as it requires me to be selfless).[11]

Derrida adds to Levinas' insight when he states in the *Gift of Death*,

> What gives me my singularity, namely, death and finitude, is what makes me unequal to the infinite goodness of the gift that is also the first appeal to responsibility. Guilt is inherent in responsibility because responsibility is always unequal to itself: one is never responsible enough.[12]

Derrida is claiming that guilt and responsibility are intrinsically intertwined, one cannot feel guilt without responsibility nor can one be responsible without also being guilty.

---

9. Jacques Derrida has examined the necessity of the mineness of responsibility in *The Gift of Death* in which he examines Patocka's *Heretical Essays on the Philosophy of History*. Dennis Keenan has done an excellent study of this work and comes to the conclusion that Derrida's reading of Patocka supports Levinas' phenomenology of responsibility.

10. Levinas, *Totality and Infinity*, 244.

11. Dennis King Keenan, *Death and Responsibility: The "Work" of Levinas* (Albany, NY: State University of New York Press, 1999) 78.

12. Jacques Derrida, *The Gift of Death*, trans. David Wills (Chicago: University of Chicago Press, 1995) 51.

What this means for an understanding of the sacrament of reconciliation should be clear. If reconciliation requires a responsibility on the part of the violator then the violator faces an impossible-possibility, the more that the violator takes on responsibility the more irresponsible he or she becomes. It is necessary to be responsible if one is to be reconciled and yet it is at the same time impossible to be responsible. Therefore, at the very first moment of the sacrament there is an aporia and this is what points to the true nature of the sacrament as mystery, it is both necessary and unfulfillable. It represents the presence of the divine (the possibility) and the absence of the divine (the impossibility).

It is often to the false assurance of guaranteed possibility that the violator is drawn. One saw this clearly in the abuse of indulgences and John Tetzel's infamous jingle "As soon as the coin in the coffer rings, the soul from purgatory springs."[13] One might ask how it becomes possible that the desire for reconciliation becomes so commercialized that it can be sold, but this economy of reconciliation is something present in the very structure of the sacrament and therefore easily distorted into a relatively simple economic exchange.

The second aporetic moment of the sacrament corresponds to the last step of the Thomistic articulation of the sacrament, the absolution, and is phenomenologically uncovered in the moment of forgiveness. Here we return to the work of Derrida and his understanding of forgiveness.[14] In the last chapter of The *Gift of Death*, entitled "*Tout Autre Est Tout Autre*" which is translated as "every other (one) is every (bit) other," he examines the possibility of Christian forgiveness through the lens of the possibility of gift. He takes a Kierkegaardian view of the Sermon on the Mount and the call to turn the other cheek. Since he has previously examined the sacrifice of Isaac, he finds the call to forgive as a similar sacrifice which requires a complete renunciation of the ethical, in order to be responsible, and yet, at the same time, a recognition of the ethical as "founding" the act of forgiveness. How can one make sense of the call to love one's enemies? Derrida explains that the problem of gift, that is the impossibility of gift, is that it is always couched within an economy of reciprocity.

13. William C. Placher, *A History of Christian Theology* (Philadelphia: Westminster Press, 1983) 183.

14. Derrida delivered a paper on forgiveness at Villanova in the Fall of 1999 for the "Postmodernity and God 2 Conference." This paper is to be published by Indiana University Press. I will depend on his work in *The Gift of Death* for my analysis of forgiveness.

The moment of gift however generous it be, is infected with the lightest hint of calculation, the moment it takes account of knowledge [*connaissance*] or recognition [*reconnaissance*], it falls within the ambit of economy; it exchanges, in short it gives counterfeit money, since it gives in exchange for payment.[15]

Jesus demands that there be forgiveness outside of the traditional economy of recompense or "justice." It is here that the history of reconciliation, as a Christian sacrament, begins. Derrida points out that Matthew's gospel repeats the idea that what is done in secret will be rewarded, "and thy father which seeth in secret will reward thee" (Mt 6:4) What has this to do with forgiveness? Forgiveness is something which must be "done in secret." That is to say it must be done outside of the economy of justice. Forgiveness is a gift which does not demand anything in return. Derrida invokes Mt 5:38-39:

> You have heard that it hath been said, An eye for and eye, and a tooth for a tooth: But I say unto you, that ye resist not evil: but whosoever shall smite thee on the right cheek, turn to them the other also.

Derrida's comments on this passage are insightful in terms of his view of forgiveness. According to Derrida,

> It is a matter of suspending the strict economy of exchange, of payback, of giving and giving back, of the "one lent for every one borrowed," of that hateful form of circulation that involves reprisal, vengeance, returning blow for blow, settling scores.[16]

There is a movement beyond justice. Forgiveness is a gift, something which cannot be thought of in terms of the economy so familiar in the "eye for an eye" justice. Yet, is it possible to give the gift of forgiveness? Is it not always the case, that one is involved in the expectation of justice? Certainly the sacrament we are examining has this call for justice within its formulation. Absolution, that is forgiveness, comes only after confession, contrition and satisfaction.

Here we see the crux of the problem the gift is not a gift, or in our terms, forgiveness is not forgiveness if the gift is within an economy, and yet the sacrament demands an economy because it demands contrition, confession and "worst of all" satisfaction. For how can there be satisfaction. We have already shown that the responsible party cannot be responsible, for in responsibility one becomes more irresponsible the

---

15. Derrida, *Gift*, 112.
16. *Ibid.*, 102.

more responsibility one accepts. From the side of the forgiver, the gift of forgiveness is not possible if it is placed within the economy of satisfaction for then it has lost the very nature of forgiveness as gift.

The sacrament is an attempt to repeat and assure the church that the impossible possibilities of both responsibility and forgiveness can be held together in a sacramental economy of faith. The symbol becomes sacrament and the guarantee of grace becomes the Church's economy of reconciliation. It is here that the true loss of the sacramental tradition begins. Instead of remaining focussed on the impossible-possibility of both responsibility and forgiveness and holding them together in a double impossible-possibility, the church affirms only the possibility, but in order to maintain the mystery claims that it is only through the church that the possibility becomes possible. Therefore it is through the clergy that the sinful member can be reconciled to the community and to God, the impossible becomes possible because the cleric is the instrument of the divine grace.

What should be emphasized is not this implicit economy of reconciliation (the focus on the possibility), but rather the recognition of the mystery (the impossible-possibility). If the church does its job, it would draw people to the sacrament, because people would recognize that here is a group of people who affirm the ambiguous nature of my lived experience. In this community, the disturbing character of responsibility and forgiveness has been held up as a symbol of the disturbing presence/absence of God. The violator and the victim will then be drawn to the community for reconciliation, because it is a place, which does not offer a false sense of security, but helps each person live with integrity in spite of the aporetic structure of existence.

PART FOUR

TOMORROW'S POSSIBILITIES:
DISCOVERING NEW *LOCI* OF SACRAMENTAL PRESENCE
IN A POSTMODERN AGE

Church as Sacrament
A Conciliar Concept and Its Reception in Contemporary Theology

Peter De Mey

Until the Second Vatican Council, Roman-Catholic fundamental ecclesiology[1] consisted in a defence of the Church of Rome by proving that she and she alone fully answered the four characteristics Jesus had in mind when installing the Church: one, holy, catholic and apostolic. Post-conciliar fundamental theologians, who recognise the difficulties of indicating a quasi-juridical church-founding act in the life of Jesus, usually develop a hermeneutical reconstruction of the Church's origin based on the post-paschal theological testimonies of the New Testament.[2] In the aftermath of Vatican II, however, a new type of justifying the Church is winning ground, namely, the *sacramental* foundation of the Church in her mission to be a sign and sacrament of the Reign of God. Its basis is the solemn declaration in the opening paragraph of *Lumen Gentium* that "the Church is in Christ as a sacrament or instrumental sign of intimate union with God and of the unity of all humanity."

The limited goal of my paper is to compare the council's conviction of the sacramental nature of the Church with the insights elaborated in ecclesiological studies of contemporary German and French Catholic theologians and to question whether the issues left unclarified by the Council have received an acceptable solution in their works.

---

1. Under the name *demonstratio catholica* it constituted the third part of the treatise on apologetics or fundamental theology. See about the recent evolution of this treatise Heinrich Döring, "Demonstratio Catholica," *Den Glauben denken: Neue Wege der Fundamentaltheologie*, Quaestiones Disputatae, 147 (Freiburg: Herder, 1993) 147-244.

2. I have especially in mind Francis Schüssler Fiorenza, *Foundational Theology: Jesus and the Church*. About his model of fundamental ecclesiology I wrote "Francis Schüssler Fiorenza over de fundering van de kerk in het Nieuwe Testament," *'Volk van God en gemeenschap van de gelovigen': Pleidooien voor een zorgzame kerkopbouw aangeboden aan Professor Robrecht Michiels*, ed. Jacques Haers, Terrence Merrigan, and Peter De Mey (Averbode: Altiora, 1999) 277-290.

1. Vatican II

A Brief History of the Idea of 'Church as Sacrament'[3]

In the documents of the Second Vatican Council, the Church is often called a sacrament. This identification occurs in the Dogmatic Constitution on the Church *Lumen Gentium* (LG 1, 9, 48, 59), in the Pastoral Constitution *Gaudium et Spes* (GS 42 & 45 quote LG 1), the Liturgical Constitution *Sacrosanctum Concilium* (SC 5, 26) and the Missionary Decree *Ad Gentes* (AG 1, 5). The council, however, did not have to invent this identification, but could refer to an early tradition. The expression *sacramentum unitatis* for Church (SC 26, LG 9) has been borrowed from a letter of one of the Latin Church Fathers, Cyprian, who inspired himself of the Deutero-Pauline letter to the Ephesians. There, *mystèrion* or the Latin equivalent *sacramentum* stands for the salvific mission of the Saviour according to God's eternal and unfathomable dispensation. When SC 5 speaks of "the tremendous sacrament which is the whole Church" (*totius Ecclesiae mirabile sacramentum*), arising from the side of the crucified Christ, this is a quote from a fifth-century oration ascribed to pope Leo the Great.

Under the influence of medieval scholastic theology and of the critique of the Protestant distinction between the visible and the invisible Church by the Council of Trent, belief in the sacramental nature of the Church disappeared into the background in favour of a more juridical approach to the Church as *societas perfecta*.

From the 1830s on the term sacrament has been applied anew to the Church in the writings of, e.g., A. Günther, J. A. Möhler and J. E. Kuhn.

---

3. See especially Leonardo Boff, *Die Kirche als Sakrament im Horizont der Welterfahrung: Versuch einer Legitimation und einer struktur-funktionalistischen Grundlegung der Kirche im Anschluß an das II. Vatikanische Konzil*, Konfessionskundliche und kontroverstheologische Studien, 28 (Paderborn: Bonifatius, 1972), chs. 3-4, 6-8; Ludwig Hödl, ""Die Kirche ist nämlich in Christus gleichsam das Sakrament...": Eine Konzilsaussage und ihre nachkonziliare Auslegung," *Kirche sein: Nachkonziliare Theologie im Dienst der Kirchenreform (FS H J. Pottmeyer)*, ed. Wilhelm Geerlings and Max Seckler (Freiburg: Herder, 1994) 163-179; Leendert J. Koffeman, *Kerk als sacramentum: De rol van de sacramentele ecclesiologie tijdens Vaticanum II* (Kampen: Van den Berg, 1986); Josef Meyer zu Schlochtern, *Sakrament Kirche: Wirken Gottes im Handeln der Menschen* (Freiburg: Herder, 1992) 19-67; Herwi Rikhof, "Kerk als sacrament: een pleidooi voor een realistische ecclesiologie," *Ius propter homines: Kerkelijk recht op mensenmaat*, ed. Hildegard Warnink (Leuven: Peeters, 1993) 19-61; A. H. C. van Eijk, "De kerk als sakrament en het heil van de wereld," *Bijdragen* 45 (1984) 295-330. Quotations from constitutions and decrees of the Second Vatican Council are from Norman P. Tanner (ed.), *Decrees of the Ecumenical Councils* (London/Washington: Sheed & Ward/Georgetown University Press, 1990).

It is possible that the dogmatic constitution *Dei Filius* of the First Vatican Council, by calling the Church – in reference to Isaiah 11:12 – "like a standard lifted up for the nations" (*ipsa veluti signum levatum in nationes*),[4] refers to this rediscovery.[5]

After a small period of disinterest in 'Church as sacrament'– in reaction to modernism the Church was again portrayed as a hierarchic society – pre-conciliar theology rediscovered this Church image for the second time. Some important witnesses to this rediscovery are H. de Lubac's 1952 *Méditation sur l'Église*, O. Semmelroth's 1953 *Die Kirche als Ursakrament*, K. Rahner's 1960 *Kirche und Sakramente*, and E. Schillebeeckx's 1959 *Christus, sacrament van de godsontmoeting*.

Importance and Limits

Why did the Council insist on this image? The old self-centred picture of the Church as a visible reality with a clear hierarchic structure had to be replaced by the de-centring notion of a sacrament, pointing both to the source and destination of what needs to be mediated: God's salvation on behalf of the world. As a sacrament the Church needs to be *signum* and *instrumentum*: she has to signify God's salvific action and at the same time to be an instrument in God's hands.

But the Church is "as" a sacrament. The hesitation expressed by the word *veluti* in LG 1 pertains to the possible confusion of the believer who is used to think in terms of seven sacraments. The council fathers also wanted to make sure that the Church deserves the name 'sacrament' only in second instance, because she pursues in a necessarily imperfect way Christ's mission to be the sacrament of God's salvation on behalf of the world. Therefore, the first line of the constitution refers to Christ as "light to the nations," and the Church is said to be "in Christ" as a sacrament. After having observed that the "visible assembly" and the "spiritual community" of the Church form "one complex reality comprising a human and a divine element," LG 8 ventures a careful comparison between Church and Christ. "No mean analogy" exists between both. The assumed human nature of Christ can be said to be the instrument of the divine Word; the social reality of the Church stands at the service of Christ's Spirit. The classic rules of analogy imply, however, a

4. Notice the contrast between the *ipsa* of Vatican I and the *in Christo* of *Lumen Gentium* 1.

5. However, the Church is not said here to signify God's salvation, but reference is made to her apologetical function as a "great and perpetual motive of credibility."

greater amount of difference than of equality. The Chalcedonian dogma insists on the unity and indivisibility of the two natures in Christ, whereas the co-operation between the human and the divine element is in the Church far from perfect.

Sacramental Ecclesiology in Lumen Gentium

Although the image of Church as 'People of God' is definitely far more popular than the one of 'Church as Sacrament', the latter occurs at some of the most pivotal places in *Lumen Gentium*. As is well known, the constitution proceeds several times from a reflection on the Church as a whole to a discussion of its distinctive groups. This transition can be observed between chapters 1-2 (The Mystery of the Church, The People of God) and chapters 3-4 (The Hierarchical Constitution of the Church and in particular the Episcopate, The Laity), as well as between chapter 5 (The Universal Call to Holiness in the Church) and chapter 6 (Religious). The contrast between the two types of chapters has some-times been explained by referring to two diverging and irreconcilable ecclesiological positions, the conciliar ecclesiology of 'Church as people of God' and the pre-conciliar ecclesiology of 'Church as mystical body'.[6] As H. Rikhof pointed out, in *Lumen Gentium* the synonymous notions of *sacramentum* and *mysterion* have been applied to the Church espe-cially in the context of those chapters (or parts of chapters) that deal with Church as a whole: Church as 'mystery' is found in the title of chapter 1 and in the opening paragraph of chapter 5 (LG 39); Church as 'sacrament' in the opening paragraphs of chapters 1 (LG 1), 2 (LG 9) and 7 (LG 48).[7]

At the four places of *Lumen Gentium* in which the Church has been circumscribed as the sacrament of God's salvific plan for the world, Trinitarian vocabulary abounds. LG 1 defines that the Church is a sacrament "in Christ." In LG 9 we hear that the Church has been called on the initiative of the Father. According to LG 48 it is the risen Christ who made the Church the all-encompassing sacrament of salvation, but "through the Spirit" who has been communicated to the disciples.

---

6. Robrecht Michiels, "Lumen Gentium: terugblik dertig jaar later: Twee kerk-beelden naast elkaar," *Een werkzame dialoog: Oecumenische bijdragen over de kerk 30 jaar na Vaticanum II,* ed. Robrecht Michiels and Jacques Haers; Nikè-reeks, 38; Publicaties van het Centrum voor Oecumenisch Onderzoek, 1 (Leuven/Amersfoort: Acco, 1997) 133-185.

7. Rikhof, "Kerk als sacrament," 39-40.

In LG 59 we read that God, on the day of Pentecost, proclaimed to Mary and the apostles "the mystery of the human race's salvation," but not "before he had poured forth the Spirit that had been promised by Christ." The Church thus has its particular place in the history of salvation, as this history has been planned and accomplished by the triune God. In LG 2 the specific role and mission of the Father, the Son and the Holy Spirit in the foreshadowing, preparation, constitution, manifestation and completion of the Church are mentioned. What has changed, however, compared to classic sacramentology, is the omission of scholastic terminology to describe the relation between Church, Christ and Trinity. Ten years earlier Semmelroth still described the institutional Church as *sacramentum tantum*, the salvific work of Christ as *res et sacramentum*, and the Triune God of whom Christ himself is the sacrament, *res sacramenti*.[8]

What the function of the Church to be an instrument of human salvation concretely implies, cannot be fully grasped from the mentioned texts in which the connection between Church and sacrament has been explicitly made. The opening paragraph, LG 1, however, clarifies the issue to a large extent. Salvation is said to consist in "the intimate union (*unio*) with God" and in "the unity (*unitas*) of all humanity." The reader is obviously reminded here of Jesus' answer to the question about the most important commandment: the equal practice of the love of God and of our neighbour (Matt. 22:34-40). The council fathers, however, decided in their final redaction of the text to mention "union with God" before "unity of humankind."[9] In an optimistic description of the "particular circumstances of our day" – the differences between the 'dogmatic' constitution *Lumen Gentium* and the 'pastoral' constitution *Gaudium et Spes* must indeed not be exaggerated – they apparently considered the second goal as almost realised. The whole of humankind, already interconnected by close "social, technological and cultural bonds", must now, by the sacramental mediation of the Church, be led to its "full unity in Christ".

In another paragraph from the same chapter, LG 5, the sacramental mission of the Church has been described by means of the biblical category of the kingdom. The Church has to continue the work of Christ, who in his proclamation, his miracles and his very person

8. Otto Semmelroth, *Die Kirche als Ursakrament* (Frankfurt a.M.: Knecht, 1953) 207-208.

9. See Giuseppe Alberigo and Franca Magistretti, *Constitutionis Dogmaticae Lumen Gentium synopsis historica* (Bologna: Istituto per le Scienze Religiose, 1975) 3.

inaugurated the kingdom of God. But her activity will never give rise
to the final breakthrough of the kingdom on earth. According to LG
5, the Church "has formed the seed and the beginning of the kingdom
on earth," while looking forward to its completion. The reference in
this paragraph to the presence and absence of the kingdom in the
earthly life of the Church, has the same function as the comments in
LG 8 about the tension between the human and divine element in the
Church and about its analogous relation to the sacrament Christ.
Through such relativising remarks the sacramental ecclesiology of
Lumen Gentium receives its realistic outlook.[10] The account of the
Church as mystery and sacrament in *Lumen Gentium* is certainly not
a triumphalistic closed story. By pointing to the incapacity of the
Church of fully accomplishing her mission to be a sign and instru-
ment of God's salvation, the council fathers seem to have uncon-
sciously anticipated the postmodern critique of ideological master-
narratives.

The Reception of 'Church as Sacrament' in the Synod of 1985

According to many commentators the extraordinary Synod of Bishops of 1985 deliberately intended to call a halt to the opinion of many
bishops and theologians in the Church, that the conciliar ecclesiology of
'Church as people of God' had to be translated pastorally into a stronger
consciousness of the common responsibility of all believers and into a
more democratic process of decision-making in the Church. Just before
and right at the outset of the Synod objections to the concept 'people of
God' had been raised in an influential lecture of Cardinal Ratzinger[11]
and in the *relatio* by Cardinal Danneels.[12] In the Final Report the concept 'people of God' has been mentioned only once, in an enumeration
of the Council's multiple images for the Church.[13]

By preferring the concept 'communion' to 'people of God' the synod
has opted for an equally biblical term, which remains also faithful to the
priority attached by *Lumen Gentium* to discussions of the entire body of
the Church. But the real reason for this preference seems to be that the
ecclesiology of communion, according to the synod fathers, is also "the

---

10. I borrow this insight from Rikhof, "Kerk als sacrament," 57.
11. Joseph Cardinal Ratzinger, "The Ecclesiology of Vatican II," *Origins* 15 (1985-86)
370-376, esp. pp. 375-376.
12. A summary appeared in *Origins* 15 (1985-86) 427-429.
13. "Synod of Bishops: The Final Report," *Origins* 15 (1985-86) 444-450.

foundation for order in the Church and especially for a correct relationship between unity and pluriformity in the Church."[14]

A second, less explicit change with regard to *Lumen Gentium* is the terminological preference for 'mystery' over 'sacrament', although the teaching of the council has been repeated that "the Church is sacrament, that is, sign and instrument of communion with God and also of communion and reconciliation of men with one another."[15] In the section of the Final Report on 'The Mystery of the Church', however, the image of 'Church as Mystery' occurs in a twofold polemic, against a purely hierarchical interpretation of Church as the 'body of Christ', and against a purely sociological interpretation of Church as 'people of God'. Commentators have wondered whether the appeal to 'Church as Mystery' in the Synod's Final Report does not function as an ideological weapon to stop "legitimate questions from the people of God."[16] Because emphasis is laid on the "eschatological character" and "universal vocation to holiness" of the Church, this mystery seems to refer to an almost unrealisable ideal.

Has the realistic conception of the Church's vocation to be a sacrament of the kingdom, which dominated the first chapter of *Lumen Gentium*, then fully disappeared in the discussion about the mystery of the Church in the 1985 Synod's Final Report?[17] Perhaps, as H. J. Pottmeyer comments, is this lack of realism only apparently the case, and does it certainly need correction. "In speaking of the Church as *mysterium* we must not remain abstract, attempting to lift the Church out of the sphere of historical developments. The mystery of the Church, the mystery of the cross and resurrection of Jesus Christ, actually indicates the Church's place within history."[18] "The designation of the Church as sacrament demands that the visible form and organisation of the Church correspond to its ground and life-principle, i.e., the mystery of the triune God, the mystery of Jesus Christ and the mystery of the Spirit's working."[19]

---

14. "Synod of Bishops: The Final Report," 448.

15. *Ibid.*, 446. Remark the substitution of 'communion' for 'union/unity'.

16. Ad Willems, "Het mysterie als ideologie: De bisschoppensynode over het kerkbegrip," *Tijdschrift voor Theologie* 26 (1986) 157-171, esp. p. 170.

17. Rikhof, "Kerk als sacrament," 49.

18. Hermann J. Pottmeyer, "The Church as Mysterium and as Institution," *Concilium* (1985/6) 99-109, esp. p. 106. Pottmeyer's article forms part of a thematic volume dealing entirely with an evaluation of the Synod of 1985.

19. *Ibid.*, 104.

2. 'Church as Sacrament' in Contemporary German Catholic Theology

Reflection on the sacramental character of the Church is particularly popular among German Catholic[20] ecclesiologists. We are fortunate to have available the 1992 *Habilitationsschrift* of the Paderborn dogmatician Joseph Meyer zu Schlochtern, *Sakrament Kirche: Wirken Gottes im Handeln der Menschen*. According to him, the most important theological contributions to the debate are:[21] Hermann Josef Pottmeyer's description of the functional relation between the Church and God's kingdom,[22] Peter Hünermann's conception of sacraments as communicative acts,[23] and Medard Kehl's attention to the presence of the Spirit in the institutional acts of the Church.[24]

J. Meyer zu Schlochtern

According to Meyer zu Schlochtern, the Church is only worthy of the qualification 'sacrament', if some or all of her activities reflect this sacramental nature. However, since it is the most typical characteristic of a

20. A recent study of the contributions to sacramental ecclesiology by modern Protestant theologians is offered in Josef Aussermair, *Konkretion und Gestalt: "Leiblichkeit" als wesentliches Element eines sakramentalen Kirchenverständnisses am Beispiel der ekklesiologischen Ansätze Paul Tillichs, Dietrich Bonhoeffers und Hans Asmussens unter ökumenischem Gesichtspunkt*, Konfessionskundliche und kontroverstheologische Studien, 47 (Paderborn: Bonifatius, 1997). See also Burkhard Neumann, *Sakrament und Ökumene: Studien zur deutschsprachigen evangelischen Sakramententheologie der Gegenwart*, Konfessionskundliche und kontroverstheologische Studien, 64 (Paderborn: Bonifatius, 1997), who on pp. 334-345 applauds Meyer zu Schlochtern's approach to the sacramentality of the Church. It must also be admitted that Wolfhart Pannenberg, in a small section on *Die Kirche als Heilsmysterium in Christus* in the third part of his *Systematische Theologie* (Göttingen: Vandenhoeck & Ruprecht, 1993) 51-62, is definitely more sympathetic to the Catholic rediscovery of 'Church as sacrament' than Eberhard Jüngel in his famous 1983 article on "Die Kirche als Sakrament?," *Zeitschrift für Theologie und Kirche* 80 (1983) 432-457.
21. With an article on the substitution of the study of the multiple metaphors of Church for the quest of a basic concept of Church – *Kirchenbegriffe, Kirchenverständnisse, Kirchenmetaphern: Zur Diskussion um den sprachlogischen Status ekklesiologischer Prädikationen* – Meyer zu Schlochtern equally contributed to a volume edited by Klaus Müller, *Fundamentaltheologie: Fluchtlinien und gegenwärtige Herausforderungen* (Regensburg: Pustet, 1998) 411-426.
22. Hermann J. Pottmeyer, "Die Frage nach der wahren Kirche," *Handbuch der Fundamentaltheologie* 3 (1986) 212-241 and Hermann J. Pottmeyer, "Zeichen und Kriterien der Glaubwürdigkeit des Christentums," *Handbuch der Fundamentaltheologie* 4 (1988) 373-413.
23. Peter Hünermann, "Sakrament – Figur des Lebens," *Ankunft Gottes und Handeln des Menschen: Thesen über Kult und Sakrament*, ed. Peter Hünermann and Richard Schäffler; Quaestiones disputatae, 77 (Freiburg: Herder, 1977) 51-87.
24. Medard Kehl, "Kirche als Institution," *Handbuch der Fundamentaltheologie* 3 (1986) 176-197. See also Medard Kehl, *Die Kirche: Eine katholische Ekklesiologie* (Würzburg: Echter, 1992, 1993³).

sacramental act that there are two actors involved, a divine and a human one, one must be able to carefully distinguish the divine and the human actor. Perhaps the most important contribution of his study are the carefully constructed questions to be solved by any future sacramental ecclesiology. In the introduction we read questions such as: "How is the claim of the Church to be a sacrament of divine salvation to be reconciled with her being created as a human construct?" "How is it to be conceived that in a human action the presence of God assumes a sacramental form? How does God's transcendence, indispensable to human agency, become real presence in the same human acting?"[25] In his conclusion Meyer zu Schlochtern asks: "How can the Church be an instance in which God's graceful compassion becomes present, when she is constructing herself as a social structure made up by human acts and decisions? How can the Church be conceived as the sacramental unity of the supernatural reality of grace and of human agency?"[26] The Church can only legitimately be called a sacrament when the relation between the real presence of the divine salvation and grace and the agency of the Church is clarified.

H. J. Pottmeyer, P. Hünermann, M. Kehl

In three other theologians' reflections Meyer zu Schlochtern perceives important impulses to link together the presence of God and the activity of the Church. He especially appreciates the fact that they restrict the sacramental reality of the Church to particular ecclesial activities.

For Hermann Josef Pottmeyer the Church is in a twofold way the sign of God's kingdom: she is sign of the presence of the kingdom in that the Spirit of Christ is already active in her, and she is sign of the kingdom's future in that she in her activities tries to remain faithful to Christ's proclamation of the kingdom. The kingdom of God is therefore for Pottmeyer at the same time the foundation of the Church's existence

---

25. Meyer zu Schlochtern, *Sakrament Kirche*, 16: "Diese Selbstauffassung in ihren Inhalten aufzuhellen ist das Hauptziel unserer Untersuchung: Wie ist der Anspruch der Kirche, Sakrament göttlichen Heils zu sein, mit ihrer Beschaffenheit als einem menschlichen Gebilde zu vereinbaren? Wie ist denkbar, daß *im menschlichen Handeln* die *Gegenwart Gottes* sakramentale Gestalt annimmt?"; p. 18: "Wie gelangt die dem menschlichen Handeln *unverfügbare* Transzendenz Gottes in ihm gleichwohl zu *realer Gegenwart?*"

26. Meyer zu Schlochtern, *Sakrament Kirche*, 389: "Wie kann die Kirche die *Gestalt der Gegenwart des gnadenhaften Erbarmens Gottes* sein, wenn sie sich als ein *soziales Gebilde aus menschlichen Handlungen und Entscheidungen* aufbaut? Wie können *das übernatürliche Sein der Gnade* und das *Handeln des Menschen* im Begriff der Kirche als deren sakramentale Einheit gedacht werden?"

(*Seinsgrund*) and of her future orientation (*Sinngrund*). Particularly in those acts in which the Church renders an explicit 'testimony' (*Zeugnis*) to the kingdom of God – the extreme realisation of such a testimony is the martyrdom (*Blutzeugnis*) – is the unity of divine and human activity realised, in Pottmeyer's opinion.[27]

According to Peter Hünermann the sacramentality of the Church is restricted to those sacramental acts that are constitutive for the Church. It are free, communicative acts which establish the communion between God and humankind in Jesus Christ anew. These sacramental acts reveal themselves at the same time as an ecclesial act and as an act of Christ's Spirit on behalf of the Church. Since it belongs to the definition of a sacramental act that it gives rise to a new birth (*Lebensvollzug*) of the Church,[28] it is clear that not all ecclesial acts must be considered as sacramental acts. Hünermann wants to restrict the notion of explicit sacramental acts to the Church's preaching in the name of Jesus and to the sacraments, above all the sacrament of the eucharist.

In order to be able to call the Church a sacramental reality her relation to Christ as the sacrament of God's love by excellence needs to be further specified. The exalted Christ is present in the Church in the power of his Spirit. According to Medard Kehl, the activity of the Holy Spirit in the life of the Church can be recognised when the Church is as an institution promoting the identification with Christ, the integration of the community and the liberation of all believers. When these conditions are fulfilled, the Church really deserves to be called 'sacrament of the Spirit'.

Meyer zu Schlochtern has learnt from these theologians that it is important to limit the sacramentality of the Church to her "constitutive acts" (*ihre konstitutive Handlungen*). He believes, however – without being able to propose a better alternative – that they were not able to clarify sufficiently how human action and the activity of Christ's Spirit are exactly mediated.[29]

---

27. See especially Pottmeyer, "Die Frage nach der wahren Kirche," 240; Pottmeyer, "Zeichen und Kriterien," 387.

28. See Peter Hünermann, "Lebensvollzüge der Kirche: Reflexionen zu einer Theologie des Wortes und der Sakramente," *Theorie der Sprachhandlungen und heutige Ekklesiologie: Ein philosophisch-theologisches Gespräch,* ed. Peter Hünermann and Richard Schaeffler; Quaestiones disputatae, 109 (Freiburg: Herder, 1987) 27-53.

29. See e.g. with regard to Pottmeyer: "Dieser Einheit kommt freilich noch kein sakramentaler Status zu, solange nicht beides, Wirken Gottes und Handeln des Menschen, *innerlich* vermittelt ist" (Meyer zu Schlochtern, *Sakrament Kirche,* 306); with regard to Hünermann: "Wie sind das Handeln der Menschen und das Wirken Gottes, das bislang als 'Ineins' oder als 'kommunikative Einheit' des menschlichen Handelns und der Wirksamkeit des Geistes Christi beschrieben wurden, exakt miteinander ver-

3. 'Church as Sacrament' in Contemporary French Catholic Theology

L.-M. Chauvet

In chapter five of *Symbole et sacrement*,[30] Louis-Marie Chauvet reflects about the Church as symbolic mediation of Christ.[31] In the first part of his book he has applied Heidegger's critique of classical metaphysics to scholastic sacramental theology. The presupposition of an immediate presence of ourselves, of things or persons outside us, or of the divine has become an impossibility for post-Heideggerian philosophy and theology. Notwithstanding the fact that the sacramental life of the Church constitutes the only access to Christ, are her symbolic mediations the presence of an absence. Chauvet reckons with a threefold symbolic mediation of Christ, "rereading the Scriptures with him in mind, repeating his gestures in memory of him, living the sharing between brothers and sisters in his name."[32]

By means of an exegesis of the story of the two disciples returning to Emmaus (Lk 24:13-35) and other Lukan texts, Chauvet explains how the faithful must overcome their fixation on the event of the crucifixion in order to be able to encounter Christ anew in the symbolic mediation of the Church. The interest of the disciples in what happened to Jesus' corpse reveals their intention to capture the object of their desire, and to hold on to their ideological knowledge about God instead of listening to God's revelation in the Scriptures.[33] The first mode of sacramental presence of the absent One is, therefore, to be found in the Church's proclamation, "according to the Scriptures," of Jesus' death and resurrection. When doing so, the Church acts as "spokesperson" and "lieu-tenant" of Christ, in the same way as He can be recognised when Church ministers celebrate the Eucharist (Lk 24:30), baptise new believers (Acts 8:36) and lay their hands on them in order to receive the Holy Spirit

---

mittelt?"(*Sakrament Kirche*, 337); and, with regard to Kehl: "Wer ist nun das wahre Subjekt der kirchlichen Vollzüge: die individuellen Subjekte, die Gemeinschaft der Kirche oder der Geist?" (*Sakrament Kirche*, 357).

30. Louis-Marie Chauvet, *Symbole et sacrement: Une relecture sacramentelle de l'existence chrétienne* (Paris: Cerf, 1987) 167-194: 'Position de la structure de l'identité chrétienne'. References are made to the English translation, *Symbol and Sacrament: A Sacramental Reinterpretation of Christian Existence* (Collegeville, MI: Liturgical Press, 1995) 159-189. The original pagination is mentioned between brackets.

31. Chauvet does not deny that salvation can be experienced in other religions, but in the Church salvation is recognised as salvation of God in Christ.

32. Chauvet, *Symbol and Sacrament*, 163 (169).

33. *Ibid.*, 168 (173).

(Acts 10:17). This is the second level of sacramental mediation of the Church. Finally, Christ is present in the Church when she "returns to Jerusalem" (Lk 24:52) to assume her mission, to be witnesses of the Messiah in word and deed (Acts 2:42-47, 4:32-35). His real body is gone, but His symbolised body is present in the Church's "interpretation of Scripture, its liturgical celebrations, and its ethical engagement."[34] Conscious of her not being identical with Christ, the Church sacramentally mediates in the three mentioned ways "the presence of the absence of God."[35]

Chauvet warns for the temptation to absolutise one of these three constitutive elements of the Christian faith,[36] comparable to the three main characteristics of human existence: cognition, recognition and praxis.[37] If the Church would hold on to a closed system of divinity, she would pay no justice to "the otherness of God, the absence of the Risen One, the unmanageability of the Spirit."[38] In the same way does an exclusivistic attention to the second and third component of faith on the one hand result in a magical interpretation of the sacraments and on the other hand in a moralistic Church, in which the Church's orthopraxis becomes the norm of her orthodoxy. The first temptation is typical for those protestant Churches who are opposed to any hermeneutical reading of the Scriptures. One meets the second temptation in (certain forms of) catholic theology, in which the efficacy of the sacraments is considered to be automatic. The third temptation is, according to Chauvet, a typically contemporary danger, not linked to a specific Christian denomination.

At the end of this chapter Chauvet pays attention to some pastoral implications of his outline of a sacramental ecclesiology.[39] I resume them in three points.

---

34. Chauvet, *Symbol and Sacrament*, 171 (177).

35. *Ibid.*, 178 (183). In this paragraph the author alternates 'Christ' and 'God' without, if my interpretation is correct, having in mind a different divine person. On p. 177 we read: "Now, as risen, Christ has departed; we must agree to this loss if we want to be able to find him." Further on Chauvet explains: "This is why to consent to the sacramental mediation of the Church is to consent to what we called above, echoing Heidegger, the presence of the absence of God." But then he prefers again the name 'Christ': "But it is precisely in the act of respecting his radical absence or otherness that the Risen One can be recognized symbolically. For this is the faith; this is Christian identity according to the faith. Those who kill this sense of the absence of Christ make Christ a corpse again."

36. *Ibid.*, 173-177 (179-182).

37. *Ibid.*, 179 (185).

38. *Ibid.*, 174 (179).

39. *Ibid.*, 180-189 (186-194).

(1) The Church can only be called a sacrament insofar as she is not occupied with herself, but with the mediation of God's kingdom to the world. But Chauvet realises that the identity of the Church hereby becomes a paradoxical one: her symbolic mediations of the kingdom cannot but be coloured by her concrete, institutional reality.

(2) Although there must be room, according to Chauvet, for a partial identification with the Church, the three characteristics of the Christian life require nevertheless a certain institutionality. This institutionality is to be considered as a gift of God's grace, which, however, does not mean that the concrete organisation of the Church is not susceptible for amelioration.[40]

(3) The sacramentality of the Church receives its primordial manifestation in the liturgical assembly (*ecclesia*) as the symbolic body of Christ. It is here that the individual believer recognises Jesus as Christ and Lord. Individual prayer and meditation presuppose the community experience of the presence of God's absence.

C. Duquoc

Christian Duquoc published in 1999 a new monograph on the Church because he was no longer satisfied with his earlier approach in his 1985 *Des églises provisoires*.[41] In the analytical first part of *"Je crois en l'Église": Précarité institutionnelle et Règne de Dieu*[42] the author no longer restricts himself to a description of the historical schisms in the history of the Christian churches, but pays attention to contemporary signs of disfunctioning as well. The second part of his book deals with the ideal Church as portrayed in bible and tradition. The qualifications 'one', 'holy', 'catholic' and 'apostolic', enumerated in the Apostolic Creed, as well as the biblical images of 'people of God', 'temple of the Holy

40. According to V. J. Miller, "An Abyss at the Heart of Mediation: Louis-Marie Chauvet's Fundamental Theology of Sacramentality," *Horizons* 24 (1997) 230-247, Chauvet has overlooked the fact that the institutionalised sacramental mediation of the Church underwent important changes throughout history and received a plurality of cultural expressions. Moreover, Chauvet does not seem to reckon with the possibility that a symbol may petrify and eventually be replaced by new symbolic expressions. "Chauvet's notion of symbolic mediation ... would favor the continuation of a distorted practice because that is what has been handed on in the tradition and has formed the identity of generations of Christians" (239).

41. Christian Duquoc, *Des Églises provisoires: Essai d'ecclésiologie oecuménique* (Paris: Cerf, 1985).

42. Christian Duquoc, *"Je crois en l'Église": Précarité institutionnelle et Règne de Dieu* (Paris: Cerf, 1999).

Spirit', and 'body of Christ', used in *Lumen Gentium,* are indeed only
fully applicable to the eschatological form of the Church as identical
with the kingdom. The visible Church is an institutionalised one and,
therefore, necessarily ambiguous.

How does the Church have to realise its unity?[43] By always looking
back at the idealistic portrayal of the unity of the community of
Jerusalem in the first chapters of the book of Acts? Recent exegesis,
however, has discovered that there existed no normative Church model
in the formation period of the New Testament. A second option would
be to hold that the unity has been realised at a specific moment of
Church history, namely, when the Church became an institution.
In this approach all internal tensions are considered as deviations, compared to this earlier (idealised) period of unity.

Personally, Duquoc prefers to describe the Church's unity by means
of the metaphor of Church as sacrament, but not without some important restrictions. A sacramental model of unity accepts in fact that the
visible and invisible are articulated in "provisional churches." But,
according to Duquoc, it would be unjustified to apply the same notion
of sacramentality, which is valid for the liturgical sacraments, to the
whole life of the Church. Whereas in the sacraments, ministers refrain
from their own personality in order to make place for the action of
Christ through his Spirit, their other activities are not completely per-
meated by God's grace. On the contrary, to invest all the ministers'
actions and decisions with sacramental authority, would mean to deny
free initiative to the believers.

Only when distinction is made between the different levels of engagement of the Spirit in the activities of the Church, can the notion of
sacrament be applied to the institutional Church as a whole.[44] It is then
no longer an overstatement to call the Church a symbol of God's
reign.[45] Through the celebration of the sacraments, those ecclesial

---

43. Duquoc, *"Je crois en l'Église,"* 125-134.

44. *Ibid.,* 129-130: "Est-il justifié de penser l'Église comme sacrement, la panoplie des
sacrements liturgiques n'étant que les formes variées de l'unique sacrement, l'institution
visible de l'Église? Je ne suis pas assuré que ce transfert de l'acte liturgique signifiant le
don de la grâce à l'Église prise en sa totalité visible ne relève pas davantage de l'hyperbole que de la métaphore: il tend en effet à qualifier toute réalité ecclésiale d'une vocation médiatrice de la grâce christique. Cette attribution ne paraît acceptable que si elle
tient suffisamment compte des différents niveaux structurant l'institution."

45. *Ibid.,* 162: "J'ai cependant fait remarquer plus haut qu'il y avait dans cette application à l'institution du concept de 'sacrement' un risque d'hyperbole. Le transfert de
son usage restreint et rigoureux à un usage plus large n'est justifié que s'il prend le sens
plus fluide de symbole."

activities in which the articulation of the visible with the invisible is most clear, the institutional Church is oriented towards God's kingdom as her transcendental goal, and is thereby relativised.[46] The same articulation "is verified analogically for the whole of the ecclesial institution."[47]

4. Conclusion

In his analysis of the use of the metaphor 'Church as sacrament' in *Lumen Gentium*, H. Rikhof pointed out that the council fathers considered the task of the Church to be a sign and instrument of God's kingdom as a realistic ideal. They were aware that the visible reality of the Church was compounded of human and divine elements, that the sacramental nature of the Church and of Christ are only analogous, and that the full realisation of the kingdom is not comprised in the sacramental vocation of the Church. The preference of the synod of 1985 for the image of 'Church as mystery' must, according to H. J. Pottmeyer, not be interpreted as a withdrawal of this realism.

The same realism motivated recent German and French theological commentators on the notion of 'Church as sacrament' to insist on the necessity of a clear distinction between the human and the divine actor in the sacramental life of the Church (J. Meyer zu Schlochtern); to emphasise that it is the concrete, institutional Church which is the bearer of this sacramental mission (Kehl, Chauvet, Duquoc); and to argue that the sacramental nature of the Church appears especially in her most constitutive acts: her testimony and proclamation (Pottmeyer, Hünermann, Chauvet), her ethical engagement (Chauvet), and, her liturgical celebration of the sacraments, above all of the sacrament of the eucharist (Hünermann, Chauvet, Duquoc).

---

46. Duquoc, *"Je crois en l'Église,"* 162-163: "Le sacrement se célèbre, en effet, dans l'institution, mais il ne travaille pas pour l'institution: il oriente vers ce qui la transcende, le Règne de Dieu ou l'Invisible. Celui-ci est l'instituant et déplace l'institution vers sa marge. Ainsi, le sacrement ne sacralise pas l'institution, mais il l'ouvre en sa forme ambiguë à ce qui, au sein d'elle-même, la dépasse et la relativise. Le sacrement forme donc l'un des noeuds de l'articulation avec l'invisible."

47. *Ibid.*, 179: "Le sacrement noue l'articulation qui, selon la diversité des actions exigeant des modes variés d'implication des sujets, se vérifie analogiquement pour la totalité de l'institution ecclésiale. Plus on s'éloigne du sacrement célébré en lequel le ministre agit *in persona Christi*, plus l'articulation est fluide, car elle laisse alors au pôle visible sa spécificité humaine en son autonomie."

Both the elaboration of the conciliar concept of 'Church as sacrament' in *Lumen Gentium* and its reception in contemporary theology (Duquoc) contain important, realistic warnings with regard to the analogical status of this metaphor. That there has been a significant reception of this conciliar notion, reassures me, however, that theologians have not yet transformed their realism in hyper-realism, in that they would no longer narrate their experiences of the presence of God's absence (Chauvet), but only deplore the absence of God's presence.

Sacramental Presence within an African Context Toward a *Theologia Africana* in Pastoral Theology

Daniël J. Louw

In his book, *On Naming the Present*, David Tracy[1] captures the essence of sacramentality, as linked to our theological attempt to connect God's presence to life issues within our human existence:

> The history of theology is the history of the ever-shifting relationship between the reality of God and that divine reality as experienced and understood from within a *logos*, i.e., a particular horizon of intelligibility. The theologian is one who attempts the nearly impossible task of correlating *theos* and *logos*.

This very challenging task of a theological hermeneutics was clearly understood by Thomas Aquinas in his *Summa Theologiae*[2] when he linked theology and our understanding of God to words and their significance: "*Ratio enim quam significat nomen est conceptio intellectus de re significata per nomen* – what we mean by a 'word' is the concept we form of what the word signifies." According to Thomas Aquinas, God-language is linked to our creaturely disposition and partial understanding. "Thus words like 'good' and 'wise' when used of God do signify something that God really is, but they signify it imperfectly, because creatures represent God imperfectly."[3] What Thomas understands is the tension between God-language and the existence of God – words and even human beings represent God and presuppose an understanding and comprehension which refer to reality, substance (*nomina diviam substantiam significant*). Yet language is always inadequate. Hence Thomas's conclusion: "... that words are used of God and creatures in an analogical way (*proportionem ad unum*), that is in accordance with a certain order between them."[4]

---

1. David Tracy, *On Naming the Present: God, Hermeneutics, and Church* (Maryknoll, NY: Orbis Books, 1994) 36.
2. Thomas Aquinas, "Knowing and Naming God," in *Summa Theologiae*, Vol. 3 (London/New York, 1963) 60.
3. *Ibid.*, 55.
4. *Ibid.*, 65.

This tension between words, their significance and reality have been revealed in a very challenging way by postmodernity with its accent on a plurality of meaning and the deconstruction of fixed concepts and understandings: "… postmodern theology is an honest if sometimes desperate attempt to let God as God be heard again; disrupting modern historical consciousness, unmasking the pretensions of modern rationality, demanding that attention be paid to all those others forgotten and marginalized by the modern project."[5] The surprising tendency in postmodern theology is that it seems that *Theos* has returned to unsettle the dominance of modern *logos*. "There can be little doubt that in modern theology, the *logos* of modern intelligibility was the dominant partner in the correlation."[6]

This unmasking of a positivistic stance in theology, with the predominant position of the *logos* over the *Theos*, poses a new interpretation of the relationship between God's presence, the significance of language and our human experience. The component of correlation, representation, significance, and symbol/metaphor, introduces the notion of sacramentality. If we assume that Tracy's assumption[7] is correct that God should enter postmodern history, not as a consoling "ism," but as an awesome, often terrifying, hope-beyond-hope; not as a speculation, but an authentic cry for his real presence in cross and negativity, above all in the suffering of all those others whom the grand narrative of modernity has set aside as non-peoples, non-events, non-memories, non-history, the following urgent question surfaces: How should God be represented and portrayed, and what role can a sacramental understanding of reality as well as a hermeneutics of interconnectedness and relatedness play in this regard? What does such an introduction imply for doing theology in an African context? What is meant by sacramentality within a *theologia africana* and what new light can African spirituality shed on the notion of God's presence? If postmodern theology is not a rival set of propositions to modern theology, but something else: a search for entirely alternative forms,[8] what new understanding of God can emerge from the hermeneutics of a *theologia africana*? Postmodernity allows us the time not to rush out new propositions on the reality of God – it rather allows one to wonder again at God's overwhelming mystery and reconsider the significance of God's presence within contextuality.

5. Tracy, *On Naming the Present*, 37.
6. *Ibid.*
7. *Ibid.*, 43.
8. *Ibid.*, 45.

1. God's Mystery and Sacramentality

The most important key words in our reflection are: analogy, correspondence, representation, spirituality (divine presence) and metaphor/symbol. With regard to sacramentality and theology, all of these concepts link transcendency to human experience and language.[9] This problem of linkage and the interplay between transcendency and immanency brings one directly into contact with the problem of sacramentality: the presence of God through signs, symbols, metaphors, language and embodiment within the context of existentiality and cosmology.

Although Thomas's thinking was influenced by metaphysical paradigms which moulded his understanding of substantiality and being (ontology), the helpful argument in his *Summa theologiae* is that the purpose of the sacraments of the church are to serve human beings' spiritual as well as physical needs.[10] Sacramentality implies that a relationship is established between the spiritual and physical dimensions. In this regard a specific sacrament signifies three things: it commemorates (memory and recall); it establishes a relationship (*communio* and communication) and prefigures (hope and expectation). In terms of Thomas's theology,[11] sacramentality helps to look back to the past to commemorate the passion of our Lord (*commemorativum Dominicae passionis*); it points to the unity of the church (fellowship and mutuality) into which human beings are drawn together ("*communio*" or "synaxis"); it prefigures that enjoyment of God which will be ours in heaven (*fruitionis Dei*).

For the purpose of this paper sacramentality[12] denotes:

(a) Representation (*Repraesentant*)
"In this life we cannot understand the essence of God as he is in himself, we can, however, understand it as it is represented by the

9. For the interconnectedness of God and reality within a sacramental paradigm, see Tjeu Van Knippenberg, *Tussen naam en identiteit: Ontwerp van een model voor geestelijke begeleiding* (Kampen: Kok, 1998) 167-168. He calls this interconnectedness the hermeneutical circle of reality, experience and "creation faith."

10. See Thomas Aquinas, "The Eucharistic Presence," in *Summa Theologiae*, Vol. 58 (London/New York, 1963) 5 – homini in vita spirituali.

11. *Ibid.*, 14-15.

12. One should reckon with the fact that in Thomas Aquinas's thinking, sacramentum has two different meanings. For the purpose of this paper we do not focus on supernatural grace and the more mechanical interpretation of the infusion of grace. Instead of infusion, the argument will be more along the lines of a pneumatic interpenetration. See also: Don S. Browning *et al.*, *From Culture Wars to Common Ground: Religion and the American Family Debate* (Louisville: Westminster John Knox Press, 1977) 122: "We focus, however, on another

perfections of his creatures; and this is how the words we use can signify it."[13]

(b) Sign and Significance (*Significationem*)

Sacramentality deals with the tension between the metaphorical meaning of words and their literal implication. In theology it is indeed true that not all words are used of God metaphorically; some are used literally.[14]

(c) Participation, Effect and Encounter (*Communio*)

The sacrament is a sign with an effect: an experience of grace and an encounter with God. The effect of sacramentality on life experiences is the liturgical[15] rite of celebration in order to enjoy God (*fruitionis Dei*). To a certain extent, a sacramental experience directs life – it keeps human beings on the way (*viaticum*) and empowers human beings to enjoy grace; and to be embraced by grace (sacramentality as the experience of *eucharist*, good grace).

(d) Disposition (*Habitus*)

Sacramentality determines our human disposition before God – it transfers human beings and reveals to them that true state before God. *Habitus* refers not to a quality you possess (have), but to a gift you receive (are).[16] This gift allows action and should be exercised by human beings in action at will.

It becomes evident that, for the purpose of linking the spiritual dimension to significant life events, sacramentality refers to an awareness of God's purposeful action among us within the context of ecclesial celebrations. The gist of my argument is captured very aptly in the following quotation:

> A sacrament, then, is a presence-filled event in which God gratuitously
> enables us to welcome the message of salvation, to enter more deeply

---

dimension of Aquinas's understanding of sacramentum This dimension is more dramatic than the somewhat mechanical infusion of grace to overcome concupiscence and immoral behavior; it invites imitation or participation in the archetypal pattern of divine action."

13. Aquinas, "Knowing and Naming God," 57.

14. *Ibid.*, 56: non igitur omnia nomina dicuntur de Deo metaphorice, sed aliqua dicuntur propie.

15. According to Regis A. Duffy, "Sacraments in General," *Systematic Theology: Roman Catholic Perspective*, ed. Francis Schüssler Fiorenza and John P. Calvin (Minneapolis: Fortress Press, 1991) 2: 183: "Liturgy is a more encompassing term than sacrament and refers to the whole range of actions and words of praise and thanksgiving that the church gives to God."

16. Thomas Aquinas, "Dispositions for Human Acts," *Summa Theologiae*, Vol. 22 (London/New York, 1963) 16 "... habitus est quo aliquid agitur cum opus est." Aquinas, "Dispositions for Human Acts," 6: "Unde dicendum est quod habitus est qualitus."

into the paschal mystery, and to receive gratefully that transforming and healing power that gathers us as the community of God's Son so as to announce the reign of God in the power of the Spirit.[17]

The basic hypothesis now is that sacramentality should be linked to pneumatology – the enjoyment of God and the celebration of life as a gift (*eucharistia*) of the Spirit within fellowship (*communio*). Sacramentality, then, is viewed less as a mechanical infusion of grace to overcome immoral behaviour. Sacramentality in a pneumatology means the interpenetration of God's indwelling Spirit in order to transform humans' basic being qualities. Gratitude and acts of justice then become proleptic marks of God's presence among us.

Sacramentality refers not so much to oath or vow (*sacramentum* understood in terms of a juridical system – *legis actiones*), but to its Greek meaning: *musterion* – the mystery of God's intentional presence.[18] Sacramentality, therefore, puts human beings in relationships with God; it establishes communion and fellowship[19] and refers to the interpenetrating presence of God within relationships as established by Christ, enfleshed by the Spirit in humans and experienced in the cosmos due to the symbolic meaning of creation. Such an understanding of the sacramental basis of life concurs with the viewpoint of Schrage:[20]

> For Paul, a sacrament is nothing other than the present reality of the Christ event. The sacramental basis of ethics as such was part of the tradition Paul inherited because the early Christians thought baptism implies Sanctification (cf. 1 Cor 6:11), but the christological emphasis is specifically Pauline.

17. Duffy, "Sacraments in General," 185.
18. Gerardus van der Leeuw, *Sacramentstheologie* (Nijkerk: Callenbach, 1949) 15-18, 236-239. – See: John P. Burgess, "Scripture as Sacramental Word: Rediscovering Scripture's Compelling Power," *Interpretation* 52 (1998) 381, for the role of Scripture in a sacramental approach, as well as the view that Scripture itself is a sacramental Word. A classic definition of sacrament is "a visible sign of an invisible grace." Perhaps we should think of the words of Scripture as "audible signal of an inaudible grace." The sacramental perspective has implications for all our human relationships. For a discussion on the link between a sacramental perspective and the marriage contract, see: John Witte Jr., *From Sacrament to Contract: Marriage, Religion and Law in the Western Tradition* (Louisville, KY: Westminster John Knox Press, 1997) 26: "As a sacrament marriage was a visible sign of the invisible union of Christ with his church."
19. Van der Leeuw, *Sacramentstheologie*, 21: "het goddelijke is in de volledige historisch-concrete werkelijkheid getreden. En daarmede is de mogelijkheid gegeven, dat deze werkelijkheid ons in gemeenschap met God brengt, of zij nu een gesproken woord of een gegeten brood is" (225). For Van der Leeuw sacramentality is the very essence of all theology. For example, it characterizes creation as a playful event in the presence of a playful God (227).
20. Wolfgang Schrage, *The Ethics of the New Testament* (Philadelphia: Fortress Press, 1988) 174.

According to Van der Leeuw[21] the reality of the resurrection moulds our human experience into a sacramental reality. Theologically speaking, sacramentality is a result of God's presence in the works of Christ.[22] Because of sacramentality, life should be viewed as a playful event (humans as *homo ludens*).

The advantage of sacramentality in theology is that it emphasizes the interconnectedness of life and its linkage with God's presence. Human experience, therefore, attains a symbolic value and significance. Our human experience and disposition become "markings" which reveal the significance of God's presence. Humans and language should thus represent God in such a way that estrangement between humans is replaced by identification, mutual participation, co-humanity and compassionate understanding. One can argue that sacramentality helps one to combat individualism by connecting God to life and human experiences. Sacramentality underlines the fact that communality should be assessed by the church as a spiritual issue which signifies meaningful experiences of God's compassionate presence and care.

Due to the fact that sacramentality deals with meaning and the theological significance of signs and symbols, it forces theology to move from a positivistic stance to a hermeneutical paradigm.

2. Sacramentality and the Notion of a *Theologia Africana*

At a methodological level, sacramentality leads to a hermeneutics of approval, acceptance, celebrative participation and embracement. It opens up a new way of comprehension. It helps to understand life as a text which reveals God's compassionate interference with human history.

However, a hermeneutical approach should avoid the danger of becoming a mere alternative for positivism. Ricoeur[23] warns against such a stance: "… the danger that we will turn hermeneutics into some sort of alternative to objective science. Under the pretext of a critique of positivism, everything that is not positivist is said to be hermeneutical." Therefore, interpretation is more than mere language

21. Van der Leeuw, *Sacramentstheologie*, 255.
22. For Van der Leeuw (*Sacramentstheologie*, 348), a theology of sacramentality ("sakramentstheologie") is both a theologia crucis and a theologia gloriae.
23. Paul Ricoeur, *Figuring the Sacred: Religion, Narrative, and Imagination* (Minneapolis: Fortress Press, 1995) 304.

– in its metaphorical discourse, interpretation deals with texts, reality and events. Ontology should not be excluded from metaphorical language and theological interpretation.

In order to avoid the danger of becoming a mere alternative to positivism, hermeneutics should take the sacred dimension of life events seriously. That life cannot be separated from a sacred and spiritual dimension is the contribution of a *theologia africana* and its understanding of spirituality.

Because the human person is a societal being within the totality of transcendental and religious powers, the *spiritual dimension* of the African view of life plays a decisive role in his/her assessment of life issues such as health and illness. "The religious dimension is vital for an African understanding of a person and should consequently be given serious attention in health, in sickness, and more importantly, in the treatment of illness."[24]

When "spirituality" is being used to describe the spirit and life view of a specific culture, it means:

– Being grasped or governed by a particular concern which is of central value to that person or a group of people. It affects a person in his/her way of thinking, acting and feeling. Spirituality thus reflects ultimate values within cultures.

– Spirituality is concerned with life as a whole. "It is not a pious behaviour but rather a commitment and involvement in a manner that gives meaning to life. Spirituality means that which influences a person to live in a mode that is truly fulfilling."[25]

To identify what exactly is meant by the concepts "African" and "spirituality" is very difficult. Every generalization runs the risk of forgetting that "African" consists of a multiple of peoples, beliefs and traditions. However, an "African spirituality" refers to certain common cultural traits and philosophical paradigms which reflect a general mind set, belief system or life approach.

According to Skhakhane[26] the community is the core of African spirituality. By "community" is meant not only the living, but also the ancestors.

24. Abraham A. Berinyuu, *Pastoral Care to the Sick in Africa: An Approach to Transcultural Pastoral Theology*, Studies in the Intercultural History of Christianity, 51 (Frankfurt: Peter Lang, 1988) 19.

25. Jerome Skhakhane, "African Spirituality," *The Church and African Culture*, ed. Mohlomi Makobane *et al.* (Germiston: Lumko, 1995) 106.

26. *Ibid.*, 110.

> African Spirituality as I understand it consists in an intimate relationship
> of people with their ancestors which relationship initiates and governs
> their activity in life in such a way that they relate to all other beings in a
> manner that guarantees harmony and peace.[27]

"Community" also includes the state of the whole family. Ackermann[28] refers to this state as the priority of community: the extended
family. Within the extended family, role assignment and the quest for
humanity are of the utmost importance. Hence the following statement
made by Bellagamba:

> A spirituality which does not incorporate all people, their events, their
> richness, their hopes and concerns, cannot speak to Africans who are
> fundamentally communal and relational.[29]

It becomes clear that, if pastoral care wants to apply the notion of
"interpathy"[30] within an African context, its first task is to understand
and interpret African spirituality. Hence the need for a pastoral
hermeneutics of care and counseling. Spirituality, even in pastoral care,
which does not relate to the struggles of humanity for a better life, for
justice, for the greater oneness of all peoples, cannot attract Africans
who have an innate sense of life and of sharing. If we accept that "spirit"
in an African spirituality means *spiritus*, a force concerned with day-to-
day human activity, the following proposition taken by Mtetwa[31] sums
up our position very aptly.

> One of the most remarkable and tangible dimensions of African Spiritu-
> ality relates to the unique notion of communality and collective solidar-
> ity that the African society exhibits in all spheres of life. There is a pro-
> found sense of interdependence, from the extended family to the entire
> community. In a very real sense, everybody is interrelated; including rela-
> tions between the living and those who have departed.

What is envisaged in an African spirituality is harmony in interpersonal relationships: *umuntu ungumuntu ngabantu/motho ke motho ka
batho* – approximately translated as: a person is a person through other

---

27. Skhakhane, "African Spirituality," 112.
28. E. Ackermann, *Cry Beloved Africa! A Continent Needs Help* (Munich and Kin-
shasha, 1993) 43.
29. Anthony Bellagamba, "New Attitudes towards Spirituality," *Towards African
Christian Maturity*, ed. Aylward Shorter (Kampala: St. Paul Publications, 1987) 107.
30. David W. Augsburger, *Pastoral Counseling across Cultures* (Philadelphia: The
Westminster Press, 1986) 29.
31. Sipho Mtetwa, "African Spirituality in the Context of Modernity," *Bulletin for
Contextual Theology in Southern Africa & Africa* 3 (1993) 24.

people[32]. Due to this view on life (communality), and because of the interconnectedness of life issues, Africans' understanding of the divine cannot be separated from what can be called: "vitalism."

Divinity is perceived in terms of *"vitalism"* as a *force* that moves and rules humanity and determines their fate in the world.[33] As a living force it penetrates everything. For an African, things exist because they participate in God. The divine Spirit penetrates everything and everywhere. "One must call this interpenetration of God a 'cosmogenic' presence of God."[34]

For example, the concept *Modimo* for the divine in Sotho-Tswana, does not refer merely to a person, but more to a *penetrating force*.

> The one quality of MODIMO which nearly approaches a human quality (but far surpasses all human manifestation thereby rendering MODIMO numinous) is being associated with "penetrating insight into men and things" as it had some human cognition.[35]

Setiloane concludes:

> As borne out in our analysis of the word in Sotho-Twana MODIMO was never conceived as a "person." It was understood to be something intangible, invincible, a natural phenomenon able to penetrate and percolate into things...[36]

This is the reason why Placide Tempels describes the divine in terms of force: "This supreme value is life, force, to live strongly, or vital force."[37] This is what Kriel calls the African's quest for power-charged objects.[38]

Still, Tempels' assessment seems to be too much a Thomistic philosophical interpretation of the divine. The divine is more than a dormant energy – (Force Vitale). Modimo is seen in terms of an existential experience – energy that is ever *active*, initiating action, and maintaining interaction.[39] The activity of this very powerful Spirit intercedes and penetrates existential experiences to the very point where humans seek to exercise

---

32. Mtetwa, "African Spirituality," 24.

33. Gabriel M. Setiloane, *African Theology: An Introduction* (Johannesburg: Skotaville Publishers, [3]1989) 34.

34. M. E. Frank, *African Notions of Sickness and Death in Pastoral Care to the Dying* (Ph.D. diss., University of Stellenbosch, 1999) 43.

35. Setiloane, *African Theology*, 25.

36. *Ibid.*, 27.

37. Placide Tempels, *Bantu Philosophy* (Paris: Présence africaine, [2]1969) 44.

38. Abraham Kriel, *Roots of African Thought: Sources of Power – A Pilot Study* (Pretoria: University of South Africa, 1989) 198.

39. Setiloane, *African Theology*, 27-28.

power over disrupting forces. Thus the conclusion of Westermann that the "craving for power is the driving force in the life of African religion."[40]

In African thought inclusiveness is crucial.[41] The divine therefore interpenetrates life as a force, becoming an integral part of Africans' struggle to survive. Due to a holistic approach and an integral spirituality, the divine is incorporated in cosmology and life events.

In conclusion, one can say that an African paradigm for God's presence within life events should reckon with the following very important perspectives in African spirituality: the duality between transcendence and immanence; the realm of ancestors[42] and the influential factor of the divine; the communality of life and the link between the divine and cosmology, as well as anthropology; the interpenetration of the divine as an encompassing Life Force; the cultural significance of the divine for co-existence and co-humanity.

As previously indicated, communality is an intrinsic component of sacramentality. If a *theologia africana*[43] forces us to interpret the presence of God in terms of communality and the influential factor of a dynamic "force" and vital embracement of all life events, the following theological question emerges: How is it possible that God as a Life Force (in terms of an African spirituality) determines every aspect of life and moulds human experience in such a way that co-humanity and communality become signs of God's embracing grace?

3. Sacramentality and God's Pneumatological Interpretation within the Context of the South African Society

The indwelling presence of the Spirit (*inhabitatio*) forces one to move further than the traditional understanding of a relational model: God *and* human being/cosmos. In a pneumatology one should go further

---

40. Edwin W. Smith, *African Ideas of God* (London: Edinburgh House Press, 1966³) 328.

41. Inclusiveness should also reckon with the problem of pluralism. See: R. S. Sugirtharajah, "An Interpretive Forward", *Asian Faces of Jesus*, ed. R. S. Sugirtharajah (Maryknoll, NY: Orbis Books, 1993) 6: "Faced with the challenge of religious pluralism to traditional Christology, recent theological thinking has broadly identified three positions in defining Christian attitudes to other religions – exclusive, inclusive and pluralist."

42. See: François Kabasélé, "Christ as Ancestor and Elder Brother," *Faces of Jesus in Africa*, ed. Robert J. Schreiter (Maryknoll, NY: Orbis Books, 1991) 103; Charles Nyamiti, *Christ as Our Ancestor: Christology from an African Perspective* (Gweru: Mambo Press, 1984) 7-23; John S. Pobee, *Toward an African Theology* (Nashville: Abingdon Press, 1979) 94-98.

43. See also David J. Bosch, *Het Evangelie in Afrikaans gewaad* (Kampen: Kok Agora, 1974).

and admit: God *in* human being/cosmos. Panentheism, then, is a metaphor for God's immediacy and presence in the cosmos through the penetrating work of the Holy Spirit. Relationality should be supplemented by interpenetration.

Van der Ven's empirical research[44] investigated the appropriateness of the three classic models in theology: theism, deism and pantheism. The survey reveals that the pantheistic interpretation of God (the unity of all existing beings with God as a driving force, a transcendent factor rather than a personal entity)[45] has a profound influence on the modern human understanding of individual and social autonomy.[46]

The outcome of Van der Ven's empirical research[47] indicates that theology should re-interpret "panentheism:" the simultaneous experience of God's immanency and transcendency. Panentheism then reflects the beauty of creation; the ecstasy of love within human relationships; the awe for the complexity of nature and the energetic force of imagination and creativity. All these elements within a cosmology should then be interpreted in terms of the dynamics of pneumatology – *a critical pneumatology of perichoresis*: the notion of God *in* humanity (not humanity *is* God, but humanity as a metaphor for the love of God).

Moltmann[48] latches onto this notion of "panentheism." God and creation cannot be separated metaphysically. Within a web of reciprocal relationships, God's "in" is a pneumatological reality.

Panentheism, understood in the light of pneumatology, does not exclude the transcendence of God. Within a metaphorical understanding, it means: the transcendence of God then is the preeminent or primary Spirit of the universe. It means that nothing exists outside God, "… though this does not mean that God is reduced to things."[49]

The penetrating effect of a pneumatological perichoresis of God *in* humanity has the following implication for a pastoral anthropology: the essence of our being human is determined by the pneumatological

---

44. Johannes A. van der Ven, "Autonom vor Gott?," *Autonomie und Glaube: Festschrift Herman Häring*, ed. Hans Küng (Kampen: Kok Agora, 1997) 301.

45. *Ibid.*, 301-302.

46. "In sieben von zehn Fällen zeigt sich daß der pantheistische Glaube Einfluß auf die individuelle und soziale Autonomie ausübt, einmal beeinflußt der theistische Glaube die soziale Autonomie, und zweimal liegt kein einziger Einfluß des Glaubens an Gott auf die individuelle und soziale Autonomie vor." *Ibid.*, 311.

47. *Ibid.*, 317.

48. Jürgen Moltmann, *God in Creation: A New Theology of Creation and the Spirit of God* (Minneapolis, MN: Fortress Press, 1993) 13-14.

49. Sallie McFague, *Models of God: Theology for an Ecological Nuclear Age* (Philadelphia: Fortress Press, 1987) 73.

principle of love and grace (the charismatic fruit of the Spirit; the pneumatic person as a metaphor of God's love for and in the world).

Interpenetration is the way through which sacramentality is embodied and enfleshed within our human context, environment and society. In terms of Thomas Aquinas's understanding of disposition (*habitus*), disposition as an act of faith should reveal the presence of God and concretize a sacramental stance in life. Due to God's interpenetration in cosmos and life, the Spirit of God creates growth: "*est quod fides est quidam habitus* – faith is a disposition, and yet it grows."[50] Enfleshment becomes real experiences of sacramentality, it exemplifies the eucharist through the virtues of charity, prudence, justice, courage, temperance, hope and faith.

In conclusion, one can say that the link between sacramentality, interpenetration and panentheism, theologically speaking, is pneumatological. As a pneumatological event, sacramentality in a *theologia africana* is linked to the dynamics of spirit-Spirit within the different dimensions of life. Hence the importance to connect God to life issues.[51]

With reference to sacramentality, a pneumatological approach helps one to understand that "presence" is a dynamic concept which refers to the human spirit, God's Spirit and actual embodiment. In terms of a "phenomenology" of the Spiritual presence of God, one can say that "The Spirit is a meaning-bearing power which grasps the human spirit in an ecstatic experience, which experience, at least momentarily or fragmentarily, overcomes all the distortions and limitations found in human life."[52] This experience is not to be thought of as a miracle in the supernaturalistic sense, but as a healing event which inspires humans (*inspiration*) and affects humans by creating infused experiences of grace and being embraced (*infusion* = outpouring of the gifts of the Spirit). In terms of our attempt to name God within postmodernity and its strategy of deconstructing, inspiration and embrace become spiritual experiences of God as our Companion for Life.

A New Pastoral Paradigm for Southern Africa?

The question at stake is: How does this panentheistic paradigm link with an African spirituality and the demand for the reconstruction of South Africa?

50. Aquinas, "Dispositions for Human Acts," 67.
51. This interconnectedness between spirit, Spirit and life has been emphasized by Paul Tillich in John C. Cooper, *The "Spiritual Presence" in the Theology of Paul Tillich: Tillich's Use of St Paul* (Macon, GA: Mercer University Press, 1997) 65.
52. *Ibid.*, 69-70.

On the one hand, Africans are sandwiched between the North-South conflict of developed and developing countries; on the other hand, Africans still rejoice in life and the communal experience of co-humanity.[53] Therefore, sacramentality within an African paradigm should reckon with both: existential vulnerability as well as life-giving co-humanity. African spirituality is structured not along the lines of a pyramid, but a circle – community and communality as the centre of religious life.[54]

Taking into consideration the encirclement by community, the implications of a *theologia africana* for our understanding of "Africanness"[55] become the following. Africanness in pastoral care should move beyond the individuation of Western thinking as well as the "pigmentocracy" of colour and race so predominant in South Africa. It should move to the paradigm of interrelatedness. A pastoral hermeneutics implies an African hermeneutics: *when you relate and identify in terms of communality and contextuality you become an Africa; when you do not relate, you become a stranger in Africa.*

What is needed in South Africa is a rediscovery of *habitus*. In terms of our argument for sacramentality, *habitus* is more than a virtue which one can possess through achievements. *Habitus* is a disposition which refers to the new quality of being due to God's interpenetrating presence in human beings. Enfleshment in society refers to the spirituality of belonging and the gift of the Spirit: unconditional love.

A hermeneutics of understanding determines belonging and communality. This is what the concept: God as our Companion for Life implies: our belonging to God and his identification in terms of relating to us. A *theologia africana* is about a hermeneutics of appropriate understanding and relating.

Within the very appealing paradigm of an *African Renaissance*, such a renaissance must not be merely a repetition of the past, in an attempt to romanticize the rural life and tribal rituals of Africa, making God a mere "Ancestor." An African Renaissance is an alternative to repetition of tradition, it is rather about a new identity regarding interrelatedness and identification. An African then is no longer a Black with the imperative:

---

53. See John S. Pobee (ed.), *Exploring Afro-Christology* (Frankfurt: Peter Lang, 1992) 6: "Africans' ontology and epistemology is still communication."
54. Bosch, *Het Evangelie in Afrikaans gewaad*, 40.
55. See also: M. William Makgoba, "Pattern of African Thought: A Critical Analysis," *Faith, Science and African Culture*, ed. Cornel W. du Toit (Pretoria: Research Institute for Theology and Religion, University of South Africa, 1998).

black is beautiful. "Black," if not attached to mere pigment and colour, becomes merely a racial issue which needs an opposite: White which then equals bad and evil with the following logical consequence: White = a stranger in Africa. Within a hermeneutics of inter-subjectivity, mutuality and equal regard, an African is that person who has the courage to take the deliberate step to understand and relate. Even a White can be a true African, and a Black without relatedness and con-textual understanding, a stranger.

In terms of the new challenge put forth by the democratization and transformation of Southern Africa, Africa should *move from the libera-tion paradigm to the reconstruction and cultural paradigm.* For the latter, God as our vulnerable Partner for Life is most fitting. Theologically speaking, it should then be a reconstruction towards co-humanity as a metaphor for God's indwelling presence within the *koinonia* of the church. God is more than a Person – through his Spirit God is the Activity of a Life-transforming Force. The world is still endowed with *Pneuma* – the resurrection power of a living God. *Modimo* is geared towards self-assertion;[56] *Yahwé* towards self-sacrifice.

In conclusion, the concept "God" in terms of African spirituality equals an entity that supersedes the parameters of a personal paradigm in terms of Western psychology: personality – the highest manifestation of the human I and subjectivity. The dynamics of a God-image which is connected to a pastoral theological hermeneutics, should take into con-sideration that the relationships: God – cosmos, God – human being, also imply energy, motivation, creativity, imagination, vitality. In terms of a *theologia resurrectionis,* Life becomes an eschatological Driving Force which determines the tension of the new aeon: already and not yet. The reason for this extension of our understanding of God is the fact that Christian hope is connected to "the riches of his glorious inheritance" and "his incomparably great power for us" – "That power is like the working of his mighty strength, which he exerted in Christ when he raised him from the dead..." (Eph 1:19-20).

To understand God as a Companion for Life, due to humans' demand for empowerment, the experience of joy and festivity as well as the demand for participation, identification, mutuality, encounter, embracement within a *theologia africana,* and a sacramental understand-ing of life events, do not imply a depreciation of God. To supplement the personal paradigm with a vitalistic paradigm (animation) does not

---

56. Bosch, *Het Evangelie in Afrikaans gewaad,* 53.

entail depersonalization or degradation to the level of things. "Companionship" refers to relationship, participation and representation. "Life" refers to the effect, dynamism, energy and animation. It is indeed true that both the terms "person" and "life" can be applied to God only analogically or apophatically; "… person indicates relationship, freedom, ineffability, mystery, the capacity to love and know and the capacity to be loved and known. God is someone rather than something;"[57] life indicates energy, vitality, motivation, driving force, animation, the sacredness of everyday events and the symbolic meaning of creation. Companionship and life together refer to the significance of God in terms of sacramentality, i.e. every human act, every event in history, every movement in nature – all of them signify God's interpenetrating presence.

In terms of a cultural and pastoral assessment, one can say that the identification with a "Superstar" can be appropriate within the context of entertainment and a culture of exaggeration and "Hollywood" adoration. In a culture dominated by show business, the play *Jesus Christ "Superstar"* was a hit. For Africa God should not become a Superstar – He should be a Companion for Life. For Africans[58] theology should not be *"show business"* – it should be *"life business"*, i.e. enfleshed in the paradigm of everyday life and communal relationships. Perhaps the notion: "God as our Partner and Companion for Life" can bring Spirit and humans nearer to one another; perhaps it can draw technology and ecology closer to one another. Perhaps it could help to reconstruct South Africa, not along the lines of a global economy with its demand for achievement and development, but along the lines of a vital pneumatology with its demand for sacrifice and communality which empowers people to be vulnerable for one another: humanity as co-humanity due to God's penetrating and indwelling Humanity.

57. Catherine M. LaCugna, "The Trinitarian Mystery of God," *Systematic Theology: Roman Catholic Perspective,* ed. Francis Schüssler Fiorenza and John P. Calvin (Minneapolis: Fortress Press, 1991) 1: 180.

58. See J. N. Kanyua Mugambi, "Christological Paradigms in African Christianity," *Jesus in African Christianity: Experimentation and Diversity in African Christology,* ed. J. N. Kanyua Mugambi and Laurenti Magesa (Nairobi: Initiatives Publishers, 1989) 137.

Exploring a *Locus Theologicus*: Sacramental Presence in Modern Art and Its Hermeneutical Implications for Theology

Gesa Elsbeth Thiessen

When Paul Tillich came face to face with the painting *Madonna with Singing Angels* by Sandro Botticelli in post-war Berlin, it was for him one of the most significant moments of his life, a moment of revelation, of sacramental presence. From then on he would integrate art, especially modern Expressionism, into his doing theology. Indeed once he even went so far as to state, that he had learned more from engaging with art than from theological books.[1] Tillich was the first theologian to claim that modern art, even without explicitly religious content, has religious dimensions as it can manifest ultimate reality.

Since Tillich, a growing number of theologians, like Horst Schwebel, Friedhelm Mennekes, Günter Rombold, George Pattison, Doug Adams, John Dillenberger, and Diane Apostolos-Cappadona have concretely engaged with visual images from a theological perspective. The issue here primarily is *not* the work of art used as a means to *illustrate* biblical-Christian truths as, for example, has happened in much Church art, particularly in the past when art served as the *biblia pauperum*. What is of interest is the appreciation and discovery of theological-spiritual dimensions in the autonomous, so-called "profane" modern and contemporary work of art and how these aspects stimulate and concur with theological and Christian concerns.[2]

In doing theology through art, art cannot be treated as a lesser partner, as *ancilla theologiae*. Rather the work of art, and the artist as an independent agent and equal discussion partner, must be recognised.[3] It

---

1. See Paul Tillich, "One Moment of Beauty," *On Art and Architecture*, ed. John and Jane Dillenberger (New York: Crossroad, 1987) 234-235.

2. For a more detailed discussion of Tillich's and Schwebel's contribution to a theology of art, as also for specific theological interpretations of works of art, and a consideration of a hermeneutics for a theology of art, see my book *Theology and Modern Irish Art* (Dublin: Columba Press, 1999).

3. Cf. Horst Schwebel who argues a similar way when he writes: "Nur wenn beide Seiten [Theologie und Kunst] bereit sind, dem anderen zu bestätigen, daß seine

is only in this way that real dialogue between and integration of contemporary art into theology can take place.

Further, it should be noted from the start that in considering the work of art as a *locus theologicus* the classical *loci theologici* – Scriptures, patristics, early Councils etc. – are, of course, not being challenged in their role as fundamental and primary sources in theology. The term *locus theologicus* then may be applied to modern visual works of art if its meaning is not limited simply to theological sources from the Christian tradition which have the consensus of all, but rather if it is seen in the context of *exploration*, i.e. when art becomes a place of theological discovery.[4]

Indeed, there is neither one language nor one method for attaining knowledge of the divine. As Rahner once put it succinctly, if theology "is not identified a priori with verbal theology, but is understood as man's total self-expression insofar as this is borne by God's self-communication, then religious phenomena in the arts are themselves a moment within theology taken in its totality."[5] It is with such a concept of theology that the arts can challenge and widen the work of the theologian.

1. Sacramental Presence

Although art, especially modern art, has usually not been regarded as a *locus theologicus as such*, it is increasingly valued as a theologically relevant source. Theology, like art, concerns itself with issues about human existence, about divine revelation, about meaning, love, truth, justice, beauty and transcendence. It is because humans have attested to the experience of revelation of ultimate reality and to glimpses of the sacred in art, hence to a sacramental presence in art, that the unsystematic, non-scientific artistic image is given its *essential* place in the work of theology. In this way one might speak of an "unsystematic systematic" theology.

Aufrichtigkeit in der Suche nach Wahrheit um keinen Punkt geringer ist als die eigene, kann es zu einem Gespräch kommen." Horst Schwebel, "Wahrheit der Kunst – Wahrheit des Evangeliums: Einer Anregung Eberhard Jüngels folgend und widersprechend," *Kirche und moderne Kunst*, ed. Andreas Mertin and Horst Schwebel (Frankfurt a.M.: Athenäum, 1988) 143-144.

4. Alex Stock, "Ist die bildende Kunst ein locus theologicus?," *Wozu Bilder im Christentum?: Beiträge zur theologischen Kunsttheorie*, ed. Alex Stock (St. Ottilien: EOS Verlag, 1990) 175-181.

5. Karl Rahner, "Theology and the Arts," *Thought: A Review of Culture and Idea* 224 (1982) 25.

Another sacramental aspect lies in the fact that theology based on visual art is an embodied theology. It is located in particularity and matter, i.e. in a concrete painting, sculpture, installation, etc. To make the visual image the source of one's theological engagement thus implies a radical "yes" to creation, to creativity, and to the capacity of the imagination. It is an affirmation of our life-giving senses, of the sensuous, of the aesthetic, of the fact that spirit, even the divine Spirit, can be glimpsed in and through the material. What is at the centre of this theology is the seemingly paradoxical assertion that ultimate reality, or, more especially, the invisible face of the always-greater God, is perceived and known in the bits and pieces of earthly existence. Doing theology through art affirms and takes as its basis the very fact that the human being learns through the senses, through experience and through the intellect.

It is the belief that, as McFague notes, the world is the body of God,[6] which pertains to a theology of art. Thus it shares a central concern with what has been stressed especially in feminist thinking, namely that life is, and theology therefore needs to be, embodied or, as one might put it, "enmattered." As we trust in an incarnate God, our theology and Christian living are concerned with both the physical and spiritual well being and healing of people and of creation. Both eco-feminist theology and a theology through art are related as they both challenge and strive to replace a dualistic perception of matter and spirit, body and soul, natural and supernatural, with a more holistic one, each from its own angle.

Prophetic and visionary, the work of art "speaks" of life in all its aspects, including death. In this way it may also convey something of the divine, whether directly through Christian iconography or in less obvious fashion, as in twentieth century works of art. Naturally, the written word does the same. However, there is a difference. While a text *describes* the beauty or ugliness, happiness or suffering of a human being, for example, which the reader has to image in her or his mind, the painting or sculpture visually *shows* that figure which can be glanced in one moment. It is this – at times confrontational and shocking – *immediacy* which provokes *instant* reactions of repulsion or attraction, disgust or delight, wonder and awe. This is its beauty and danger. Real engagement with visual art demands more than a glance, it demands to

---

6. Cf. Sallie McFague, *The Body of God: An Ecological Theology* (London: SCM, 1993) 207-212.

go beyond one's immediate reactions. What is required, precisely because of the sensuous, seductive nature of art, is a discipline of seeing.[7] As the process of reading is foundational to word theology, the process of *seeing* is the basis for doing theology through visual art. Disciplined, intensive seeing is essential in order to appreciate the work of art not merely in terms of its sensuous quality on the one hand or its moral and sacramental dimension, for example, on the other, but rather to be illumined by it as a whole, i.e. by its intertwined aesthetic, spiritual, intellectual and ethical dimensions. It is this act of seeing, of engaging with the material image, which fundamentally expands traditional theological method. Nevertheless, it functions in many ways analogous to reading/hearing. In a theological *see*ing of art one becomes open to, experiences and interprets visions of the transcendent, of the divine, of the *deus absconditus* and of the *deus revelatus* in Christ, bodied forth in surprising, gentle, challenging, shockingly immediate, or meditative fashion.

In all our efforts to truly see and to treat and acknowledge the work of art as a *locus theologicus*, it is vital to be aware thus of the tension that exists between the artistic image and the written word. The tension lies in the very fact that, as Rahner rightly observed, the arts cannot be translated entirely into other modalities. It is precisely this tension, which provides the ground for and gives life to doing theology through art. But tension in this context is not negative. As long as the written word and the visual work of art can be distinguished, and as long as they *both* express reality and ultimate reality, intimate relations between the two can be explored and expand our horizons.

2. Images and the Imagination in Theology

While many leading theologians, like Rahner, Tillich, von Balthasar, Francis Schüssler Fiorenza, McFague or Tracy have acknowledged the importance of the creative imagination in religious experience and in theology, it is, however, true that on the whole the voice, paint, or tunes of the artists, i.e. of those in whose work imagination plays a particularly important role, have been left out of the theological enterprise.

---

7. John Dillenberger, *A Theology of Artistic Sensibilities – The Visual Arts and the Church* (London: SCM, 1987) 244.

Despite the modern affirmation of the importance of creative imagining, and the gradual shift away from aligning the scientific with the rational, and the imaginative with the non-rational,[8] residues of these schisms are still with us. The aim therefore is to recognise more properly the importance of the creative imagination, to actively uncover, discover, appreciate and use the pictorial image as a source of gaining religious and theological knowledge.

McFague, in her advocating of a constructive, metaphorical theology, emphasises the necessity of trying out "new pictures that will bring the reality of God's love into the imaginations of the women and men of today."[9] Such a theology "insists on a continuum … between image and concept, the language of prayer and liturgy and the language of theory and doctrine." Since, as she points out, this theology is heuristic and speculative by nature due to its trying out of new models, metaphors and images, it is a theology of risk, namely the risk of ending up with nonsense rather than truth. However, one would agree with her that theology needs to take those risks. Theology needs to develop and explore new images, it needs to walk untrodden, difficult paths in order to remain relevant to people's lives and to its own life and *raison d'etre*. In line with McFague, it is to be suggested that theological engagement with works of art needs to be seen in similar creative and somewhat heuristic terms.

A theology, which risks trying new and challenging images, symbols and metaphors becomes relevant and exciting, as it aims towards inclusiveness and is open to transformation, to possibility – the possibility of imagining in new ways, of celebrating and interpreting the past (tradition) and present, and anticipating the future. As the imagination essentially has to do with the *possible*, there is, in fact, a profound link between the imagination and eschatology. Art becomes a medium of imaging the here and the not yet, an anticipation of the *eschaton*. This may not necessarily happen through wonderful visions, as, for example, in Monet's *Waterlilies* or Robert Natkin's beautiful colourful abstract

8. James P. Mackey (ed.), *Religious Imagination* (Edinburgh: Edinburgh University Press, 1986) 4. In this context see also Mackey's article "Theology, Science and the Imagination: Exploring the Issues," *Irish Theological Quarterly* 52 (1986) 1-18. Mackey argues that the imagination is not only propaedeutic to analytic intellect but that it is essential to our being in and envisioning the world, including the empirical sciences, as it enables us to really see "what is and what can be, so that seeing truly we might truly live."

9. Sallie McFague, *Models of God: Theology for an Ecological Age* (Philadelphia: Fortress Press/London: SCM, 1987) xii.

works, but even in the bleakest of pictures as in Picasso's *Guernica* or
Jack B. Yeats's *Grief* or Lovis Corinth's *Red Christ*, which precisely
through their manifestation of what *is* anticipate and point us to a
world that *could* be, a world that cries and longs for redemption.

Through the imagination one is enabled to conceive of the possible,
of an ultimate wholeness in ever-new ways. It allows one to envision
that nature and grace, immanence and transcendence, the sacred and
the secular are distinct, yet interdependent, ultimately striving towards a
dynamic whole. The imagination creatively can transcend dualisms
through its power to connect opposites, to juxtapose and hold in creative unity light and darkness, bringing together what otherwise may be
regarded as disjointed or irreconcilable. And in this way, also, it is the
imagination that makes possible and builds dialogue between theology
and the arts.

3. Hermeneutical Considerations

In the age of postmodernity, of pluralism, which is as evident in theology as in other spheres of life, theology is much concerned with
hermeneutical and methodological questions.[10] Naturally, in trying to
develop a theology of and through art, it is essential to consider a
hermeneutics since the interpretation of works of art from a theological
perspective is central to this theology.

Since the early 1960s the great claims of modernism, i.e. its faith in
growth and progress, its reliance on the power of reason, its belief in
meta-narrative, meaning and truth, are increasingly doubted in recognition of the estranged, meaningless, atomised and fragmented make-
up of human existence.[11] While on the one end of the post-modern
spectrum, deconstructivist, nihilist doubts of truth and values –
reflected in superficial life-styles with instant gratification and lack of
commitments – are to be found, there is a constructive critique of
modernity which searches for liberating, holistic forms of life. In this

---

10. Cf. Werner Jeanrond, *Text and Interpretation as Categories of Theological Thinking*,
trans. Thomas J. Wilson (Dublin: Gill and Macmillan, 1988) xviii. Cf. David Tracy, *The
Analogical Imagination: Christian Theology and the Culture of Pluralism* (London: SCM,
1981) 67-68. Cf. Michael P. Gallagher, "Post-Modernity: Friend or Foe?," *Faith and Culture in the Irish Context*, ed. Eoin G. Cassidy (Dublin: Veritas, 1996) 74-75.
11. Michael P. Gallagher, *Clashing Symbols: An Introduction to Faith-and-Culture*
(London: Darton, Longman and Todd, 1997) 88-90.

context the prophetic, i.e. the voices from the margins, from the arts, from contextual theologians and the mystical, i.e. negative theology which stresses religious experience and refrains from universalist claims, assume growing importance in theology and in the quest for meaning.

Doing theology through art thus may be considered in contextual terms as it takes the specific situation, the experience, the subjective, prophetic voices and images of the artists as its basis. Like other contemporary theologies it cannot and must not deny, but rather grapple with, the reality of doubt, destruction, cynicism, relativism and estrangement. Indeed, it is precisely here that a humble search for truth, meaning, authenticity and the God who is love arises. The work of art becomes a source of theological interpretation, i.e. for theological understanding and knowledge. Although the media of communication in theology and visual art differ – the written word on the one hand, and the material work on the other – there are hermeneutical similarities between the methods of (theological) interpretation of works of visual art and of texts.

Frank Burch Brown, a leading scholar in the realm of theological aesthetics, rightly notes that whereas theology "in its most typical classical mode strives to be logically consistent, coherent, comprehensive, conceptually precise, and propositional," art explores "fictively, metaphorically, and experientially what formal theology cannot itself present or contain."[12] Metz, not unlike Burch Brown, points out that modern Catholic theology has been largely characterised by a "deep schism between theological system and religious experience."[13] He stresses that "the most important achievements in theology and Church history stem indeed from a scientifically 'impure' theology in which biography, fantasy, accumulated experience, conversions, visions, prayers were indissolubly woven into the system."[14] Certainly, in the foundational biblical texts, as in later spiritual and theological writing, revelation of the divine is recorded and made transparent through narrative, poetry, doxology, etc. from and through the subjective religious experience of the writers

---

12. Frank B. Brown, *Religious Aesthetics: A Theological Study of Making and Meaning* (Princeton: Princeton University Press, 1989) 166-167.

13. Johann Baptist Metz, *Glaube in Geschichte und Gesellschaft: Studien zu einer praktischen Fundamentaltheologie,* 4th ed. (Mainz: Matthias-Grünewald, 1984) 196-197.

14. *Ibid.,* 196-197. "Biographisch soll eine solche Theologie heißen, weil die mystische Biographie der religiösen Erfahrung, der Lebensgeschichte vor dem verhüllten Antlitz Gottes, in die Doxographie des Glaubens eingeschrieben wird" (196).

and/or of those of whom they write. God's self-communication therefore happens through and is dependent on stories and images.[15] Similarly the modern work of art – also through symbol and imagery – can
be an expression and interpretation of the artist's religious experience
and faith in paint on canvas. The task is therefore not only to interpret,
but rather to be aware that the text or work of art for interpretation
itself already presents the artist's or writer's interpretation of her or his
experience and *Weltanschauung*.

In the actual interpretation then of a work of art it is important to
remember that interpretation does not imply the elimination of one's
own preconceptions in order to find one true reading. Rather, as
Gadamer puts it, one makes use of "one's own preconceptions so that
the meaning of the text [the work of art] can really be made to speak for
us,"[16] i.e. the fusion of the horizon of the author (or artist) with that of
the interpreter. Through this process we may be transformed, enriched
and encouraged to see differently or in a new way.[17]

As the personal dimension in interpretation implies the danger of
subjectivism, the aim is to achieve comprehensive, imaginative, responsible, personal *and* objective interpretations, always *grounded in the work
of art itself*. Also Lonergan's observation that objectivity requires
"authentic subjectivity" ought to be remembered here.[18] Moreover, what
has been established already by the community of interpreters – theologians, art historians and critics – must be sufficiently and properly taken
into account.

Further, the *pre*-interpretation (*pre*-understanding) stage, i.e. the very
selection of artists and of works, already confirms the involvement and
significance of the interpreter's horizon. Indeed, this stage is already a
stage of interpretation or pre-understanding, as here the interpreter

15. Heinrich Freis, "Mythos und Wissenschaft," *Christlicher Glaube in moderner
Gesellschaft*, ed. Franz Böckle, Franz-Xaver Kaufmann, Karl Rahner, and Bernhard
Welte; Enzyklopädische Bibliothek, 2 (Freiburg: Herder, 1981) 36-37. "Der Mythos ist
Rede in Anschaulichkeit, in Bildern und Symbolen. Auch in diesem Betracht besteht
eine Zuordnung zur Offenbarung. Ihre Vermittlung kann der Bilder und Gleichnisse
nicht entbehren. Denn es gibt kein Wort ohne die es begleitende Vorstellung."
    16. Hans-Georg Gadamer, *Truth and Method* (New York: Crossroad, 1984) 358.
    17. Cf. Paul Ricoeur, *Hermeneutics and the Human Sciences: Essays on Language,
Action and Interpretation*, ed. and trans. John B. Thompson (Cambridge: Maison des
Sciences de L'Homme and Cambridge University Press, 1981) 143.
    18. Bernard Lonergan, *Method in Theology* (London: Darton, Longman and Todd,
1972) 53, 265. Lonergan's basic methodological imperative asks of the interpreter to be
"attentive," "intelligent," "reasonable," and "responsible."

discerns and decides, even if somewhat more intuitively and less conceptually developed, which artist and/or work (author/text) will be of theological relevance to his or her discussion.[19]

The painter's "language," unlike the writer's, is paint on canvas, and the expression of personal faith and religious experience within the painted image and one's reception of it is, one might argue, less direct, in some ways less clear, than words. Paradoxically, on the other hand and at the same time, it is more direct because of its sensuous nature, its colour and lines and especially because of its immediacy as the work can be seen in its totality at once. Hence the work of art *possibly* may be a little more open to mis-interpretation.[20] Further, one's reaction to visual art, in comparison to texts, poetry and literature, occasionally *may* be more emotional due to the expressive, immediate, confrontational, sensuous and frequently highly experiential nature of (contemporary) artistic images. The interpretative, reflective act that follows may be influenced (unconsciously) by this first emotional response. As such an emphatically emotional reception could be the very part which makes the interpretation an interesting one, but it may also be in danger of being simply too subjective, even arbitrary. This calls for a continuous awareness and an application of a balanced, reasonable and comprehensive interpretation.

Moreover, the contemporary painter's depiction of specifically biblical and Christian subject matter will be his or her reaction to, and therefore interpretation of, the story as told in the Scriptures. Being confronted with it, the interpreter may draw connections between the painter's appropriation of the story and the narrative itself, and then draw his or her conclusions. Thus the interpretation of a work of art with Christian subject matter, which in itself presents an interpretation of the biblical subject, is once removed from the way one encounters and interprets the biblical text as such. It is this that makes the "reading" of works of art with Christian iconography both enriching, due to the artist's interpretation of it, and limiting, also because of the artist's interpretation, i.e. the individual particularity of his or her rendering of the theme. In the context of text understanding a similar situation arises when the biblical text is not directly received through one's own

---

19. Cf. Werner Jeanrond on the role of prior understanding in *Theological Hermeneutics: Development and Significance* (London: Macmillan, 1991) 5-6.

20. Cf. Anne Sheppard, *Aesthetics: An Introduction to the Philosophy of Art* (Oxford: Oxford University Press, 1987) 112-113.

reading, but rather through someone's retelling of or sermon on it, i.e. through an interpretation of it.

Having engaged in my own studies in extensive theological discussions of paintings, I would conclude – with caution since it may not always apply – that the less obviously religious is the subject matter of the work, the more open and personal an interpretation *may* result. Abstraction instead of figuration encourages this more personal response even further. Also, emphatic use of symbolism invites rather complex interpretations. The reason for this lies in the multivalent nature of the symbol itself, i.e. in the fact that it participates in what it symbolises and at the same time points beyond itself, in its mysterious and revelatory power of disclosing and concealing, its stirring the imagination and its transforming effect.[21]

Conclusion

Visual images, positive and often negative, confront the human being daily and are becoming increasingly more powerful through the media of television, computers and advertisement. It is high time then for the theological world and the Churches to treat and value the artistic image – paintings, sculptures, installations, films – as a relevant source of and in theology. It is both paradoxically and obviously in the concrete materiality of the work of art that human beings may continue to glimpse *something* of the incomprehensible, unimaginable Other, the God of creation, "the glory of Christ who is the image of God" (2 Cor 4:4), the God of freedom and love. In this way art, especially contemporary art, will not only play an increasingly important role in theology, but hopefully it will gain and regain its place and importance in church life, i.e. in places of worship. Art then, like theology, may yet offer something different, something life-giving and life-affirming, a critical view of our existence, a call to change and a source of hope.

21. Avery Dulles, *Models of Revelation* (Dublin: Gill and Macmillan, 1983) 136-138. Cf. also Dulles on theology being fundamentally concerned with communication through symbols, in *The Craft of Theology: From Symbol to System* (Dublin: Gill and Macmillan, 1992) 17-39.

Writing the Body in Postmodern Theology

Michele Saracino

It is not too strong to suggest that the issue of embodiment has been *the* question in Christian theology for two thousand years.[1] Nevertheless, in current discussions about Christian anthropology there seems to be some uncertainty related to the notion of corporeality. Even with the phenomenological insights of Husserl and Merleau-Ponty, the theological task of interpreting the relationship between being subject and being embodied is complicated. In this essay, consequently, I attempt to demonstrate that postmodern thought, concretised in the work of Emmanuel Levinas, can help resolve the problem of understanding embodied subjectivity. The way in which Levinas deals with such notions of incarnation, sacrifice, and gender can facilitate more life-affirming ways of discussing the sacramentality of the Christian subject.[2] As he describes the subject as postured or positioned by the demand of the Other, we can begin to imagine the body being written for the Other, for God.

Arguably, the task of developing a theological anthropology that effectively mediates sacramentality with postmodern interpretations of the body proves to be painstaking.[3] Although the notion of the body-subject as the site of sacrament is not a new idea, the questions raised by postmodern thought complicate any attempt to speak about the human subject as the site of God's presence.[4] Postmodern thought, moreover, is

---

1. See Philip A. Mellor and Chris Shilling, *Reforming the Body: Religion, Community, and Modernity* (London: Sage, 1997). In their theoretical analysis of the body, Philip Mellor and Chris Shilling claim that Catholicism is indeed a hallowed eating community in which "sacred knowledge was encountered *through* the body" (78).

2. It is significant to note, however, that at no point does Levinas refer to the subject as 'sacramental' in the Christian sense of the word.

3. Some postmodern questions regarding the body include: 1) How does body relate to knowledge? 2) Is there such thing as a normative body or are bodies merely texts, signs, and canvases to be invented? and 3) How is embodiment related to the construction of gender, race, and class? As I cannot attend to all these queries in this short essay, I will limit my comments to an analysis of how the body is a sign of the subject's relationships with and responsibilities to others, how the body is the site of God's presence.

4. Indeed, a reading of the subject as a site of sacrament can be found within the work of French theologian, Louis-Marie Chauvet. He asserts that the body of the Chris-

complexified by insights related to the fields of feminist studies, critical
race theory, and cultural anthropology. As I cannot attend adequately to
the many issues raised in these disciplines, I will limit my analysis to the
issue of essentialism or biological determinism. I focus on the question
of biological determinism in feminist and critical race theory because
many theologians and believers are concerned that the theological conversation about sacramentality is plagued with essentialist assumptions.[5]
For our purposes, essentialism can be defined as the conflation of ontology and destiny with biological capacities.

   In an effort to understand how essentialist assumptions about body,
gender, and race affect theological explanations of sacramental anthropology, I will construct a hermeneutical grid. In this grid, I emphasise
primarily the work of Emmanuel Levinas, and secondarily the ideas of
Luce Irigaray and various other North American and European theologians and philosophers. Through an analysis of this grid, I hope to show
the complexity of the charge of essentialism in theological discourse.
Four key points will be made. First, I will show that the theological
understanding of the body is related to the interpretation of humanity's
engagement with suffering, mortality, and sacrifice. Second, I will illustrate that in philosophy and theology the notions of giving and sacrifice
are wedded to assumptions about gender and otherness. Third, I will
investigate how the charge of essentialism is a symptom of the larger
problem of fearing otherness. Fourth, even as we deconstruct the trap of

---

tian believer is instrumental to his/her reception of grace. He writes: "The liturgy is not
a matter of 'ideas' but of 'bodies' or, better, 'of corporeality'." Chauvet, "Editorial:
Liturgy and the Body," in *Concilium: Liturgy and the Body*, vol. 3, ed. Louis-Marie
Chauvet and François Kabasele Lumbala (Maryknoll: Orbis Books, 1995) viii. This volume of *Concilium* effectively demonstrates the important role of the embodied subject
in receiving sacrament. By referring to the body as a sign, this volume of *Concilium*
shows that corporeality can be interpreted as sacramental.

   5. See Susan A. Ross, *Extravagant Affections: A Feminist Sacramental Theology* (New
York: Continuum, 1998). This Roman Catholic theologian questions the Church's presuppositions about body and gender in its reading of sacramentality. She wonders how
"a tradition which venerates material" is "hostile" to bodies, women's bodies in particular (9). What's more, she is concerned as to why women's bodies are not understood just
as revelatory as men's bodies (63). Ross argues that traditional sacramental theology is
grounded in essential or natural categories – an issue, of course, that has ramifications
for the issue of women's ordination. Ross splits the Church's position on body and gender into two schools: the Vatican model and post-conciliar theology (125). According to
Ross, the Vatican model reads women as essentially maternal and receptive, while post-
conciliar theology seems to ignore women's experience altogether. Obviously both
approaches to understanding the body are inadequate; thus, theologians need to explain
more consistently the connection between body and sacramentality.

essentialism, I will argue that theologians need to envision alternative ways for understanding sacramental subjectivity beyond the confines of gender and race. One such way of interpreting sacramental subjectivity is through the notion of the body-subject being written or positioned in a posture of shouldering the Other.

By understanding the sacramental body-subject in terms of writing, we capture the play between the subject's freedom and his/her responsibility. In other words, if we understand the body-subject as a script, we can argue that flesh does not imprison the human person, rather the mortality and suffering connected with corporeality invites the subject into a posture of being *for-the-Other*.[6] As we write ourselves and are written through our dealings with the Other, our bodies become the locus of God's presence. In shouldering the Other, we become sacramental subjects.

My first point is regarding the question of how the body is related to the ideas of suffering, mortality, and sacrifice. For Christians, the meaning of the body is overdetermined: there is the human body of the believer, the ecclesial body, the mystical body of Christ, and the human, suffering body of Jesus. As Christians are understandably overwhelmed by references to the body, there seems to be no adequate understanding of the role of the human body in theology. Even though Levinas's work is not intended to lead to any constructive theology, his ethical concerns about body prove to be a rich resource for understanding the relation between body and sacramentality in a postmodern context. Writing out of a cultural milieu that remembers the horrors of Auschwitz, Levinas imagines an ethics that takes seriously the mortal plight of the embodied subject and Other. Consequently, the thrust of both his Talmudic and philosophical writings is grounded in a concern for those who suffered throughout history. For Levinas, suffering is concrete, tangible, embodied, and corporeal.

We know from his early writings on Edmund Husserl that Levinas was intrigued by Husserl's emphasis on the body. Following Husserl's lead, Levinas argues that "to be embodied is to be a *subject* in a way that

---

6. I use the phrase '*for-the-Other*' to signify Levinas's idea of normative subjectivity. Levinas claims that subjectivity is not rooted in the world of the self, rather is grounded in obligation and opening *for-the-Other*. He employs the phrase, *for-the-Other*, in some texts, including the essay "Notes on Meaning," *God Who Comes to Mind*, trans. Bettina Bergo (Stanford: Stanford University Press, 1998) 152-171. While, in his work *Otherwise Than Being or Beyond Essence*, trans. Alphonso Lingis (Boston/The Hague: Nijhoff, 1981), Levinas refers to this same approach as the "one-for-the-other."

differs from the subjectivity of the idealist analyses."[7] Here idealism is interpreted as a theory that understands consciousness as moving away from the body. In order to counter the idealist understanding of the subject, Husserlian phenomenology explains consciousness as moving toward and through the body. Consequently, one's consciousness cannot be separated from one's flesh. Even though he commends Husserl for his contribution to the notion of an embodied subject, Levinas, nonetheless, is convinced that in its preoccupation with "the theoretical, a privilege of representation, of knowing; and, hence, of the ontological meaning of being," Husserl's work is too intellectualist.[8]

Levinas, therefore, moves beyond Husserlian phenomenology and wields a phenomenology similar to that of Maurice Merleau-Ponty. Merleau-Ponty's phenomenology fosters both an ambiguous and incarnational approach to consciousness and relationships.[9] His interpretation of the body is dynamic, rather than static. Merleau-Ponty explains the human person as a 'body-subject', who engages and transforms the life-world, instead of as a lump of matter that merely occupies space. In her commentary on Merleau-Ponty's *Phenomenology of Perception*, Monika Langer explains the subject's action in the world as an "incarnate intentionality" in which the body "inhabits space and projects itself towards a perceptual world."[10] As the site of incarnate intentionality, the body-subject is not an inactive receptor of sensory associations, rather is an embodied subject vigorously embracing the world[11]. For Merleau-Ponty, the body-subject's engagement with the world is often complicated and ambiguous because s/he can never separate him/herself from

7. Emmanuel Levinas, "Reflections on Phenomenological 'Technique'," *Discovering Existence with Husserl*, trans. Richard A. Cohen and Michael B. Smith (Evanston: Northwestern University Press, 1998) 104.

8. Emmanuel Levinas, "Nonintentional Consciousness," *Entre Nous: On Thinking-of-the-Other*, trans. Michael B. Smith and Barbara Harshav (New York: Columbia University Press, 1998) 124. Levinas's critique of Husserl dates back to his dissertation, in which he accuses Husserl of intellectualism, yet at the same time, commends him for paying attention to relationships in intentionality analysis; see Emmanuel Levinas, *The Theory of Intuition in Husserl's Phenomenology*, trans. André Orianne (Evanston: Northwestern University Press, 1973).

9. See Maurice Merleau-Ponty, *Phenomenology of Perception*, trans. Colin Smith (London: Routledge, 1992).

10. Monika M. Langer, *Merleau-Ponty's Phenomenology of Perception: A Guide and Commentary* (Tallahassee/Basingstoke: Macmillan, 1989) 48.

11. Merleau-Ponty's phenomenology can be read as implying that the incarnate subject gives bodily for others through his/her gestures; see Emmanuel Levinas, "On Intersubjectivity: Notes on Merleau-Ponty," *Outside the Subject*, trans. Michael B. Smith (London: Athlone, 1993) 96-103.

the experience of society. Ambiguity here is not something to be avoided; in fact, Merleau-Ponty urges human beings to revel in the ambiguity of corporeal subjectivity. Relying on Merleau-Ponty, Levinas interprets subjectivity in terms of an "incarnate existence."[12] It is in the cooperative, coexistence of mind and body, that consciousness and matter enact incarnation. From this brief survey, we can grasp that from very early in his career, Levinas was concerned with the unified, wholistic existence of subjectivity, with an anthropology of incarnation. Pushing Merleau-Ponty's work beyond the questions of reflection and signification, Levinas paves the way for reading embodiment as a type of writing, in which the subject is positioned, postured, and written by the demand of the Other.[13] Simply put, for Levinas, incarnate existence emerges in the subject's obligation *for-the-Other*. Accordingly, being human is not disconnected from one's body; rather being human emanates from one's bodily encounter with the world. Sacramentality surfaces in interpersonal relations.

As the subject takes shape or is written in interpersonal encounter, the threat of the mortal deaths of both s/he and the Other mount. Levinas contends (in contrast to Martin Heidegger) that this mortality marks the subject's relationship to the Other. Levinas writes:

> This approach of death indicates that we are in relation with something that is absolutely other, something bearing alterity not as a provisional determination we can assimilate through enjoyment, but as something whose very existence is made of alterity. My solitude is thus not confirmed by death but broken by it.[14]

According to Levinas, when a person dies naturally, s/he confronts such otherness. This mortal situation is exacerbated further in murderous and violent situations. In such predicaments, the impending and unjust death of the Other enlivens the subject to substitute his/her own body *for-the-Other*. Since, for Levinas, death is beyond representation and anticipation, the subject's obligation to the Other cannot be

---

12. Emmanuel Levinas, "The Ruin of Representation," *Discovering Existence with Husserl*, trans. Richard A. Cohen and Michael B. Smith (Evanston: Northwestern University Press, 1998) 117-118.

13. For a more rigorous analysis of how Levinas departs from the thinking of Merleau-Ponty, see Emmanuel Levinas, "Meaning and Sense," *Basic Philosophical Writings*, ed. Adriaan Peperzak, Simon Critchley, and Robert Bernasconi (Bloomington: Indiana University Press, 1996) 33-64.

14. Emmanuel Levinas, "Time and the Other," *Time and the Other [and additional essays]*, trans. Richard Cohen (Pittsburgh: Duquesne University Press, 1987) 74.

predicted; as a result, the subject is placed in a vulnerable and risk-filled position. The only certainty in such a scenario is that the subject answers the demand of the Other in a complete embodied response by posturing *for-the-Other* to the point of death. This posturing is a sort of writing in that meaning is signified as the Other calls forth this radical posture from the subject.

In an effort to concretise the dangerous posture of the incarnate subject, Levinas rewrites ordinary language to connote excessiveness and to create the effect in which skin is not an armour or "hide nor covering, camouflage, uniform, adornment. It is [rather] a surface of exposure, zone of susceptibility, of vulnerability, of pain and abuse."[15] It could be argued that these thick and fleshy sketches of humanity are profane and pornographic. Nevertheless, Levinas's project does not attempt to scandalise the body of the subject; rather it strives to demonstrate how the body-subject has a mortal responsibility for others, at any cost. He writes: "Incarnation is an extreme passivity; to be exposed to sickness, suffering, death, is to be exposed to compassion, and, as a self, to the gift that costs."[16] Indeed the body is indispensable for subjectivity as it is the site of passivity, pain, ageing, sacrifice, and gift. This same body, similarly, is the site of joy, pleasure, creation, and responsibility. The connection between pain and pleasure is wedded by the posture of giving at all costs.

Clearly, one person's substitution of him/herself for another is an exemplar performance of being subject.[17] Christians realise this poignant fact in the death and resurrection of Christ. Less understood, however, is Levinas's as well as the Church's rationale for linking the excessive giving of the subject to the female gender. The question of gender leads us to the second point in my analysis. By exploring Levinas's gendered language, we can learn something about our own (Christian) assumptions about sacrifice. On one level, Levinas imagines the responsible subject in terms of fecundity; and on another level, he explains the subject's attraction to the Other in terms of the feminine, the Woman.[18]

---

15. Alphonso Lingis, *Deathbound Subjectivity* (Bloomington: Indiana University Press, 1989) 138.

16. Levinas, *Otherwise Than Being or Beyond Essence*, 195, n. 12.

17. For a glimpse into how Levinas interprets death beyond self-interest, see Levinas, "Dying For...," *Entre Nous: On Thinking-of-the-Other*, 207-217.

18. Emmanuel Levinas, *Totality and Infinity: An Essay on Exteriority*, trans. Alphonso Lingis (Pittsburgh: Duquesne University Press, 1969) 155.

In the first case, the procreative or fecund role of humanity becomes a key trope for understanding the posture of being *for-the-Other*. Indeed, for Levinas, the fruit of the engagement between subject and Other, that is, the result of the subject's desire for the Other, is fecundity. Alterity extends toward the future in the procreation of a child. The possibility of the subject's openness to the future, nevertheless, materialises not only in the production of a child, but also in the proliferation of more relations and additional responsibility. Clearly, Levinas's notion of fecundity reflects no easy translation to motherhood. Still, in Western culture the connection between motherhood and fecundity is obvious. Moreover, in Levinas's later work, he upholds maternity as the "ultimate sense of this vulnerability," of being *for-the-Other*.[19] In such a relationship, the mother is a hostage of the child and substitutes herself for the welfare of the child. Reading Levinas in the Western landscape, one could argue that by performing or mimicking the substitution between mother and child, the human subject is exposed and postured *for-the-Other*. This subject cannot rest or hide within the confines of the body; rather s/he is exposed as responsible to the point of death.

As Levinas employs the notion of fecundity to capture the excessive giving of the subject, he utilises the idea of paternity to concretise the separation between subject and Other. Levinas is concerned with maintaining a distance between subject and Other in order to respect the Other's alterity. Hence, Levinas imagines the father as different from the offspring son; and, at the same time, the bond of paternity solidifies the obligation between them. As Levinas describes a relationship among fecundity and offspring, a heterosexual and spousal metaphor emerges.

Connected to the way he genders the relationship between subject and Other, Levinas eroticizes and feminizes the Other. He describes the mystery and receptivity of the Other by exploiting the rhetoric of femininity. Levinas claims: "The Other whose presence is discreetly an absence, with which is accomplished the primary hospitable welcome which describes the field of intimacy, is the Woman."[20] Even as he rejects the facile conflation of the feminine with otherness and the masculine with subjectivity, he still employs phrases that have feminine connotations when speaking about responsible subjectivity.[21] For instance,

19. Levinas, *Otherwise Than Being or Beyond Essence*, 108.
20. Levinas, *Totality and Infinity*, 155.
21. Levinas explicitly rejects the facile conflation of femininity with otherness, *ibid.*, 279.

he exercises such phrases as 'overflowing' and 'voluptuosity' in order to emphasise the mystery of the Other. Voluptuosity refers to the inexhaustible depth of the subject's enjoyment of and desire for the hiddenness of the Other. This voluptuosity "transfigures the subject himself, who henceforth owes his identity not to his initiative of power, but to the passivity of the love received."[22] What's more, the term 'voluptuosity" marks the relation of the Other to the subject, and at the same time underscores the distance of the Other from the subject. The alterity that maintains the closeness and distance between subject and Other materialises in a heterosexual and spousal bond. Again, according to Levinas, this bond is fecund and leads to more relationships; thus, as the subject's love "aims at the Other," a child is created.[23]

Even as we are mindful of Levinas's good intentions and admirable project, it is easy to become irritated by the way he collapses the notion of femininity with the gesture of hospitality, especially since feminist critics have long critiqued the over-association of the notions of passivity and femininity.[24] Similarly, in hearing Levinas's deliberate use of gendered language, Christians may wonder about their own gendered, that is, feminine description of the serving role of the laity in the Church. Why indeed, in this age of postmodernity, when we are cognisant of the implications of sexist language, does Levinas use this tired trope of femininity in order to identify the ethical posture or what I interpret as the sacramental character of the subject? For even as Levinasian scholars are intent on pinpointing the complexity of his thought in regard to gender play, when read in a Western milieu, the boundaries between the identities of male and female and roles of mother and father become obfuscated. This ambiguity is welcomed by some readers of Levinas and rejected by others. Some, including myself, think that this slippage between Levinasian language and cultural expectation regarding the questions of gender and giving for others is positive or advantageous in that it highlights the reality that all humans are obliged to become exposed to and deposed *for-the-*

22. Levinas, *Totality and Infinity*, 270.
23. *Ibid.*, 256.
24. Simone de Beauvoir is an example of a feminist thinker who critiques an immanentist and passive reading of women. See Simone de Beauvoir, *The Second Sex*, ed. H. M. Parshley (New York: Vintage, 1980). In the introduction to that work, she comments on how Levinas links subjectivity with gender: "I suppose that Levinas does not forget that woman, too, is aware of her own consciousness, or ego. But it is striking that he takes a man's point of view, disregarding the reciprocity of subject and object. When he writes that woman is mystery, he implies that she is mystery for man. Thus his description, which is intended to be objective, is in fact an assertion of male privilege" (xl).

Other. On the other hand, some readers find Levinas's thought frustrating and problematic because it seems to support the logic that all women are relational, ethical, and ultimately sacrificial. Such frustration with the dominance of gendered language in the discussion of sacrifice leads us to my third point: the charge of essentialism.

Even though French feminist thinker Luce Irigaray's theory is largely framed within psychoanalytic rather than philosophical discourse, we still would be wise to attend to her concern that Levinas's thought leads to essentialism or equates women with their biological and cultural affinities for mothering, caring, domesticity, and hospitality. While pondering the issue of essentialism, Irigaray interrogates Levinas's understanding of femininity and wonders how otherness can be understood outside of this landscape of gender.[25] She attempts to create a presence for women, linguistically, that has been negated by male presence and female absence. Put another way, the objective of her project is to locate a position for women as subjects, rather than merely as others. Contesting the attitude in "dominant discourse" that women are "always off-stage, off-side, beyond presentation, beyond selfhood," Irigaray strives to create a space and medium in which women can present themselves, write themselves into being.[26]

Nevertheless like Levinas, Irigaray relies on effusive and baroque metaphors of relationship as well as rich carnal images of women's bodies in order to illustrate the presence of women as subjects. One must question whether Irigaray, similar to Levinas, runs the risk of determining women's identity on the basis of biology. Simply put, are Levinas and Irigaray's theories of subjectivity and otherness grounded in an insidious essentialism? Again, the essentialism of women involves the conflation of a woman's role and destiny with her biological capacities. Many theorists worry about philosophy being essentialist because it reduces a person to his/her biology and denies personal identity in any other sphere of life. One could read both Levinas's and Irigaray's theories as essentialist because of the way in which they seem to connect bodily function with destiny and ontology. Nonetheless, I hope to show that their work, when accurately interpreted, is more deconstructive and performative than reductionist.

---

25. See Luce Irigaray, "Questions to Emmanuel Levinas: On the Divinity of Love," *Re-Reading Levinas*, ed. Robert Bernasconi and Simon Critchley (Bloomington, IN: Indiana University Press, 1991) 109-118.

26. Pam Morris, *Literature and Feminism: An Introduction* (Oxford: Blackwell, 1993) 116.

My argument assumes that the language used to describe the subject, Other, and the relationship between the two parties does not lead to essentialism. Instead, such language re-envisions and re-scripts the person and relationship in question. In other words, as Levinas and Irigaray speak about subjectivity and womanhood, they further develop the meanings of those terms. American cultural critic, Jane Gallop, affirms that in Irigaray's discussion about the body, Irigaray reimagines what it means to be embodied. Her fleshy narration of femininity reproduces and presents yet anew the body-subject of the woman.[27] Furthermore, when Irigaray was asked whether she was part of any women's liberation movement, she answered: "I am trying ... to go back through the masculine imagery, to interpret the way it has reduced us [women] to silence, to muteness or mimicry, and I am attempting, from that starting-point and that same time, to (re)discover a possible space for the possible imagery."[28] Irigaray's aim, therefore, is not to reduce women to one specific role or type, but rather to open women to alternative ways of being human.

Speaking about human beings as embodied and gendered does not limit the way we think about women or others, unless we allow one image to totalize the subject. This totalization or reduction of the subject can lead to idolatry and to the confusion of ontology with description. Levinas's and Irigaray's intentions are not to make any reductionist assertions about being, rather to illustrate the various dimensions of being and ways of performing subjectivity.[29] Furthermore, the way in which they both play with sexual iconography does not result in essentialism, but expresses Levinas's and Irigaray's respect for the complexity of being human. The ambiguity in both their theories allows the role of being for others and the notion of woman to be constantly contested

27. Jane Gallop, *Thinking Through the Body* (New York: Columbia University Press, 1988) 91-99.

28. Luce Irigaray, *This Sex Which Is Not One*, trans. Catherine Porter with Carolyn Burke (Ithaca: Cornell University Press, 1985) 164.

29. Often thinkers, feminist and otherwise, attempt to avoid essentialism by forcing the rhetoric of equality. Cultural theorist, Daniel Boyarin points to this problem of avoiding essentialism at the cost of reifying the body through an analysis of androgyny in the traditional Christian account of gender. He contends in the discourse of Rabbinic Judaism, that sexual difference is not an accident or due to sin, rather is part of the destiny of the human. He argues against all those invested in a sense of Christian androgyny as a supreme or ideal sense of the human. Accordingly, such rhetoric, Boyarin claims does not "destabilize gender," but re-enacts an insidious dualism. See Daniel Boyarin, "Gender," *Critical Terms for Religious Studies*, ed. Mark C. Taylor (Chicago: University of Chicago Press, 1998) 126.

and challenged, to be endlessly written. Feminist thinkers refer to this endless play in meaning as *écriture féminine*. We can define *écriture féminine* literally as 'feminine writing' or writing that encourages women's experience, desire, and bodies to come into being. Often *écriture féminine* is performed by the language of excess, sacrifice, and gift. It is important to note that feminine language is not limited to female writers; rather, it encompasses any writing that focuses on the excess and fecundity that is characteristic of subjectivity. Accordingly, we can grasp how Levinas's work is evidence of *écriture féminine*. In fact, any theory that rejects the binaries of male versus female and subject versus Other and engages an ethic of openness, excess, gift, and sacramentality can be interpreted as *écriture féminine*.

Significantly, feminist thinker Arleen Dallery highlights a key point about Irigaray's writing about the body, which we can extend to Levinas's work as well as to the Church's use of gendered language.[30] Concurring with the supposition that Irigaray's writing is performative, Dallery explains how Irigaray's *écriture féminine* resists essentialism. She argues that those who resist performative writing and claim that it is literalist or essentialist are fearful and uncomfortable with otherness. In other words, in accusing someone of being essentialist, one shows his/her antipathy toward difference. Dallery further asserts that "the antiessentialist [i.e. one who opposes Levinas and Irigaray] forgets that the body is a sign, a function of discourse."[31]

Stating that the body serves as a sign does not undermine the reality of it. On the contrary, proposing that the body is a sign underscores the fact that human corporeality is imbued with cultural meaning. When we overlook the fact that the subject's body functions as a sign, we end up collapsing the body or body part with one specific cultural meaning. Therefore, it is imperative that we do not confuse a person's being, that is, ontology with cultural meaning. With this said, we should feel more comfortable when studying otherness and less fearful about the gendered imagery used in philosophical and ecclesial discourse.

Still, some may want to imagine other metaphors for understanding subjectivity and difference beyond the language of gender. This creative

---

30. Arleen Dallery, "The Politics of Writing (the) Body: Écriture Féminine," *Theorizing Feminism: Parallel Trends in the Humanities and Social Sciences*, ed. Anne C. Herrmann and Abigail J. Stewart (San Francisco/Boulder: Westview, 1994) 288-300.

31. *Ibid.*, 297. Many of the anti-essentialist claims, Dallery argues, come from American and British feminists who are enmeshed in rights language and equality feminism.

effort should be acceptable, since we are aware that body language is not
intended to be interpreted literally. As we return to Levinas's work, it
becomes obvious that the trope of fecundity, while not devised to be
understood literally, does denote a particular role: mothering. The
metaphor of motherhood for understanding the sacramental or giving
subject is limiting on two levels: primarily, because only women can
physically bear children; and secondarily, because women can have children only during their fertile years. The figure of maternity excludes
other people, including men, children, and the elderly, from imagining
themselves as open, receptive, and sacramental.[32] Consequently, feminist
thinker, Catherine Chalier, argues that the generosity of being *for-the-
Other* must transcend the metaphor of maternity. She asserts that while
maternity is a significant way in which women are open to otherness,
openness goes beyond one act, function, or set identity, such as motherhood[33]. Here, Chalier calls our attention to the fact that the notion of
fecundity is limiting because it refers merely to an event or possibility,
rather than to an open-ended disposition or posture. The notion of
mother, moreover, is rooted in spousal imagery, which is inextricably
connected to sexist assumptions about marriage and sacrifice.[34] Ultimately, fecundity as a metaphor for giving *for-the-Other*, for sacramental
subjectivity is indeed myopic.

It is crucial to realise that the risk of essentializing difference not only
surfaces in discussions of gender, but also in the construction of race: a
phenomenon that may be more obvious in the American context, but
nevertheless is evident in the global landscape. Theologian and cultural
critic, Victor Anderson explores issues that arise when theorists essen-
tialize or reify racial categories. He explains how culture has compart-
mentalised and distilled experiences of some black persons under the
static concept of blackness, regardless of whether these experiences
are fact or fiction. Anderson defines the cultural reification of black
experience as ontological blackness: "a covering term that connotes

32. The way in which we privilege fecundity as a role and age span is evident in the
North American culture which values youth, mothers, and career women, over senior
women. For example, senior women are in danger of being marginalized by the hegemonic male gaze, which renders beauty in terms of youth and fertility. Frida Kerner Furman carries out an enlightening study of the ways in which older women both inter-
nalise and externalise the dominant cultures assumptions and attitudes about age and
gender in her work. See Frida Kerner Furman, *Facing the Mirror: Older Women and
Beauty Shop Culture* (New York: Routledge, 1997).

33. Catherine Chalier, "Ethics and the Feminine," *Re-Reading Levinas*, 119-129.

34. Ross, *Extravagant Affections*, 114.

categorical, essentialist, and representational languages depicting black life and experience."[35] These images and feelings conjured by the monolithic concept of blackness have been created by whites. Anderson challenges this reductionist attitude and laments that blackness constructed in relation to the normative whiteness "constitutes a fundamental natural inequality."[36] Regretfully, Anderson wonders if humanity can transcend the static concept of blackness or if such an essentialist reading will type blacks permanently. His analysis encourages theologians to question how bodies stigmatised by racial stereotypes are thwarted from being understood as good, valuable, and sacramental.

The reification of racial categories, hence, presents theologians with a dilemma. If one reject's a connection between cultural identity and experience, blackness could become relegated to a myth or metaphor. Yet if one focuses too much on ethnic identity, the particular person becomes reduced to commonsense assumptions about his/her race. Systematic theologian, M. Shawn Copeland, in an essay entitled, "Collegiality as a Moral and Ethical Practice," grapples with racist attitudes toward black scholars.[37] In both constructing and analysing a hypothetical case scenario involving an African-American female academic, Copeland questions whether people of colour can transcend the reductionist conceptions that surround race. Struggling with the paradox of race in American universities, she suggests that if the black scholar is merely a symbol of her race, then she is "never a particular person."[38] Alternatively, she is the embodiment of a static concept of blackness, a placeholder who "bears the burden of her race and the race bears the burden of her performance."[39] Here the academic is reduced to any and all of Western preconceived notions about blackness. Poignantly, even as this black female scholar is to educate a culture, biased notions about her race and gender prevent her from being true to her talent and fulfilling her tasks.

The flip side of this dilemma involves erasing racial difference altogether. Exegeting Frantz Fanon's psychoanalytic theory, critical theorist, David Theo Goldberg discusses how the black body is constructed as

35. Victor Anderson, *Beyond Ontological Blackness: An Essay on African American Religious and Cultural Criticism* (New York: Continuum, 1995) 11.
36. *Ibid.*, 78.
37. M. Shawn Copeland, "Collegiality as a Moral and Ethical Practice," *Practice What You Preach: Virtues, Ethics, and Power in the Lives of Pastoral Ministers and Their Congregations*, ed. James F. Keenan and Joseph Kotva Jr. (Franklin: Sheed & Ward, 1999) 315-332.
38. *Ibid.*, 320.
39. *Ibid.*

"racially marked," while the white body poses as "racially invisible."[40] The bodies of whites perform as if they were naked, undressed, pure, racially unmarked, and normative. Alternatively blacks are marked, costumed, and dressed in this hegemonic blackness which refuses to allow for any particularity of the person and judges that person by a biased concept. In this scenario the person is at once a symbol and anonymous. On one level, as we have learned from Copeland, individual persons of colour serve as symbol for all blacks; and on the other level, blacks as individuals are rendered anonymous.[41]

Clearly, it is dangerous to correlate ontology with experience or biology. To avoid this problem in understanding anthropology, theologians have to engage difference beyond the superficial connotations attached to gender and race. Only then can sacramental subjectivity, that is, being *for-the-Other* become a reality. Arguably, Levinas's thought implies a critique of essentialism. He explains: "The Other is this, not because of the Other's character, physiognomy, or psychology, but because of the Other's very alterity. The Other is, for example, the weak, the poor, 'the widow and the orphan,' whereas I am the rich or the powerful."[42] In his claim that difference is not a monolithic category, we can begin to comprehend how the position of alterity constantly shifts, thus complicating the dichotomous way in which we often configure diversity. The only normative dimension of the Other, therefore, is the responsibility that s/he places on the subject's shoulders.

As we attempt to move away from the sticky metaphors of gendered and racist language, we need to devise more life-affirming and inclusive ways of valuing our bodily responsibility for others without falling into the trap of essentialism. This endeavour to find more inclusive metaphors for sacramental subjectivity, leads us into the fourth and last point of my investigation. Since the position of the Other is ever changing, we need to develop a metaphor that illustrates the subject's relation to the Other as a fluid and dynamic process. One concrete way to interpret the subject as giving, sacramental, and open *for-the-Other*, is in terms of shouldering. Significantly, this reference to the notion of shouldering originates in Levinas's explication of the subject's separation, that

---

40. David Theo Goldberg, *Racial Subjects: Writing on Race in America* (New York: Routledge, 1997) 83.

41. For an important analysis of the anonymity of blackness, see Lewis R. Gordon, "Existential Dynamics of Theorizing Black Invisibility," *Existence in Black: An Anthology of Black Existential Philosophy*, ed. Lewis Gordon (New York: Routledge, 1997) 69-79.

42. Levinas, *Time and the Other*, 83-84.

is, his/her independence from and proximity to the Other. *In Humanisme de l'autre homme*, Levinas explains how one cannot shift responsibility from one's shoulders, for the closer the distinctive subject becomes to the Other, the more s/he is responsible *for-the-Other*.[43]

There are various figures in myth and culture that relate to the notion of shouldering. In Greek mythology, it was the Titan, Atlas, who bore the burden of shouldering the world – his punishment for losing the battle to the Gods. Shouldering the world confined his freedom and prohibited him from again rebelling against the Gods. From this myth developed an understanding of freedom as power over people, and responsibility was interpreted as a burden and punishment. Many Westerners have a similar perspective; and, individualism thrives on personal rights, but refuses to realise fully the connection between rights and responsibilities. Nonetheless, we learn from the Judeo-Christian worldview that being obligated to another person to the point of substitution does not limit freedom but creates authentic freedom. Juxtaposed with Atlas, who complains about having to bear the world on his shoulders, the sacramental subject freely shoulders the world in one moment.

Systematic theologian, M. Shawn Copeland further explains how the practice of shouldering the oppressed and marginalized is a concrete task demanded of all Christians, regardless of their gender, age, and

---

43. Emmanuel Levinas, *Humanisme de l'autre homme* (Montpellier: Fata Morgana, 1972) 50. It is significant to note that Didier Franck references Levinas uses of the shouldering metaphor in his essay, "The Body of Difference," *The Face of the Other and the Trace of God: Essays on the Philosophy of Emmanuel Levinas*, ed. Jeffrey Bloechl (New York: Fordham University Press, 2000) 3-29. There, he comments on Levinas's ambiguous reference to corporeality in *Existence and Existents*, trans. Alphonso Lingis (The Hague: Nijhoff, 1978) 29; and implies that the presence of corporeal images in Levinas's work disrupts Levinas's argument by assuming that the body is somehow prior or constitutive of existence. Franck writes, "But to speak of the existent's relation to existence as one of 'body to body" (*corps à corps*) – is this not to suggest that the existent has a position in existence by virtue of having a body" (9). Franck's concern, nevertheless, does not seem to undercut my argument. For in Levinas's writings, surely, there are numerous ambiguous references to the body. The text which I have referenced in particular, *Humanisme de l'autre homme*, was written almost thirty years later than *Existence and Existents*. And in *Humanisme de l'autre homme*, Levinas asserts that the Other anticipates the subject by placing weight on his/her shoulders, in other words, by making a demand of the subject. Levinas's reference to bearing the weight on one's shoulders is a metaphor for ethical subjectivity, that unlike the notion of the voice has corporeal implications and unlike the notion of the face has communal demands. This metaphor of shouldering should not be understood literally, which I think Franck does, but instead as a trope for capturing the material dimension of intersubjectivity beyond fecundity.

social location.[44] Responsibility as standing for and with the oppressed, "shoulder-to-shoulder" explodes our commonsense knowledge of what it means to be *for-the-Other*.[45] By understanding shouldering this way, we can take into consideration the particular differences of each person and tie them to a posture of responsibility. Hence, the term shouldering holds both the notion of an embodied, distinct individual in tension with the idea of a person who is responsible for and interchangeable with others. At the same time, shouldering avoids essentialist presuppositions, yet remains attentive to difference. Quite effectively, the trope of shouldering underscores the subject's obligation to the Other, without relying on insidious gender stereotypes as well as without erasing difference. Indeed, it is precisely in the liminal space between self and Other that the subject becomes incarnate.[46] In other words, the self only becomes the sacramental subject through his/her bodily stance *for-the-Other*. Shouldering demonstrates a sacramental relationship with others.

In this essay, although I interpret more than a few thinkers on the question of sacramental subjectivity, the point that I endeavoured to make is simple. As theologians discuss subjectivity as sacramental, they have to be attentive to the issues raised by feminist, critical race, and postmodern theorists, such as essentialism. What's more, I attempted to show that the charge of essentialism is forgetful that the body is a sign imbued with cultural meaning. In other words, we often collapse ontology and description. Alternatively, I asserted that if we read the body as a sign, we can break free of the fear of a debilitating essentialism; and, we can revision and rewrite sacramental subjectivity. One such way of rewriting subjectivity is in terms of the notion of shouldering that I developed through the work of Levinas and Copeland. Ultimately, the subject who shoulders the Other to the point of death simultaneously signals the presence of God and writes him/herself as sacrament.

44. Copeland refers to the importance of shouldering in her work, "The New Anthropological Subject at the Heart of the Mystical Body of Christ," *Proceedings of the Fifty-Third Annual Convention* (Catholic Theological Society of America) 53 (1998) 25-47.
    45. *Ibid.*, 44.
    46. Levinas, *Totality and Infinity*, 164.

Even the Postmodern Story Has a Body
Narrative, Poetry and Ritual

Scott Holland*

> *The tongue is both an organ of language and taste.*
> Maurice Merleau-Ponty

Introduction

The incomparable work of David Tracy understands theology within the theoretical context of "the materiality of writing."[1] Resisting any theology that views scripture as mere testimony to past presence rather than *as writing*, and situating his hermeneutics within a theology of material culture in the world behind the text, in the text, and in front of the text, he understands how the metaphorical and poetic languages of scripture and faith refer not only to a sensuous, living world in front of the text but also to articulate flesh, to the human body. Tracy's attention to material culture, and to *the materiality of writing* in particular, challenges many modern assumptions that language is rooted in ideation not physicality. It applies a hermeneutics of suspicion to any easy notion that the agent's rational intent comes before form or that idea comes prior to embodiment and imaginative activity. Indeed, if the surpluses and excesses of meaning in the metaphorical language of faith stories lead us not merely to more texts but also to the world as text and to the body as text, then it seems that a well-integrated theology must move from a hermeneutics of the text to a hermeneutics of the gesture. This essay in the genre of a theopoetic exploration and reflection begins to bring narrative, poetry and ritual together within the theoretical and theological context of the possibilities of sacramental presence in a postmodern world come of age.[2]

* A parallel yet expanded version of this essay is part of a book length manuscript in progress on narrative theology and ritual performance. It will be titled, *How Do Stories Save Us?*

1. David Tracy, "Writing," *Critical Terms for Religious Study*, ed. Mark C. Taylor (Chicago: University of Chicago Press, 1998) 391.
2. I have published several theological articles that enter into some conversation with postmodernism, some on narrative, some on poetry, and some on ritual. However, this

Paul Ricoeur's former student, Jacques Derrida, writing on the visual arts, has confessed, "It is true that only words interest me."[3] Indeed, in most postmodern theory, it is the linguistic text and not the author nor his or her material culture which becomes the body of theory. It is well known that that in the postmodern imagination the author was killed in Paris, embalmed at Yale, and pronounced dead again and again in English departments and divinity schools from Paris to New Haven to Durham.

The body of the text has also dominated contemporary conversations in theology. While the hermeneutics of Paul Ricoeur is more attentive to the world in front of the text, that is, the intertextuality of the narrative text, author, authorial context and audience than his deconstructive students, his radical Huguenot Protestantism – where the Word-Event is central – whispers through all his theory. It has been correctly observed that the work of the Catholic theologian David Tracy is a "theological performance of the hermeneutics of Paul Ricoeur." Tracy does turn to the work of Eliade to explicate and exegete a phenomenology of the sacred, nevertheless, his hermeneutic remains deeply indebted to his former Chicago colleague Ricoeur.[4] In most contemporary hermeneutic or narrative theologies, whether pure or impure, anti-correlational or correlational, there is the assumption that one can move from text to ethical action, from story to morality, without much conscious attention to ritual, liturgy, sacrament or spirituality.

Interestingly, David Tracy has been stuck, by his own admission, on how to move on to book three of his projected trilogy: the work on practical theology. Likewise, Paul Ricoeur has failed to fully produce his promised "poetics of the will." In his insistence that one must move from text to ethical action Ricoeur senses that something else must be addressed. A poetics of the will?

In the rich history of both Catholicism and Protestantism, "orthodoxy" has never been understood as mere cognitive correctness in either

---

essay seeks to begin to bring these themes together. In the long process of my research and writing in the area of narrative theology it became evident to me that even as the text returns us to an embodied world, so a hermeneutical, narrative theology carries us to a liturgical and sacramental theology. See Scott Holland, "How Do Stories Save Us?," *Louvain Studies* 22 (1997) 328-351, and Scott Holland, "Signifying Presence: The Ecumenical Sacramental Theology of George Worgul," *Louvain Studies* 18 (1993) 38-55.

3. Jacques Derrida, "The Spacial Arts: An Interview with Jacques Derrida," *Deconstruction and the Visual Arts*, ed. Peter Brunette and David Wells (London: Cambridge University Press, 1994) 19.

4. See Holland, "How Do Stories Save Us?"

theology or ethics; it has been concerned with right worship. This is no small matter, for it implies that there may in fact be a ritual, liturgical, sacramental, indeed aesthetic, "consummation of theology,"[5] which spills over into productive public life, not simply from the surplus of meaning in the text, but from the poetics *and* performance of the prayer, the liturgy, the hymn, the homily, the Eucharist – *the performance of doxology*. Theology in the Hebrew and Christian traditions in the end yields to a doxology against all idolatry and ideology, even the idols of dogma and ethics.

Recently, the fields of narrative theology and hermeneutical theology have been vigorously challenged by the innovative discipline of ritual criticism.[6] Ritual critics remind us that every story, every text, happens some*where* and in some*body* as well as some*time*.

Drawing from ritual critics such as Ronald Grimes and sacramental theologians such as George Worgul, my evolving work suggests that the self is performatively constituted as well as narratively constituted. I claim that "ritual knowing" is not epistemologically inferior to "narrative knowing" on the way to naming ourselves and rendering God's name in history, for even the stories of God are told and enacted some*time*, some*where* by some-*body*.

The Embodied Mind

Those who read postmodern thought know that the earlier postmodern "linguistic turn" in critical theory gradually evolved into a "narrative turn" which is now clearly becoming an intense *turn to the body*. Phenomenologically, this is because, as Merleau-Ponty always knew, the tongue is both an organ of language and taste.[7] Theologically, this is because the Creator God of Genesis is both *poet* and *potter*.

5. In this context I have been fascinated by Catherine Pickstock's *After Writing: On the Liturgical Consummation of Philosophy* (Oxford: Blackwell, 1998). However, I find her and her "radical orthodox" colleagues [see *Radical Orthodoxy* (London: Routledge, 1999)] to bound by the theology, sacramentology and philosophy of the late Middle Ages. I am more attracted to the understanding of liturgical and ritual innovation outlined in Nathan D. Mitchell's study, *Liturgy and the Social Sciences* (Collegeville, MN: The Liturgical Press, 1999).

6. See Ronald L. Grimes, *Ritual Criticism: Case Studies in Its Practice, Essays on Its Theory* (Columbia: University of South Carolina Press, 1990).

7. Maurice Merleau-Ponty, "La Conscience et l'acquisition du langage," *Bulletin de psychologie* 18 (1964) 226-259. Also see Monila M. Langer, *Merleau-Ponty's Phenomenology of Perception: A Guide and Commentary* (Tallahassee: Florida State University Press, 1989).

Ricoeur and Tracy, in their rich conversations with postmodernism, have demonstrated that the quest for philosophical understanding and theological meaning demands hermeneutical detours, for the only path of the self to itself is through the other. Consciousness must pass through the unconscious (the semantics of desire); intuition must pass through critical interpretation (the hermeneutics of suspicion); reason must pass through language (linguistics and rhetoric); and reflection must pass through imagination (poetics).

Following yet extending their fine work, I am contending through this theopoetic reflection what every good poet, priest and preacher already knows: all narratives must pass through the body – *the hermeneutics of gesture* – for "Even the Postmodern Story Has A Body." My evolving work and its attention to the body pries open space for the postmodern return of the strong author (poet, priest, prophet, mystic – for William James taught us that "religious thought is carried on in terms of personality") and this embodied space likewise provides both mystical and carnal possibilities for the postmodern return of God, even, at least in moments of grace, through a consummation of the signified and signifier on the tongue.

I suppose I am prepared to argue that "since we are not Greeks," metaphorically speaking, the body knows as much as the soul.[8] Let me explain. George Lakoff and Mark Johnson have recently published their capstone work collecting important and even astonishing empirical research on the history and nature of human perception, consciousness and cognition. Their study will be received with great satisfaction by ritual critics, sacramental theologians, poets and preachers. It is a huge and happy book and it is titled, *Philosophy in the Flesh: the Embodied Mind and Its Challenge to Western Thought.*[9]

Lakhoff and Johnson's findings can be summarized under the three central theses of the book: First, most thought is unconscious. Second, abstract concepts are largely metaphorical. The richness of life is found in the rule of metaphor. Third, the mind is inherently embodied. Thought requires a body – not in the trivial sense that you need a physical brain with which to think, but in the profound sense that the very structure of our thoughts comes from the nature of the body. The mind is inherently

8. In the statement, "since we are not Greeks," I am speaking in the language of poetic excess linking this line with the poetic assertions of Yeats and Cairns later in this essay. Thus, this is not philosophical history but metaphorical exaggeration.

9. George Lakoff and Mark Johnson, *Philosophy in the Flesh: The Embodied Mind and Its Challenge to Western Thought* (New York: Basic Books, 1999).

embodied. This conclusion of cognitive science is so important for sacramental theology that I must say a bit more about it before I extend my
claim that a theopoetics and a hermeneutics of gesture finally meet on
the tongue of language and taste. Consider this summation of Lakoff and
Johnson on the embodied nature of thought:[10]

- Reason is not disembodied, as the tradition has largely held, but arises
  from the nature of our brains, bodies, and bodily experience. This is not
  just the innocuous and obvious claim that we need a body to reason;
  rather, it is the striking claim that the very structure of reason itself
  comes from the details of our embodiment. The same neural and cognitive mechanisms that allow us to perceive and move around also inform
  our conceptual systems and modes of reason. Thus, to understand reason we must understand the details of our visual system, our motor system, and the general mechanisms of neural binding. In summary, reason
  is not in any way a transcendent feature of the universe or of disembodied mind. Instead, it is shaped crucially by the peculiarities of our
  human bodies, by the remarkable details of the neural structure of our
  brains, and by the specifics of our everyday functioning in the world.
- Reason is evolutionary, in that abstract reason builds on and makes use
  of forms of perceptual and motor inference present in "lower"animals.
  The result is a Darwinism of reason, a rational Darwinism: Reason,
  even in its most abstract form, makes use of, rather than transcends,
  our animal nature. The discovery that reason is evolutionary utterly
  changes our relation to other animals and changes our conception of
  human beings as uniquely rational. Reason is thus not an essence that
  separated us from other animals; rather, it places us on a continuum
  with them.
- Reason is not "universal" in the transcendent sense; that is, it is not
  part of the structure of the universe. It is universal, however, in that it
  is a capacity shared universally by all human beings. What allows it to
  be shared are the commonalties that exist in the way our minds are
  embodied.
- Reason is not completely conscious, but mostly unconscious.
- Reason is not purely literal, but largely metaphorical and imaginative.
- Reason is not dispassionate, but emotionally engaged.

These empirical findings from cognitive science confirm what every
priest and poet knows: the body is cognitive, not stupid; and likewise,
the mind is embodied. Further, these findings link language to the body,
especially the movement of metaphor and the dance of poetry. They
also suggest much about the human movement from narrative to lyric
to drama.[11]

10. Lakoff and Johnson, *Philosophy in the Flesh*, 4.
11. For a very satisfying study tracing the creative movement of "narrative, lyric and
drama" in the religious construction of the self see Frederick J. Ruf's *Entangled Voices:*

The Primal Origins of Art and Religion

My own work has emphasized the emergence of theopoetics beyond a reified metaphysics, systematics and dogmatics, joining theologians like David Tracy in announcing the return of God in our postmodern condition.[12] Theology in our postmodern condition must be understood as a poetics, not a metaphysics. I am of course not suggesting that all theology must be written in verse, although that might be lovely indeed. I am, however, arguing that whether theology is inscribed in the genre of poetry, in the form of narrative, or in a thicker, theoretical style of prose, it remains a *poiesis*: an inventive, imaginative act of composition performed by authors.

The grand preacher, poet and philosopher Ralph Waldo Emerson was making much the same point when he suggested that we must work by art, not metaphysics. Unhappy with both moral philosophers and philosophical theologians, Emerson declared that philosophy would one day be taught by poets.[13] This call to theopoetics is not novel. Consider the dated yet timely words of the preacher-poet Samuel Taylor Coleridge:

> We need not wonder that it pleased Providence that the divine thoughts of religion should have been revealed to us in the form of poetry: and that at all times, poets, not the slaves of any particular sectarian opinions, should have joined to support those delicate sentiments of the heart … which may be called the feeding streams of religion.[14]

Poets have been teaching me much recently about the tongue as an organ of both language and taste. Like most modern and postmodern thinkers, I am tempted by the primacy of the text and by the pleasures of imaginative textual production. "Imaginative construction!" This can almost falsely imply that language precedes both the world and the body. Indeed, in my earlier work on theology as imagination, I constructed too much on an epigraph by Robert Ganzo: "Invent, there is no lost feast at the bottom of memory!"[15]

Genre and the Religious Construction of the Self (New York: Oxford University Press, 1997). Another important treatment of the self as formed not merely in discourse but through performance is Calvin O. Schrag's Gilbert Ryle Lectures, *The Self After Postmodernity* (New Haven: Yale University Press, 1997).

12. Scott Holland, "Theology is a Kind of Writing: The Emergence of Theopoetics," *Cross Currents* 47 (1997) 317-331.

13. *Ibid.*, 319.

14. Samuel T. Coleridge in *Biographia Literaria,* cited in Kathleen Norris, *Amazing Grace: A Vocabulary of Faith* (New York: Riverhead Books, 1998) 380.

15. "Theology is a Kind of Writing," 317.

A poet, who is also a smart theorist, challenged me on this point by asking, "Are you quite sure?" She helped me see again what I already knew. Although all knowledge and memory is composed, there is a feast at the bottom of memory: a carnal knowledge, a bodily intelligence, a primal pulse, an animal faith, an *eros* toward God and the world; indeed there is a Eucharistic hunger under all our loves and longings and losses. Herein are the origins of art and religion. This claim is confirmed in the work of Ellen Dissanayake as she explores the origins and meaning of art.[16] Dissanayake contends that art was central to human evolutionary adaptation and that the aesthetic faculty is a psychological component of every human being. She argues that art is closely linked to the origins of religion and to the rituals of birth, death, transition and transcendence.

The astonishing work of anthropologist Roy Rappaport, which he completed on his deathbed, confirms and extends the findings of Dissanayake on the bio-historical origins and evolutionary interconnections of art, ritual and religion.[17] Some critics have suggested that Rappaport's final work is the most important and original social scientific study of the foundations of religion and culture since Durkheim. Combining cognitive and adaptive approaches to the study of human behavior he examines the centrality of ritual and religion in evolution and argues that they are co-extensive with the invention of language and thus with culture. Indeed, Rappaport establishes the centrality of ritual for what it means to be human. Importantly, his work is "real anthropology" in contrast to the highly philosophical, disembodied anthropology that informs much postmodern theory and theology. His project demonstrates that ritual is not merely an alternative way to express certain things; on the contrary, he shows that certain things can be expressed *only* in ritual.

Like Dissanayake, Rappaport is attentive to the evolutionary links between art, ritual and religion, or what he calls "art and grace." As an anthropologist he is interested in the neurological union of opposites in human biology, history and culture. This includes the union of the discursive and non-discursive and the sacred and the profane. He writes that the union of opposites, the vision of some harmony with

16. Ellen Dissanayake, *Homo Aestheticus: Where Art Comes From and Why* (Seattle: University of Washington Press, 1992).

17. Roy A. Rappaport, *Ritual and Religion in the Making of Humanity* (Cambridge: Cambridge University Press, 1999).

the universe in the midst of conflicts and contradictions, is what R. Otto called approaching "the holy" but what he, following William James and Gregory Bateson, calls "grace." In this anthropological understanding, grace is related to integration, especially what is to be integrated in the diverse parts of the mind, the multiple levels of experience that at one level is termed consciousness and at another level is called the unconscious. Here Rappaport quotes Bateson, "For the attainment of grace, the reasons of the heart must be integrated with the reasons of reason."[18] Concluding a brilliant career as an anthropologist, Roy Rappaport suggests that reason, ritual, religion and art cannot be pried apart in any epistemology that takes seriously the complexity, contradictions and wonder of human behavior and the making of meaning, which is to say the artful making of culture.

A poet and theological thinker, Catherine Madsen, insists that knowledge is more than something merely constructed. She writes,

> Knowledge at its best is not transmitted in increments, but comes whole into the mind, and then must be filled in, thickened in density, to achieve its potential: it is not like a wall built of separate stones but like a child's body, feeding. Knowledge is carnal. It is metabolized, not acquired; perhaps at that level it is not even "constructed."[19]

As Jorge Luis Borges insists, "Thinking, analyzing, inventing are not anomalous acts; they are normal respiration of the intelligence." Let all that has breath praise the Lord." "Taste and see that the Lord is good."

The good work of theology is the embodied work of narrative, lyric and drama. Narrative language desires dramatic performance; Poetic language hungers.[20] Rather than take my readers through more theory and theology proper, which preceded this chapter and which will indeed follow this chapter, I want to invite the reader into the pleasure of the text, some poetic texts, as we consider this claim that language is hungry because it is "indeed of the body." This hunger, as we shall see, is both Eucharistic and erotic. Let us consider some poetic "fragments."

18. Rappaport, *Ritual and Religion*, 383.
19. Catherine Madsen, "Intellectual Light," *Cross Currents* 49 (1999) 299-302.
20. See the collected essays, *Concilium: Liturgy and the Body*, vol. 3, ed. Louis-Marie Chauvet and François Kabasele Lumbala (Maryknoll: Orbis Books, 1995). Also see Jonathan Bishop, *Some Bodies: The Eucharist and Its Implications* (Macon, GA: Mercer University Press, 1992).

Theopoetic Fragments

David Tracy has recently written that "fragments" rather than systems or totalities are indeed the marks of the spiritual situation of our times[21]. He observes that there are at least three kinds of contemporary thinkers for whom the category of "fragments" is important: first, the radical conservatives who view fragments with regret and nostalgia as markers of all that remains of what was once a unified culture; second, the post-modernists in their love of extremes tend to see fragments as a welcome emancipation from the reigning totality systems of rationality and onto-theology; the third group of thinkers interests Tracy most for they see fragments "theologically as saturated and auratic bearers of an infinity and sacred hope, fragmentary of genuine hope in some redemption."[22] He sees Walter Benjamin and Simone Weil as suggestive representatives of this third group.

In her *Spiritual Autobiography*, Simone Weil records two personal epiphanies of sacred presence in her fascinating yet tormented spiritual journey. One occurred at Assisi while praying where Francis once prayed in the chapel of Santa Maria degli Angeli. The other epiphany came through a poem she memorized which, in her words, "took on the virtue of a prayer." Weil had been drawn to the so-called metaphysical English poet-priests. During her recitation of a poem by George Herbert she had an experience much like her epiphany at Assisi through which she declared, "Christ came down and took possession of me." She calls the encounter "a real contact, person to person, here below, between a human being and God." She confesses feeling "the presence of Love."[23]

The poem by George Herbert is entitled "Love," which is his theo-poetic synonym for "God" or "Lord" or "Christ" "Sacred Presence." Consider the words of the poet-priest:[24]

---

21. David Tracy, "Fragments: The Spiritual Situation of Our Times," *God, The Gift, and Postmodernism*, ed. John D. Caputo and Michael J. Scanlon (Bloomington: Indiana University Press, 1999) 170-184.

22. *Ibid.*, 173.

23. Cited by Doris Grumbach in her *The Presence of Absence: On Prayer and an Epiphany* (Boston: Beacon Press, 1999) 52.

24. I am using here the modern translation of Herbert's text from the collection, *George Herbert: The Country Parson, The Temple*, edited with an introduction by John N. Wall, Jr., with a preface by A. M. Allchin; Classics of Western Spirituality (New York: Paulist Press, 1981) 45.

"Love"

Love bade me welcome; yet my soul drew back,
    Guiltie of dust and sinne.
But quick-ey'd Love, observing me grow slack
        From my first entrance in,
Drew nearer to me, sweetly questioning,
        If I lack'd any thing.

A guest, I answer'd, worthy to be here:
        Love said, You shall be he.
I the unkinde, ungratefull? Ah my deare,
        I cannot look on thee.
Love took my hand, and smiling did reply,
        Who made the eyes but I?

Truth Lord, but I have marr'd them: let my shame
        Go where in doth deserve.
And know you not, sayes Love, who bore the blame?
        My deare, then I will serve.
You must sit down, sayes Love, and taste my meat"
        So I did sit and eat.

George Herbert's "Love" concludes his collection of poems, *The Tem-ple,* with an expression of almost reckless grace, which I shall suggest, integrates the beauty of holiness on the tongue of taste and language. Herbert was perhaps the greatest poet-priest writing in the school of great master John Donne. T. S. Eliot has noted that in the preaching and poetry of Donne, thought seems in control of feeling. However, in Herbert, he suggests, feeling seems in control of language[25]. This pro-. duces a more "intimate" tone of speech, Eliot argues. It also produces a graceful image of "talking and tasting."

In a lovely, engaging lecture at The University of Chicago at a con-ference titled, "Mystics: A Conference on Presence and Aporia,"[26] Regina Schwartz accented Herbert's "Love" poem. Her lecture – "From Ritual to Poetry: A Mystic Eucharist" – discussed a movement from "from ritual to poetry" in the work of Herbert and other metaphysical poets. She noted the emergence of the "Eucharistic" significance of poetic language itself, especially in Herbert, beyond rites and rituals. There is a "Eucharistic" dimension in the linguistic expression itself.

---

25. Thomas S. Eliot, *George Herbert* (London: The British Council and the National Book League by Longmans, Green & Co., 1962) 17.

26. Mystics: A Conference on Presence and Aporia, Kent Hall, The University of Chicago, 13 -14 May 1999. These papers are scheduled for publication.

Thus, she argued, we see an aesthetic movement from ritual to poetry as a locus of sacred presence.

I agree. The metaphysical poets were fine preachers because of their theopoetic understanding of the sacramental possibilities of artful language, of the Word-Event. Poetic language is able to do more with the dance of the signified and signifier than is possible in propositional or purely descriptive language. A number of recent books are making this claim about the sacramental possibilities of language. I am thinking especially of Philip Ballinger's *The Poem as Sacrament* and Theresa DiPasquale's *Literature and Sacrament: The Sacred and the Secular in John Donne.*[27] This work really echoes the earlier theory of Nathan Scott. Scott, a religion and literature specialist and an Episcopal priest, wrote widely on "visions of presence in poetry" and on "the poetics of belief." In poetic or metaphorical language the signified and signifier at times seem to embrace and kiss in moments of artful manifestation.

Yet in the end is not the manifestation of sacred presence experienced in both the sacrament of Word *and* ritual? Consider the embodied, phenomenological movement of Herbert's poem. It is saturated with grace. As the poet encounters Divine Love, he does not merely rest in the assurance communicated in the language of love nor does his meditation end in the artful liturgy of love. Love's invitation is far more carnal and corporeal. Love "takes his hand" and says, "taste my meat." He did indeed sit and *EAT!* In the liturgy of life the tongue is an organ of both language and taste.

Spiritually awake poet William Butler Yeats seemed to understand how talk and taste meet on the tongue, how in artistic moments, indeed, in graceful movements, we cannot know the dancer from the dance, because "we are not Greeks." Consider this famous fragment from his "Among School Children:"[28]

27. Philip A. Ballinger, *The Poem as Sacrament: The Theological Aesthetics of Gerard Manley Hopkins* (Leuven/Grand Rapids: Peeters Press/Eerdmans, 2000). Theresa M. DiPasquale, *Literature and Sacrament: The Sacred and the Secular in John Donne* (Pittsburgh: Duquesne University Press, 1999). Nathan A. Scott, Jr., *The Poetics of Belief* (Chapel Hill: University of North Carolina Press, 1985). Also see the following: L. William Countryman, *The Poetic Imagination: An Anglican Spiritual Tradition* (Maryknoll, NY: Orbis Books, 1999) and Douglas F. Ottati, *Hopeful Realism: Reclaiming the Poetry of Theology* (Cleveland: The Pilgrim Press, 1999). Also, Andrew M. Greeley makes similar arguments about poetic language in *Religion as Poetry* (New Brunswick: Transaction Publishers, 1995).

28. William Butler Yeats, *Selected Poems and Four Plays,* edited with an introduction by M. L. Rosenthal (New York: Scribner Paperback Poetry, 1996) 121.

Plato thought nature but a spume that plays
Upon a ghostly paradigm of things;
Solider Aristotle played the taws
Upon the bottom of a king of kings;
World-famous golden-thighed Pythagoras
Fingered upon a fiddle-stick or strings
What a star and careless Muses heard:
Old Clothes upon old sticks to scare a bird...

Labour is blossoming or dancing where
The body is not bruised to pleasure soul,
Nor beauty born out of its own despair,
Nor bleared-eyed wisdom out of midnight oil.
O chestnut tree, great rooted blossomer,
Are you the leaf, the blossom or the bole?
O body swayed to music, O brightening glance,
How can we know the dancer from the dance?

How indeed? The distinguished American poet Scott Cairns, like
Yeats, is interested in a spirituality where the body is not bruised to
pleasure the soul nor is the dancer removed from the dance. His new
collection of work is entitled *Recovered Body*. His poem, "Loves," is
subtitled, "Magdalen's Epistle," and in it he explores incarnational love
through Mary's voice. Here is a fragment of that lengthy poem:[29]

I have received some little bit
about the glib divisions which
so lately have occurred to you
as right, as necessary, fit –

That the body is something less
than honorable, say, in its
appetites? That the spirit is

something pure, and – if all goes well –
potentially unencumbered
by the body's bawdy tastes.

This disposition, then, has led
to a banal and pious lack
of charity, and, worse, has led

more than a few to attempt some
soul-preserving severance – harsh
mortifications, manglings, all

---

29. Scott Cairns, *Recovered Body* (New York: George Braziller Publisher, 1998) 66-
67.

> manner of ritual excision
> lately undertaken to prevent
> the body's claim on the *heart*
>
> or *mind*, or (blasphemy!) *spirit* –
> whatever name you fix upon
> the supposed *bodiless.*
>
> I fear that you presume – dissecting
> *the person* into something less
> complex. I think you forget
>
> you are not Greek. I think that you
> forget the very issue which
> induced the Christ to take on flesh.
>
> All loves are bodily, require
> That the lips part, and press their trace
> of secrecy upon the one
> beloved …

Because we are not Greeks, Cairns contends, all loves are bodily and require that the lips part and press their trace of secrecy upon the one beloved. Some saints and mystics through the centuries have in fact believed that the lips are the holiest of all the body's members because through them pass not merely the language and kisses of love, but the Eucharist. The body knows as much as the soul. Cairns is currently at work on some essays tracing his own spiritual journey into what he is calling a "sacramental poetics."[30] He claims that his own work as a poet led him to reflect beyond literature into the experience of sacramental presence. Interestingly, his spiritual autobiography validates the claim I am making about the "hunger" of poetic language. Raised in the Baptist Church, Scott Cairns now worships in communion with the Russian Orthodox Church because the rich, poetic language of the liturgy consummates on the tongue where talk and taste meet and signified and signifier together dwell in the beauty of holy mystery.

I turn now to a beautiful poem by the Mennonite-Brethren poet Jean Janzen. True to her Anabaptist heritage, Janzen sees that sacred presence and Eucharistic satisfaction of our holy and fleshly hungers are found outside of temples made with human hands in a sacramental universe. Churchly sacraments open one who eats and drinks to another hunger,

---

30. I have been in correspondence with Scott Cairns about this and I hope to run the essay in which he reflects upon poetry and his spiritual journey in the Fall 2001 issue of *Cross Currents.*

a holy desire, indeed, to a eucharistic *eros* toward the world. Those who love God must also love the world, filled as it is with such pain and such indescribable beauty. You can not merely theorize it or even describe it; *you have to eat it.*[31]

Wild Grapes by Jean Janzen

Grandfather, dying in November,
asked for wild grapes from
a distant creek. He remembered them,
sweet under the leaves, sent Peter,
his eldest, on horseback.
Through the window the light,
golden as broth, filled his bedside cups,
and the dusty air shimmered.

I have known others, who, at the end,
crushed the flesh of nectarine against
the dry palate, or swallowed bits
of cake, eyes brimming.

What to drink in remembrance
of each morning that offered itself
with open arms? What food
for the moments we whispered
into its brightness?

Grandfather, the last pain-filled days,
dreamed cures. He who loved God,
who would go to him, but who also
loved this world, filled as it is
with such indescribable beauty,
you have to eat it.

As I finish this theopoetic reflection, a new book has arrived on my desk, Antonio Damasio's *The Feeling of What Happens.*[32] Damasio is a professor of neurology and the author of the award winning book, *Descarte's Error,* which has been translated into seventeen languages. This new work explores the centrality of body and emotion, beyond and perhaps even before language and reason, in the making of human consciousness. It parallels the findings of Lakoff and Johnson. The distinguished neurologist begins his book with a poetic epigraph which sets

---

31. Jean Janzen, *Snake in the Parsonage* (Intercourse, PA: Good Books, 1995) 57. Used with permission.
32. Antonio Damasio, *The Feeling of What Happens: Body and Emotion in the Making of Consciousness* (New York: Harcourt Brace & Company, 1999).

the tone for the following four hundred pages of scientific and humanistic investigation into the nature of consciousness. I will conclude where Damasio begins:

> Or the waterfall, or music heard so deeply
> That it is not heard at all, but you are the music
> While the music lasts. These are only hints and guesses,
> Hints followed by guesses; and the rest
> Is prayer, observance, discipline, thought and action.
> The hint half guessed, the gift half understood, is Incarnation.

T. S. Eliot, "Dry Salvages" from *Four Quartets*

List of Contributors

Marie L. Baird is a professor of theology at Duquesne University in Pittsburgh (USA). She specializes in spirituality and the philosophies of Emmanuel Levinas and Eric Voegelin.

Craig A. Baron is a Ph.D. in Theology at Duquesne University in Pittsburgh (USA). He is also an instructor of theology at Duquesne University and Wheeling Jesuit University specializing in fundamental theology and Christology.

Desiree Berendsen has a Ph.D. in fundamental theology from the Free University of Amsterdam (the Netherlands). She has studied theology at the Free University of Amsterdam and philosophy at the University of Amsterdam and finished her dissertation on religious anthropology in November 2001.

Jeffrey Bloechl was an associate researcher at the Katholieke Universiteit Leuven (Belgium) for the research project on 'Postmodern Sacramento-Theology' (1997-99) and is presently Edward Bennett Williams Fellow and professor of philosophy at College of the Holy Cross in Worcester (USA).

Lieven Boeve is a professor of fundamental and dogmatic theology at the Faculty of Theology, Katholieke Universiteit Leuven (Belgium), and a guest professor at the Faculty of Theology and Canon Law, Université Catholique de Louvain-la-Neuve (Belgium). Currently he is also the coordinator of the research group 'Theology in a Postmodern Context' [www.theo.kuleuven.ac.be/ogtpc].

Peter De Mey is a postdoctoral fellow of the Fund for Scientific Research-Flanders and lecturer in dogmatic theology at the Faculty of Theology of the Katholieke Universiteit Leuven (Belgium).

Patrick Terrell Gray is currently a Th.D. candidate in historical and systematic theology at The General Theological Seminary in New York City. He is also Assisting Deacon at All Saints' Episcopal Church, West Newbury, Massachusetts (USA).

Scott Holland teaches peace, public and cross-cultural theologies at Bethany Theological Seminary in partnership with Earlhan School of Religion in Richmond, Indiana (USA). He is an active minister in the Church of the Brethren and a contributing editor to *Cross Currents*.

Thomas M. Kelly is assistant professor of theology and coordinator of the Study Center on Religion and Public Life in the New Hampshire Institute of Politics at Saint Anselm College in Manchester (USA). He specializes in contemporary systematic theology.

Paul J. Levesque teaches in the Department of Comparative Religion at California State University, Fullerton. He was a Theodore T. Basselin Scholar in the School of Philosophy at The Catholic University of America and holds the Ph.D. in Religious Studies from the Katholieke Universiteit Leuven (Belgium).

David J. Livingston is professor in the Religious Studies Department at Mercyhurst College in Erie (USA). He specializes in the areas of theological anthropology and ethics. His forthcoming book addresses the possibility of forgiveness and reconciliation in situations of domestic violence.

Daniël J. Louw is professor in pastoral theology and pastoral counselling. He is head of the Department of Practical Theology and Missiology at the University of Stellenbosch (South Africa).

Michael Purcell lectures in systematic theology in the Faculty of Divinity at the University of Edinburgh (Scotland). His current research interests focus on the work of Emmanuel Levinas and its theological appropriation.

John Ries has studied and taught philosophy and theology at a number of universities in the USA and Europe. He obtained his Ph.D. in theology from the Katholieke Universiteit Leuven (Belgium) and was an associate researcher there working on the research project 'Postmodern Sacramento-Theology' (2000). At present, he teaches philosophy at Molloy College, Rockville, New York (USA).

Dennis Rochford is professor of systematic theology at Australian Catholic University and coordinator of the Masters programme. His Ph.D. in religious studies from the Katholieke Universiteit Leuven examined the theological project of Edward Schillebeeckx to bridge Christian faith with contemporary culture.

Michele Saracino received her Ph.D. from Marquette University in Milwaukee (USA) and currently is a professor in the Department of Religious Studies at Regis College in Weston (USA).

Gesa Thiessen is Associate Lecturer at All Hallows College and at the Milltown Institute of Theology and Philosophy (Ireland).

PRINTED ON PERMANENT PAPER • IMPRIME SUR PAPIER PERMANENT • GEDRUKT OP DUURZAAM PAPIER - ISO 9706

N.V. PEETERS S.A., KLEIN DALENSTRAAT 42, B-3020 HERENT